I
LOVE
THE RED SOX

JON CHATTMAN, ALLIE TARANTINO
& RICH TARANTINO

TRIUMPH
BOOKS

This book is available in quantity at special discounts for your group or organization. For further information, contact:

Triumph Books LLC
542 South Dearborn Street, Suite 750
Chicago, Illinois 60605
(312) 939-3330
Fax (312) 663-3557
www.triumphbooks.com

Printed in U.S.A.
ISBN: 978-1-60078-679-2
Design and editorial production by Prologue Publishing Services, LLC
Photos courtesy of AP Images unless otherwise indicated

For Nelson de la Rosa

CONTENTS

FOREWORD

There are similarities between Red Sox and Yankees fans, in that they're both crazy. Period. They're die-hard. The one thing with Red Sox fans I always thought was nuts was that you could see a family of six, from Grandma down to a little baby boy wearing Papi T-shirts, and they're going to go out to dinner—that's the way they're rolling. That's it. And with Yankees fans, you're going to see someone with a pinstripe jersey on, a Jeter jersey, open-buttoned, with a white shirt underneath and a Yankees hat on anywhere, anytime, whether out at dinner or walking the streets. They're garbed up. Yankees and Red Sox fans are crazy. They're ready to roll. If you want to use the word *passionate*, great; if you want to use the word *crazy*, great. Whatever they are, it's both. Before I got to Boston in 2003, I didn't know anything about the rivalry. You hear about it, with the Bucky Dent home run and the Bill Buckner ball through his legs, big deal. Growing up in L.A., I was more interested in the Giants/Dodgers rivalry. It was just another rivalry from where I stood. Then, by the time I left Boston, I realized why it's such a big deal.

The Yankees are always the dressed up, tall, clean-shaven, wealthy organization. There are Yankees fans all over because of their history and the great players they've had, like Gehrig and Mantle and Ruth. The Boston Red Sox, we were always kind of like the bad-body, grinding, scruffy, blue-collar type team. I would always say to the Yankees' reporters, "This isn't a rivalry. How could this be the best rivalry in sports? They're not even sharing any of their titles." Twenty-six to nothing, that's not cool. There's nothing cool about that unless you're a Yankees fan, right? I always said that it's not a rivalry until we win. We have to win to make it a rivalry. Now it's a rivalry. After we won in '04—and in '03 we were right there—they knew we were coming. Obviously now the Sox have won a couple of World Series to the Yankees' one since 2000, so now the rivalry's developed more. But still, before we had won for the first time in 86 years, we were like, "They're way better than us!" Realistically, there wasn't a rivalry before then. I actually like East Coast baseball better than West Coast baseball now because of the passion. The fan base is on another level. When you lose, the sky is falling; when you win, it's huge, so I just think the passion's greater on the East Coast.

By the time I left, I realized I understood the Yankees–Red Sox rivalry part of it—it's the passion of the two cities, the fans' attachment, the media focus that creates all this. The players don't hate each other. We respect each other. I never hated Derek Jeter; playing against him, we always respected his play, we wanted to be like him. This may be different—not every player thinks the way I think—but I actually loved, loved the bitterness the fans showed toward us in a Boston uniform when we went to the Bronx. I loved it when the fans were all over me, I loved them hating me, I loved the whole "Cowboy Down" thing—I appreciated that. That's passion. I had fun with the fans. I talked back, I yelled back, I made gestures back, but that was all part of it. When you go watch an event, you want some tension. It's like Reggie Miller making those three-pointers against the Knicks at the Garden in 1994 with

Kevin Millar played first base/outfield for the Red Sox from 2003 to 2005 and hit .282 with 52 homers and 220 RBIs, helping the Sox to claim their first World Series championship in 86 years in 2004.
Photo courtesy of MLB Network

Spike Lee and him going at it. That's what it's about. I understood that. When the Yankees came into our house, the fans would chant Jeter-this, Jeter-that or whatever it was to get into their heads, that's the way Boston rolled. Red Sox fans blow it out of the water, that's a fact. The Red Sox games are hard to get a ticket to, but the fans are going to be there. They're going to be there, miserable or angry, but they're there. There were times when I played in front of 10,000 or 12,000 people in Baltimore, and it stunk. And deservedly so—we stunk. But even if the Red Sox stink, the fans are still going to be there. They always appreciate you. I've had fans come up to me in Hawaii, in Seattle. I mean, coast to coast, Red Sox Nation is everywhere.

It's the most unique organization, being a part of it, because it's such a small city, but it's connected. If you're out, they're always going to send a drink over; they're always going to say something. What makes me feel good now is that they're always thankful. "Thank you, thank you, thank you for what you've done," when really all I did was be who I was and play the game that I played and loved to play. But they're really thankful. They're sending over a shot of Jack Daniel's—and I'm not a big drinker, I'm perceived as a big party animal— but you're going to get a shot of Jack Daniel's somewhere or someone's going to pick up your bill. And you know what? That's pretty neat because they're a full-on stranger, really, but I always said it was like we had four or five million family members. It's such a small city, but with three and a half million people in it, it's like family when you win.

—Kevin Millar

INTRODUCTION

You can have Ohio State vs. Michigan, Celtics vs. Lakers, and Evel Knievel vs. the Snake River Canyon, I'll take Red Sox vs. Yankees as the greatest American sports rivalry. For more than eight decades it was the hammer vs. the nail. Like Humphrey Bogart talking to Peter Lorre in Casablanca *when the Yankees were asked if they despised the Sox they could only say, "If I gave you any thought I probably would." Then 2004 happened and everything changed. Red Sox fans earned new bragging rights. No longer needy and pathetic, they became like the Yankee fans they once loathed. Now it's not just Red Sox vs. Yankees, it's All of Baseball vs. Red Sox and Yankees.*

—Dan Shaughnessy
sports columnist/associate editor, *Boston Globe*

There are Pepsi people and there are Coca-Cola people. You might prefer one over the other or, perhaps, like both. But either will probably do in a pinch. The same can be said about milk chocolate vs. dark chocolate, boxers vs. tighty-whities, and so on. When it comes to baseball, however, fans either love the New York Yankees or hate them. There is no in-between. In Boston, using the word *hate* is the biggest understatement ever—like saying Lady Gaga dresses only mildly different than your grandmother. So much has been made about the rich history of the Yankees, and why shouldn't there be? The ticker-tape franchise is the most successful in sports history with their 27 world championships, near-annual playoff finishes, and worldwide "appeal." Throw in a bottomless batch of baseball legends who've worn pinstripes, and it's easy to see why so many people root, root, root for the...Yankees.

But while the Bronx Bombers have welcomed fans on a worldwide bandwagon, another team in the AL East is nearly as rich in history, adoration, and has far more character. So let's ignore the Yanks, their titles, their "Joba Rules," their arrogance, and their fan base, which every chance it gets jam those 27 rings down our throats. Let's talk about the Boston Red Sox, whom we're sure current Yankees fans would've been rooting for, had they lived anytime between 1912 and 1918.

So much has been made about the franchise selling Babe Ruth eons ago, but too little has been made about the importance of the team ever since. The Sox define everything that's good about this country. They earn their victories, losses, successes, and failures and never give up. Neither does their fan base.

Ask any Massachusetts native, and they'll tell you about a moment in time that personifies the team, whether it's Carlton Fisk's dramatic, hands-flailing home run or Kevin Millar's "idiots" never-lose battle cry. Red Sox Nation is a proud group who will cheer and bleed for their team whether they're good, bad, or atrocious. How many Sox fans stopped rooting for the Sox after Buckner botched Mookie's ball in the 1986 World Series? How many decided to jump ship after Bucky Dent sent the Sox packing in 1978? How many people became Yankees fans after A-Rod was traded to the team? How many became Sox fans because they signed Alex Gonzalez? Get the picture, yet?

Boston fans pour out onto Huntington Avenue Grounds after the Red Sox defeated the Pittsburgh Pirates in the first-ever World Series in 1903. Photo courtesy of Getty Images

Yes, whether the Sox are a crew of overachieving underdogs like they were in the "impossible" run of 1967, or a group of idiots destined for greatness in 2004, Sox fans root their team on largely because of their relatable, working-class hero mentality. Because of this anti-Yankees corporation vibe, it's easy to love the Red Sox and their passionate fans.

If any team's fan base deserves an honorary baseball card or an unofficial roster spot, it's the Sox. Back in 1903 when the Sox weren't even the Sox yet, the "Royal Rooters" got inside the Pirates' minds by singing "Tessie" repeatedly. The Sox won that first World Series ever played. The more things change, the more they stay the same. Some 10-plus decades later, fans were at it again, sporting blonde girl masks to distract Alex Rodriguez, who at the time was romancing movie star Kate

Hudson. Some call it annoying, we'll call it funny, original, and zealous.

But the reason the Sox are the Sox is because they're the Sox. From superstars like Cy Young and Ted Williams to "Yaz" and "Youk," some of the finest players to ever wear a uniform have played in Boston, and those name-drops fail to scratch the surface. You can't mention the team without noting heavy-hearted, high-impact players like Pesky, Tiant, Wakefield, and too many other names to list here.

The Sox can be the top dog, the mid-carder, or down and out, and you love them the same. You can always identify with their players, and you know no matter what, the team will figure things out. It might not be this year, last year, or next year, but it'll happen.

1

RED SOX MOMENTS WE LOVE

What's the best thing about being a Sox fan? That sense of tradition and the family connection to the team that is passed down from generation to generation—borderline brainwashing. But hey, I'm brainwashing my kids all the time when it comes to what teams they're gonna like.

—Ken Casey
lead singer, Dropkick Murphys

Big or small or in-between, moments in Red Sox history are appreciated and emblazoned in the hearts of Red Sox Nation forever. It can be as monumental as singing away Pirates' World Series dreams in 1908 or as minor as greeting the aforementioned A-Rod with dumb-blonde masks at Fenway; you won't find a more loyal bunch of passionate fans than the Nation.

Sox Moments and the Nation go hand in hand. Fans will recount epic stories of Fisk flailing his hands for a ball to stay fair in 1975 as often as you'll hear them recall a big Rich Garces pivotal strikeout in a forgotten game. Moments are moments in Boston, but let's be honest, some are just so much bigger than the game.

Red Sox Nation celebrates World Series rings, sure, but also celebrates key moments in history that didn't end up with the gold. That's a difference between the Sawx and that other franchise with Jeter. While the Sox don't feel like they're entitled to a World Series win every year, Yankees fans—and the organization they go nuts over—do. The Yankees fans can't appreciate a good season unless it ends with the last win in October.

We all know the majority of Yankees fans: the ones who weren't rooting for them when Clay Parker was in the bullpen or "Pags" was at the hot corner. It's a fan who has only been a fan since the 1996, 1998–2000 run, who grew tired of the lack of titles in the 2000s, but came right back in 2009.

Many authentic Yankees fans (we mean the ones who became Yankees fans because their grandfathers used to take them to the old park) don't even like going to Yankee Stadium anymore because the new breed of fan is better represented there than they are. And let's not even talk about those insulting ticket prices, which keep the middle-class fan out of the ballpark. But we digress. Let's get back to those amazing moments where the Sox beat the odds, earned a few milestones, and made us forget about winning the whole damn thing—almost.

THE FIRST FIVE TITLES
WE HAD A DYNASTY, TOO

The two leagues didn't agree upon the first "modern" World Series between Boston and the Pittsburgh Pirates until August of 1903. Leading up to the inaugural series, the Red Sox franchise then known as the Pilgrims used six pitchers on the season, five of whom pitched more than 175 innings. They

BOSOX HURLERS WHO ACED THE YANKEES

Buck O'Brien, 1912 (4–0): 20 of Buck's 29 career victories came in the summer of 1912

Smoky Joe Wood, 1912 (5–0): 29–5 against the rest of the league, not too shabby

Babe Ruth, 1917 (5–0): the Bambino capped off his final 20-win season (24) with a 5–0 record vs. his future team

Jack Kramer, 1948 (5–0): went 18–5 in debut with Sox

Mel Parnell, 1953 (5–0): undefeated vs. World Series champs in second 20-win season for Sox

Josh Beckett, 2011 (4–0): made a career of killing Yankees, 2011 regular season just icing on the cake

RED SOX

were led by Cy Young, who won 28 of his career-record 511 during the regular season. Buck Freeman led Boston and the majors with 13 dead-ball home runs heading into the best-of-nine series against Honus Wagner and the Bucs. The "Flying Dutchman" hit .355 on the season but could only manage a .222 average against the "Cyclone" and the rest of the rubber-armed Boston rotation. Cy Young even managed to knock in the same amount of runs (3) as Wagner when he struck with a crushing Game 5 triple. While Yellow Fever was running rampant, this would be the start of an early 20ᵗʰ century Red Sox renaissance.

In a World Series that saw a tie game on account of darkness, the 1912 Red Sox won their second title in franchise history behind the pitching efforts of Smoky Joe Wood. Wood went 34–5 with 10 shutouts during the regular season, so it was no surprise that he would be victorious three times in the series against the formidable New York Giants. The Giants

Smoky Joe Wood warms up at the Polo Grounds prior to the 1912 World Series vs. the New York Giants. The Sox won the series 4–3. Photo courtesy of Getty Images

were three outs away until Fred Snodgrass dropped a routine fly ball, setting up a Boston victory. The first season the Red Sox played in Fenway Park was memorable due in part to an offense that included Hall of Famers Tris Speaker and Harry Hooper as well as Red Sox stalwart Duffy Lewis.

A year after the Boston Braves swept the Philadelphia A's in the World Series, the Boston Red Sox needed just one extra game to defeat the Philadelphia Phillies in the 1915 Fall Classic. After falling to Phillies great Pete Alexander in Game 1, the Red Sox won four straight one-run games behind the pitching of Rube Foster, Dutch Leonard, and Ernie Shore. The 1915 Series stands out for a couple of debuts: Woodrow Wilson became the first president to attend a game; and, more importantly, a 20-year-old named Babe Ruth pinch hit in his first postseason at-bat. While the Bambino would get just that one at-bat in picking up his first ring, it's most likely that almost 100 years later more kids know him than our 28th president.

The Red Sox accomplished their only back-to-back championship seasons when they defeated the Brooklyn Robins in 1916 with a five-game Series victory. Babe Ruth starred in Game 2, pitching all 14 innings in a 2–1 win. The Boston games took place at Braves Field, which held more people. Despite hitting .176 for the series, Larry Gardner led the team with two home runs and six RBIs. Future Yankees manager Casey Stengel batted .364 in the losing effort.

The soon-to-be cursed Red Sox won their fifth title in the now-infamous season of 1918. While most Yankees fans spent the better part of the late 1990s and early 2000s chanting, "Nineteen eighteen!" there is probably very little they can tell you about the team other than the fact that Babe Ruth pitched for them. As we all know, the Red Sox would take a 5–0 title lead over the Yankees only to see the Bombers rattle off 26 titles before Boston would win again. The Red Sox hit zero home runs and batted .186 in front of approximately 20,000 fans per game in the best-of-seven Series. You'd almost think the Curse was already in effect, but they were playing the Cubs, who were in the infancy of their current Series futility. Carl Mays and

Babe Ruth each won two games, and the series remains the only Fall Classic to entirely take place in September due to wartime restrictions placed by the government. The Red Sox would win three series in four years, but eight-plus decades of frustration, heartache, and Yankees headaches was about to begin.

THE OTHER DIMAGGIO HIT STREAK

> *Watch them as they whirl, careen*
> *Over the fields of verdant green*
> *Rulers of the batting eye*
> *Where the gaudy triples fly*
> *In the sunset's shining glow*
> *Who is it that steals the show?*
> *Vincent, Dominic, and Joe*

—Grantland Rice

Dom DiMaggio was the youngest of nine children, three of whom were successful major leaguers. Papa Giuseppe and Mama Rosalee must've been very proud to have raised three all-star center fielders. While Joe D. is well known for his Yankees exploits, marriage to Marilyn Monroe, and his hit streak, about 56 Yankees fans could tell you that the Boston Red Sox hit-streak record belongs to Joltin' Joe's bro, the "Little Professor." Coming in at a modest 34 games, the leadoff-hitting Dominic saw an ironic end to his streak in 1949 when the ball hit in his final at-bat landed in the mitt of the Yankee Clipper.

Dom DiMaggio batted .352 during the streak in a season in which the Red Sox finished one game behind the Yankees. On the streak, he told Alan Schwarz, "Hitting streaks didn't matter to me, even when I hit in another 27 in 1951. It's just

RED SOX

RED SOX-YANKEES TRADES
THAT DID NOT INVOLVE BABE RUTH*

August 13, 1997: The Red Sox trade Mike Stanley and Randy Brown to the Yankees for Tony Armas and Jim Mecir.

March 28, 1986: The Red Sox trade Mike Easler to the Yankees for Don Baylor.

March 22, 1972: The Red Sox trade Sparky Lyle to the Yankees for Danny Cater and Mario Guerrero.

August 3, 1967: The Red Sox trade Pete Magrini and Ron Klimkowski to the Yankees for Elston Howard.

June 12, 1962: The Red Sox traded Tom Umphlett and cash to the Yankees for Billy Gardner.

March 14, 1957: The Yankees traded Bill Renna to the Red Sox for Eli Grba and Gordie Windhorn.

May 15, 1934: The Red Sox traded Freddie Muller and $20,000 to the Yankees for Lyn Lary.

May 15, 1933: The Red Sox traded Marv Olson, Johnny Watwood, and cash to the Yankees for Dusty Cooke.

August 1, 1932: The Yankees traded Gordon Rhodes to the Red Sox for Wilcy Moore.

June 5, 1932: The Yankees traded Ivy Andrews, Hank Johnson, and $50,000 to the Red Sox for Danny MacFayden.

May 6, 1930: The Yankees traded Cedric Durst and $50,000 to the Red Sox for Red Ruffing.

May 5, 1925: The Yankees traded Ray Francis and $9,000 to the Red Sox for Alex Ferguson and Bobby Veach.

continued

December 10, 1924: The Yankees traded Mike McNally to the Red Sox for Howie Shanks.

January 30, 1923: The Yankees traded Norm McMillan, George Murray, Camp Skinner, and $50,000 to the Red Sox for Herb Pennock.

January 3, 1923: The Yankees traded Al DeVormer and cash to the Red Sox for Harvey Hendrick and George Pipgras.

July 23, 1922: The Yankees traded Chick Fewster, Elmer Miller, Johnny Mitchell, Lefty O'Doul, and $50,000 to the Red Sox for Joe Dugan and Elmer Smith.

December 20, 1921: The Yankees traded Rip Collins, Roger Peckinpaugh, Bill Piercy, Jack Quinn, and $100,000 to the Red Sox for Bullet Joe Bush, Sad Sam Jones, and Everett Scott.

December 15, 1920: The Yankees traded Del Pratt, Muddy Ruel, Hank Thormahlen, and Sammy Vick to the Red Sox for Harry Harper, Waite Hoyt, Mike McNally, and Wally Schang.

Courtesy www.baseball-reference.com

a statistic. And the only statistic that matters to me is hitting .300." The youngest DiMaggio would finish his career at .298, as his streak goes by almost as unnoticed as Ted Williams' record of reaching first base safely in 84 consecutive games. The bespectacled Dom started as a right fielder in his rookie season of 1940, but he would quickly move to center field (a position he would only give up to serve the country during wartime). During his rookie campaign, he faced the Yanks and his older brother in a five-game series. The DiMaggios combined for 20 hits (11 from the Little Professor).

After returning from battle, the Sox reached the 1946 World Series against the St. Louis Cardinals. But Dom popped his hamstring reaching second on a double, and the Sox had to play a sub. As Red Sox luck would have it, the Cardinals' Enos Slaughter would score on his "mad dash" from first on a ball that would've been fielded by DiMaggio had he not been nursing his hammy. A seven-time All-Star and league leader in runs, triples, and steals, Dom never embarrassed the DiMaggio name.

DiMaggio has remained a borderline Cooperstown Hall of Famer but in 1978 was inducted into the Italian-American Sports Hall of Fame, followed by induction into the Boston Red Sox Hall of Fame in 1995. DiMaggio lived to the age of 92 and, in his post-retirement days, led a group that would eventually evolve into the Baseball Players Union. As a successful businessman, he formed a group that attempted to purchase the Red Sox when Tom Yawkey passed away in 1976. While Ted Williams' 84-consecutive games reaching base and Joe DiMaggio's 56-game hit streak may be untouchable, the Little Professor's achievements, while approachable, were clearly significant. But Dom DiMaggio's legacy has been ensured in a "Teammates" statue with fellow West Coasters turned Red Sox (Ted Williams, Johnny Pesky, and Bobby Doerr) located at Gate B of Fenway (the intersection of Van Ness and Ipswich Streets).

IMPOSSIBLE DREAM

Imagine if the Little Red Riding Hood got eaten, Sleeping Beauty never woke up, and Snow White's prince was a no-show. That's essentially how it felt when the fairy tale season of 1967 ended with the Sox losing to the Cardinals in the World Series 4–3 after an improbable, "impossible dream" run. Even so, that memorable season remains one of the most, if not *the most*, impressive teams ever, considering the Sox were expected to dwell near the cellar as they had for the previous seven seasons.

Following two atrocious seasons—1965 and 1966—in which Boston lost 100 and 90 games, respectively, fans treated Fenway like a Taco Bell bathroom: staying away to avoid another stinker. With just one marketable player in Carl Yastrzemski, new manager Dick Williams was assigned to make the most of a team of never-weres, and did he ever. The tough-as-nails manager preached fundamentals and powered his team to overachieve and remain in the playoff hunt all season long.

Much to major league baseball's and the fans' surprise, the headline-free Sox made headlines and rocked the baseball world thanks to a career year from Yaz and breakthrough seasons from others. Aside from Captain Carl, who put up a Triple Crown/MVP year with 44 homers and 121 RBIs, the Sox got a whole lot of hits from fan favorites Rico Petrocelli and Tony Conigliaro, the latter of whom had his season tragically cut short in August. (Conigliaro was hit by a pitch in the cheekbone, and suffered severe damage to it and his retina.) Perhaps the biggest surprise was pitcher "Gentleman" Jim Lonborg, who dominated AL hitting more than shoulder pads did women's jackets in the 1980s, and came out of nowhere to become the first Sox star to win the Cy Young Award.

Even more impressive than individual stats was how the Sox managed to rise above the pack despite injuries and military-related departures to stay in the thick of a five-team race (White Sox, Twins, Tigers, and Angels) down the stretch. The hearts of Fenway faithful, who broke attendance records that season, must've been in their throats when the final weekend of the season came down to three teams (White Sox, Twins, and Tigers) competing with the Sox for the top spot. Yes, there was no Selig wild-card here, so whoever finished first won the pennant and went directly to the Series. By the time the last day arrived, the White Sox were out, the Tigers fell to the Angels, and Lonborg pitched the Sox to a series sweep of the Twins to take the pennant. They didn't win the Series until 2004, but the "improbables" of 1967 deserve to be mentioned in the same breath as those "idiots."

A GAME 6 TO REMEMBER

At 12:34 AM, in the 12th inning, Fisk's histrionic home run brought a 7–6 end to a game that will be the pride of historians in the year 2525, a game won and lost what seemed like a dozen times, and a game that brings back summertime one more day. For the seventh game of the World Series.

—Peter Gammons, *Boston Globe*

GNR's *Chinese Democracy* aside, some things are worth waiting for. Game 6 of the 1975 Fall Classic sure was for Sox fans. With three rainy-day delays, momentum shifted back to the Sox, who were down to the mighty Cincinnati Reds three games to two. With ace Luis Tiant back on the mound, the Sox were pumped up and ready to take down the Big Red Machine. But El Tiante wasn't the story on that breezy October 21 evening at Fenway. In one of the best games ever played in the World Series or anywhere (MLB Network considers it No. 1 of all-time), the Sox—in a must-win game—defeated the Reds in an epic 12-inning game.

Carlton Fisk wills the ball he hit off of Reds reliever Pat Darcy to stay fair. It did, clearing the Green Monster and giving the Red Sox a 7–6, 12-inning victory in Game 6 of the 1975 World Series and forcing a decisive Game 7.

In a game that had it all—more ups and downs than John Travolta's career and more exciting highlights than the entire 2008–2011 seasons, the Sox overcame George Foster's go-ahead two-run double in the seventh thanks to Bernie Carbo's game-tying three-run shot in the bottom of the eighth. By the bottom of the ninth, it seemed the Sox would force a Game 7 when they loaded the bases with no out. But Denny Doyle got thrown out at the plate following a shallow fly ball (third-base coach Don Zimmer—yes, him—alleged he had said "No no no" not "Go go go") to help kill the rally. In the 11th, Joe Morgan nearly sucked the life out of the crowd when he smashed a shot that Dwight Evans leaped up and somehow grabbed.

All of this set the stage for 12th-inning heroics by one of the most reliable Sox players of all-time. With Pat Darcy on the mound, Carlton Fisk drove a 1–0 pitch deep to left field, striking the foul pole right over the Green Monster. Captured on television and replayed forever after, Fisk waved his arms repeatedly to the right to try to will the ball to stay fair, as he jumped along the first-base line. The ball stayed fair, and the Sox lived to play another game. Sure, they would fall to the Reds in heartbreaking fashion in Game 7, but nothing can take away what Fisk and the team accomplished the night before.

BRUNO'S OUT-OF-THIS-WORLD CATCH

During his major league career, right fielder Tom Brunansky was known more for his slugging (271 career home runs) than for his fielding (62 errors). Yet on October 3, 1990, "Bruno's" ninth-inning, game-saving, season-preserving catch earned him a place in Red Sox immortality. If you are a Red Sox Nation member in your late twenties, this snag of White Sox shortstop Ozzie Guillen's line drive may have been your introduction to forthcoming great Red Sox moments. Earlier in the season, Boston received Brunansky in a trade for All-Star reliever Lee Smith. Bruno would hit 15 home runs in just under 130 games, but his future "web gem" was yet to come. With Jeff Reardon on the hill and two outs on the books, a scrawny Sammy Sosa singled to center. Reardon then plunked

Scott Fletcher, putting the tying run on first. The Toronto Blue Jays were in hot pursuit, and they suddenly became the biggest Guillen fans in the world and Canada. He sliced a liner to right field, where Brunansky made his heroic dive, which was followed by a Fenway eruption of division-winning joy. The win would be the last of the season for the Sox, who were swept in the ALCS by the A's (who coincidentally were swept in the 1990 World Series by the Reds). However, in 2010 the sliding catch was entered into the Red Sox Hall of Fame Memorable Moments, preserving its place in Sox lore forever.

PEDRO AND TEDDY BALLGAME SHINE IN '99

In July of 1999 Fenway Park hosted Major League Baseball's All-Star Game for the third time. Despite being held smack dab in what would eventually be known as "the Steroid Era," Pedro Martinez was in the midst of one of the all-time greatest seasons ever for a pitcher. But more on him later.... Ted Williams was in the house, and Boston hearts were ready to be warmed. Assisted by one of the greatest hitters of the 1990s, Tony Gwynn, "the Splendid Splinter" made his final Fenway appearance to throw out the ceremonial first pitch of the game. All-Stars gathered around and honored "Teddy Ballgame," who stole the show and gave a fitting memory to Red Sox fans of the pending century.

When the actual game began, Pedro was ready to dominate the National League's top hitters. In the first inning, he fanned three former NL MVPs: Barry Larkin, Larry Walker, and Sammy Sosa. He began the second by fanning Mark McGwire. Big Mac was followed by Matt Williams reaching base on an error. As Jeff Bagwell was busy striking out,

Pedro Martinez delivers to home plate in Game 3 of the 1999 ALCS against the New York Yankees at Fenway Park. The Sox pummeled the Yankees 13–1 Photo courtesy of Getty Images

Williams was caught stealing. Inning over. While this was happening, future teammate Curt Schilling was roughed up for two early runs. The AL won 4–1, and Martinez was named All-Star Game MVP. Martinez won the AL Triple Crown for pitchers by leading the league in strikeouts (313), ERA (2.07), and record (23–4, best in winning percentage and wins). He easily won the Cy Young Award as the Red Sox earned the AL wild-card. Pedro was the Game 1 starter, leaving early with a bad

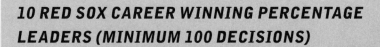

10 RED SOX CAREER WINNING PERCENTAGE LEADERS (MINIMUM 100 DECISIONS)

.760 **Pedro Martinez,** 117–37
.691 **Jon Lester,** 76–34
.674 **Joe Wood,** 116–56
.659 **Babe Ruth,** 89–46
.641 **Josh Beckett,** 84–47
.640 **Tex Hughson,** 96–54
.634 **Roger Clemens,** 192–111
.632 **Cy Young,** 192–112
.629 **Lefty Grove,** 105–62
.623 **Ellis Kinder,** 86–52

back in a loss against the Cleveland Indians. After Bret Saberhagen wet the bed, giving up six runs in 2⅔ innings in an 11–1 Game 2 defeat, the Sox found themselves facing elimination.

Perhaps in a sign of things to come in the next century, Boston reeled off three straight wins (including a 23–7 Game 4 trouncing, in which John Valentin helped himself to seven RBIs off of Bartolo Colon and two relievers). But the most electrifying performance of the series belongs to Pedro Martinez. After Saberhagen once again stunk up the park and Derek Lowe didn't help much, the Sox found themselves in an 8–7 free-for-all after just three innings. Jimy Williams made an emergency call for Pedro from the pen. Pedro responded in typical fashion with six innings of remarkable no-hit ball. The win sent the Sox into their first ever ALCS with the Yankees. It was a forgettable five-game loss, but the stage was set for the next decade. Game on!

DOWN GOES ZIMMER

*In my lifetime, the most exciting days of the Red Sox–Yankees
rivalry were the 1970s, when both teams were truly hungry
for World Series glory, and the players (few if any of whom
were actual millionaires) genuinely hated each other. As
enjoyable as it was to see Pedro put Zimmer on his ass in
'03—if nothing else, it seemed like karmic retribution for
Zim's grotesque mismanagement of the Red Sox rotation in
'78—Red Sox–Yankees "brawls" in the 21ˢᵗ century typically
make me think of British Lords slap-fighting over perceived
breaches in yachting etiquette.*

*But the enduring rivalry and enmity between Thurman
Munson and Carlton Fisk, the ferocious May '76 donnybrook
at Yankee Stadium where Graig Nettles sent Bill Lee to the
disabled list for six weeks with a busted shoulder, the nail-
biting one-game playoff at Fenway Park in '78, or even the
way that nearly every major turning point in the Bronx Zoo
soap opera of '77–'78 seemed to occur against the Red Sox…
that, my friends, is the stuff that a classic rivalry is made of.*

— Dan Epstein
author of Big Hair and Plastic Grass: A Funky Ride
Through Baseball and America in the Swinging '70s

Cain vs. Abel. Ali vs. Frazier. Alf vs. Random Cats. In our
history there have been countless epic battles that have reso-
nated with us—none of which have been as unexpected and
arguably as humorous as the fight between Pedro "Who's Your
Daddy?" Martinez and bench coach/couch potato Don Zimmer. The unusual fight during Game 3 of the 2003 ALCS was
a no-contest that pitted a star Red Sox pitcher against a former Red Sox manager (he managed the team in the one-game

> *It's definitely a postseason vibe when you play [the Yankees]. There is electricity in the ballpark, whether it's in Boston or New York. It's something that everyone can understand, even watching it on TV. You can feel the electricity every time you play those guys. You feel like you are in a World Series for those 19 games just because of the rivalry among the fans—not even including that you were a game or two apart and trying to win a division title.*
>
> **—Bronson Arroyo**

playoff involving Bucky "Fuckin'" Dent.) Even Pete Rose couldn't bet on this happening.

The geriatric smackdown all started after the All-Star pitcher threw behind Yankees outfielder Karim Garcia's head in the top of the fourth inning. The umpire awarded Garcia first base (graze = HBP) and warned both dugouts. Following that, Garcia slid hard into second baseman Todd Walker, leading to a heated exchange between the two and a near-bench clearance. Then in the home inning, Boston backwash Roger Clemens threw up and in to Manny Ramirez. Man-Ram raised his bat at the Rocket, and the benches emptied.

It was at this time when Zimmer charged Martinez at full speed as if the Cy Young Award winner had just stolen the last bowl of Quaker Oats. Channeling his inner Mikhail Baryshnikov, Petey danced around the then-72-year-old, took him by his ginormous head, and threw him down to the ground—face first. Zimmer stayed in the game, one which the Yankees won (after another Garcia fight with a grounds-crew member in the bullpen), and came out of it with a small fine, a smaller cut across his nose and one largely bruised ego. In a press conference the following

day, Zimmer, aka Joe Torre's batboy, cried and told both Yankees and Red Sox fans that he embarrassed himself. He sure
did. This "Rumble in Fenway—Cocoon Edition" was the most
anticlimactic outcome of a fight since Mike Tyson took Michael
Spinks down in 1988.

2004: BEST. SEASON. EVER.

> *Amongst all the joy and what have you…and the bedlam in
> the clubhouse, there was Gabe Kapler, a fan favorite and
> one of the hardest workers, who was just standing back and
> observing. He told me this is one of those moments you have
> to just take it all in.*
>
> —Jerry Trupiano, former Red Sox radio announcer

It could've lingered. It could have stopped their momentum.
It could have fueled "the Curse" even further. The "ghosts"
could've gotten in their heads like they always seemed to.
Instead, the Boston Red Sox used their sudden, tragic loss
to the Yankees in Game 7 of the 2003 ALCS as ammunition
against the AL East perennial frontrunners in 2004. Showing
no signs of what wrestlers making comebacks refer to as "ring
rust" from the year before, or any year for that matter, the Sox
were armed and ready when it came time to play ball in 2004
following the homer from the ho-hummer Aaron Boone.

Stacked with a team that on paper and on the field were better than the best the Bombers had in 2003, the Sox knew how
good they were, and wanted to get better. In a winter that saw
GM Theo Epstein cut ties with Grady "Take Pedro Out" Little,
put enigmatic superstar Manny Ramirez on waivers and fail to
trade him for A-Rod (who ended up in the Bronx), and attempt

to displace fan favorite Nomar Garciaparra (and again, fail), the Sox knew they needed to make some bold moves to compete with Steinbrenner's ever expanding Costanza-like wallet.

The wunderkind, who had already brought Big Papi and Kevin Millar to the team, made his first splash when he wined and dined ace pitcher Curt Schilling in the then-Diamondback's home on Thanksgiving. He eventually lured him to Boston to join a rotation that already included Cy Young Award-fanboy Pedro Martinez, veteran Tim Wakefield, and workhorses like Derek Lowe and Bronson Arroyo. More importantly, Epstein kept the All-Star out of pinstripes.

After that impact move, Epstein bolstered the bullpen with a proven closer in Keith Foulke and hired new manager Terry Francona, who may not have won in Philadelphia but was notoriously known throughout the Bigs as a good manager and an even better man. With the final pieces in place, the Sox seemed primed and ready to take down, as Sox president Larry Lucchino termed it, "the Evil Empire." They were also ready to shake the "Curse of the Bambino" by simply not paying any serious attention to it at any point in the season.

Everyone knows the outcome of the 2004 season, but even before they came from behind to beat the Yankees and win a record eight-straight postseason games, the season seemed to be one for the history books well before October. The Sox started the season by taking three of four games against the Yankees at Fenway, and then swept the team a week later. In April the Sox had a 15–6 record and seemed to have a different hero each night—it could be a David McCarthy pinch-hit, walk-off homer to win or a come-from-behind victory featuring five homers in an eventual rout. But while players like Schilling, Ramirez, Damon, and Ortiz had monster seasons, the Sox faltered mid-season and lost some momentum. Plagued by injuries and spotty play, the team fell—at one point—eight games behind the Bombers. But they rebounded by late July thanks to a few punches and shrewd business moves.

On July 24, the Sox salvaged a game against their biggest rivals by hitting the Yankees hard—literally. Following a famous brawl in which Jason Varitek made Alex Rodriguez eat his catcher's mitt, Bill Mueller hit a game-winning drive

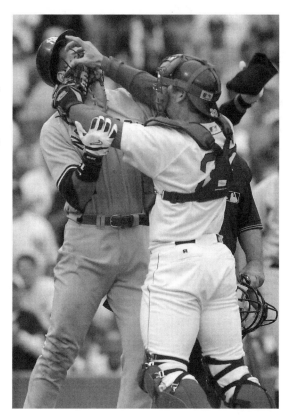

Red Sox catcher Jason Varitek educates Yankees third-bagger Alex Rodriguez on a point of etiquette during a dust-up on July 24, 2004. Photo courtesy of Getty Images

off the usually untouchable "Sandman" Mariano Rivera. A week later, Epstein decided to give the Sox another shot in the arm. At the MLB trading deadline, the ambitious young exec traded away fan favorite but disgruntled superstar Nomar Garciaparra to the Cubs in exchange for Orlando Cabrera from the Expos and Doug Mientkiewicz from the Twins. In addition, he traded a prospect to the Dodgers for speedy outfielder Dave Roberts. With the new trio in the lineup (and contributing right off the bat), the Sox ended up winning 22 out of 25

RED SOX

10 RED SOX POSTSEASON WALK-OFFS

1915 World Series, Game 3
Duffy Lewis singles off Philadelphia's Pete Alexander, 2–1
1916 World Series, Game 2
Del Gainer singles off Brooklyn's Sherry Smith, 2–1
1975 World Series, Game 6
Carlton Fisk homers off Cincinnati's Pat Darcy, 7–6
2003 ALDS, Game 3
Trot Nixon homers off Oakland's Rich Harden, 3–1
2004 ALDS, Game 3
David Ortiz homers off Anaheim's Jarrod Washburn, 8–6
2004 ALCS, Game 4
David Ortiz homers off New York's Paul Quantrill, 6–4
2004 ALCS, Game 5
David Ortiz singles off New York's Esteban Loaiza, 5–4
2007 ALDS, Game 2
Manny Ramirez homers off Los Angeles' Francisco Rodriguez, 6–3
2008 ALDS, Game 4
Jed Lowrie singles off Los Angeles' Scot Shields, 3–2
2008 ALCS, Game 5
J.D. Drew singles off Tampa Bay's J.P. Howell, 8–7

games and finished with a 98–64 record—just three games shy of the AL East title and good for the AL wild-card.

Just as the 2004 regular season was arguably the best season the team ever played—at least from a dramatic standpoint— there's no question the postseason was the best they'd ever been a part of. But, as had so often been the case in their history, the Sox didn't make it easy on themselves or their fans. After sweeping the Anaheim Angels in the first round of the playoffs, thanks to solid pitching and explosive bats, the Sox started the ALCS giving their fans solid anxiety and likely explosive diar- rhea. In the first three games, the Sox looked overmatched and underplayed. Game 1 saw Schilling battling an ankle injury and getting rocked by those expensive Yankees bats. Game 2 brought their offense to a standstill courtesy of Jon Lieber, of all people. Game 3's return to Fenway didn't change anything. As a matter of fact, the team was routed by a score of 19–8—former Yankee Ramiro Mendoza fittingly got the "L."

As the New York media feasted on the 3–0 Yankees start and an inevitable return to the World Series, the Sox players—labeled "idiots" by Millar throughout the season for their carefree and less-than-groomed demeanor (Damon = Jesus)—didn't let it phase them. "Don't let us win tonight," was a warning Millar spewed to the cameras with a cheesy grin before Game 4. His threat wasn't an empty one.

In the ninth inning of Game 4—with the Yankees on the verge of yet another trip to the World Series, the Sox started their epic uphill climb. The tide started to turn, and the Yankees spirits started to fade when Roberts pinch-ran for Millar after he was walked by Rivera in the ninth inning. Roberts narrowly

The Red Sox celebrate their first world championship in 86 years in St. Louis after sweeping the Cardinals 4–0 in the 2004 World Series.

stole second and scored the tying run for the Sox when Mueller singled him home. Ortiz would go on to hit a walk-off homer off Paul Quantrill in the 12th inning to force Game 5.

Game 5 felt like déjà vu all over again for the franchise that always expects things to go their way because it always does. In another extra-inning stunner, the Sox came back to beat the Yankees and Rivera. In the eighth inning, Tom Gordon allowed a lead-off homer to Ortiz, and after the next two batters got on base, Rivera—who up until the series had blown just three saves in 65 postseason appearances—came in and gave up the tying run again. In the 14th, Damon and Ramirez set the stage by drawing walks. Big Papi came up and did it again: another game-winning hit.

Game 6 propelled the series even further into MLB history. Following a mediocre Game 1, Schilling pitched through likely unbearable ankle pain. With his white sock filling with blood, Schill shut the door on the Yankees by pitching masterfully, and forced a Game 7. With million-dollar bust Kevin Brown on the mound for New York, the Sox took the Bombers out of the game from the start. Eventual ALCS MVP Ortiz hit a two-run homer in the first, Damon hit two homers—one grand slam—and Derek Lowe held the Yanks to a handful of runs. By the end of the night, the Sox handily defeated them 10–3 to help give birth to the biggest choke in sports history.

Shaking the biggest proverbial monkey off their backs, the Sox seemed destined to win it all for the first time in 86 years. The St. Louis Cardinals, who had defeated the Sox in the 1967 Fall Classic, didn't stand a chance after that four-game spanking of the Yankees. Game 1 opened at Fenway and was a slugfest that ended with the Sox edging out the Cards 11–9. Game 2 of the Series featured another vintage Schilling performance. With shots and stitches in his tendon-torn ankle, Schill, staining another sock, pitched one-run, six-inning ball in yet another Sox victory.

While the series shifted to Busch Stadium for Game 3, the song remained the same. Martinez was magnificent, holding Albert Pujols and the Cards to just three hits in seven shutout innings. The Cards may have had a chance early against Petey, but opposing pitcher Jeff Suppan cost his team by blundering on the base paths and getting hung out to dry on the third-base line in the third inning.

It seemed the end of the book was already written, but the Cards played Game 4, anyway. Damon led off with a homer off of Jason Marquis, and the Sox never looked back. Lowe, who triumphed in that *other* Game 7, silenced the birds by pitching seven innings of three-hit ball. Throw in a Trot Nixon two-run double, flawless relief from Bronson Arroyo, Alan Embree, and Foulke, and the Sox rolled to a 3–0 win, set New England ablaze, and ended the so-called "Curse."

As Epstein said that night, "We can die happy. I just hope everyone out there who has been rooting for the Red Sox the last 86 years is enjoying this as much as we are."

We did.

MORE ON THE BLOODY SOCK

The sports world has been witness to its fair share of painfully dramatic moments. For instance, do you remember where you were when Michael Jordan willed the Chicago Bulls to an NBA Finals victory over the Utah Jazz with a 103-degree fever? Or when Washington Redskins quarterback Joe Theismann's leg was snapped like a Slim-Jim on *Monday Night Football* by New York Giants linebacker Lawrence Taylor? Of course Jordan would eventually win the championship that year and sadly Theismann's career was ended, but enough about them. This is a Red Sox book, and surely you remember where you were when arguably the most dramatic franchise moment of all-time occurred. Right before our eyes on

October 19, 2004, in the moment that is now simply remembered as the "bloody sock" game, Boston hurler Curt Schilling
gave new meaning to the team's namesake. With the team
down 3–2 in the series, the eventual three-time World Series
champion had without a doubt the most satisfying moment of
his illustrious career—playing through an injured ankle, forcing a Game 7, and eventually leading to the greatest comeback
in the history of team sports.

No fan or sportswriter could have predicted what Schilling
would accomplish, given that he had a horrible outing in

*Curt Schilling is fired up
after getting a Yankees
batter out, despite a right
sock drenched with blood
from an ankle injury. His
performance at Yankee
Stadium in Game 6 of
the 2004 ALCS forced a
deciding Game 7, which the
Sox won easily, 10–3.
They went on to sweep the
St. Louis Cardinals in the
World Series.* Photo courtesy
of Getty Images

Game 1 of the ALCS after tearing his ankle during the ALDS. Still, he gave his team a lift when he sucked it up and pitched Game 6, bloody sock and all.

After disposing the Yankees in memorable fashion, the Red Sox went on to sweep the St. Louis Cardinals for their first championship since 1918. Schilling, who boasts the game's greatest postseason winning percentage with at least 10 decisions (.846, 11–2), was not about to miss another chance to make postseason magic. Schilling, along with his Cooperstown-bound right Franken-ankle, managed to pitch seven strong innings of one-run ball before turning the game over to Bronson Arroyo and Kevin Foulke, assuring that this legendary red sock was ready to take a championship duck-boat ride from Boston to immortality.

THE REDEMPTION OF BILL BUCKNER

> *The Bill Buckner game stung. After that game, after he booted that ball and the game went into toilet, my uncle [Jack Rogers], who was the team's traveling secretary, was leaving to take the team back to the hotel. He was probably 70-something. Out of the center-field gate, a Molson bottle was thrown from the upper deck and it hit him on the top of the head. He had to go to the hospital and had two black eyes. Talk about adding insult to injury.*
>
> —John Slattery, actor, *Mad Men*

As champagne was being chilled in the visitor's dugout and pitcher Bruce Hurst was prematurely being announced as MVP of the Series, the Red Sox were just one strike away from becoming world champions for the first time since 1918…well, that was until the most famous grounder in the history of the game reared its ugly head and was embedded into our minds forever.

"A little roller up along first...behind the bag! It gets through Buckner! Here comes Knight, and the Mets win it!"

And, as they say, the rest is history, as legendary broadcaster Vin Scully's call during Game 6 of the 1986 World Series was heard by millions upon millions of Red Sox Nation members all over the world. The Mets won the game that fateful night, October 25, 1986, by the score of 6–5, thus tying the series and setting up an inevitable Game 7 win that would set the Sox back for years.

With our hearts crushed and our tears flowing as if we had been dumped by the homecoming queen after the first dance, we only had one person to blame, and just like that, Bill Buckner—the man single-handedly responsible for the most talked about E3 in history—became public enemy No. 1. Although the Sox blew a three-run lead in the decisive final Series game, if you look up *scapegoat* in the dictionary, chances are you will see a picture of Buckner.

There are those who defend Billy Buck, and rightfully so. Despite a .289 lifetime average over a stellar 22-year career, this error defines his baseball existence. The game was already tied after Boston relievers blew a two-run, two-out lead, but as the Curse of the Bambino clouds loomed on that fall night in Queens, it was the one-time All-Star who let the Sox's Series hopes literally slip right between his legs. And fans and the media talked it up for the next two decades.

On April 8, 2008, with a little help from two titles in four years, we finally forgave Buckner for his sins and welcomed him back with open arms as he threw out the first pitch to fellow '86er Dwight Evans before a sold-out crowd at Fenway Park. (Meanwhile, the Mets continue to milk the Game 6 collapse some 25 years later and counting.)

Despite the standing ovation, Buckner's eyes welling up, and the 2007 banner being unveiled, we honestly couldn't help but remember one of the best jokes ever written about this once-tragic figure and the biggest miscue in Boston sports history, which includes the Tim Duncan NBA Lottery fiasco of 1997. Did you hear Bill Buckner tried to commit suicide after the World Series? He stepped in front of a bus, but it went between his legs.

Anyway, these days Buckner, when not saving babies on *Curb Your Enthusiasm*, and Mookie Wilson have teamed up and become a collector's wet dream by autographing everything from bats to balls and 8 x 10s commemorating the biggest blunder in MLB history not called Jose Canseco. If fans can come away with any sort of solace in the face of defeat, it's that although they blew a chance to win the title and deliver a championship to Yawkey Way in 1986, the Bombers crapped the bed throughout the '80s and early '90s.

THREE YEARS LATER... AN EPIC '07

In 2004 seasoned veterans like Curt Schilling, Manny Ramirez, and Johnny Damon helped put the kibosh on the so-called "Curse of the Bambino" to lead the Sox to their first World Series championship since 1918. In 2007, however, it was a crop of rookies who stalled Yankees fans from milking another significant drought by giving Boston their second title in just three years. More on them later...

After a surprisingly lackluster 2006 campaign in which the team missed the postseason for the first time since 2002 and placed third in the AL East, GM Theo Epstein was a man on a mission that winter. With scrappy longtime favorite Trot Nixon departing for Drew Carey country (that's Cleveland, people), Epstein picked up slugger J.D. Drew after he opted out of his Dodgers contract. In a move that had some people shaking their heads, the Sox signed the oft-injured star to a five-year, $70 million deal.

Drew came up big in some spots (you'll read about what you already know later in this section), but failed to play to the back of his baseball card. As a matter of fact, many of Epstein's off-season acquisitions were perceived big splashes at the time but ended up being a few jumps in the pool short of a belly flop. Signing shortstop Julio Lugo (taking over for Alex Gonzalez, who fled to the Reds) to a four-year deal proved to be a bit of a misstep since Lugo barely hit his fighting weight. (A late season deal for former closer aficionado Eric Gagne also misfired, but that's all we'll say about that Canuck.)

To take the pool metaphor further, the biggest splash Epstein made during the off-season wasn't exactly a cannonball, either. His Sox beat out the rival Yanks and their Monopoly money for exclusive rights to negotiate with Japanese ace Daisuke Matsuzaka. Ultimately, the BoSox signed the pitcher to a six-year contract worth $52 million. Yes, Dice-K hasn't lived up to his hype, but he did have some key wins in 2007. Dice-K, Lugo, and Drew had their moments, but let's get to those rookies who somewhat defined the season. Dustin Pedroia was named the team's starting second baseman after one-hit wonder Mark Loretta left for the Astros, and after a dreadful April, skeptics started wondering if letting Loretta walk was the right move. Then May happened. From there, Pedroia put on a "laser show" and ended up with a .317 batting average, eight homers, and 50 RBIs. He was named the American League's Rookie of the Year, and hit a ton in the postseason. We'll get to that in a few…

Pedroia wasn't the only rookie to glisten in 2007. Center fielder Jacoby Ellsbury made his debut in late June and made everyone forget all about Coco Crisp, who almost made everyone forget all about Johnny Damon. In just 33 games, the speedy outfielder hit .353 with 41 hits and nine stolen bases. He also showed some pop, and that stellar play led to big at-bats in the postseason.

Rounding out the trio of star rookies was Clay Buchholz, a hard thrower who made his debut at 23 on a hot August afternoon in Boston. The starting pitcher did a decent job in his first outing (striking out five in six innings and giving up three earned runs), but it was his second start that will forever live in Sox Nation infamy. On September 1, the Lumberton, Texas, native mowed down nine Orioles, and became just the second rookie in MLB history to hurl a no-hitter. He may have been left off the postseason roster, but he pitched four winning games with the team and sported a 3–1 record with a 1.59 ERA and created a magical moment in what became a magical season.

Okay, let's get to all that magic…

RED SOX

TOP 10 GAMES AT FENWAY

1. **October 21, 1975:** The first postseason night game in Fenway history was epic, ending in historic fashion. Carlton Fisk homered off Pat Darcy in the 12th inning to lead the Sox to a Game 6 victory in the World Series against the Big Red Machine.
2. **September 11, 1918:** The Sox win the 1918 World Series with a 2–1 victory over the Cubs. They wouldn't win the big show again until...oh forget it, why bring that up?
3. **October 17, 2004:** Down to their last inning in the 2004 ALCS, the Sox came back against the usually reliable Mariano Rivera. Pinch runner Dave Roberts stole second and scored the tying run on a single by Bill Mueller. David Ortiz would set the stage for a Sox comeback and Yankees choke by hitting a walk-off homer in extra innings.
4. **October 1, 1967:** The "Impossible Dream" Red Sox clinched the AL pennant on the last day of the season with a 5–3 win over the Twins.
5. **June 21, 1916:** Rube Foster throws the first Sox no-hitter over—you guessed it—the New York Yankees.
6. **October 21, 2007:** For the first time, the Sox clinch the ALCS at home, winning their 12th AL pennant with an 11–2 victory over the Indians. They'd go on to win their second Series in four years.
7. **April 29, 1986:** Roger Clemens, back when we liked him, struck out a record 20 batters in a 3–1 win over the Mariners.

continued

8. **October 16, 1999:** In Game 3 of the ALCS, Pedro Martinez shuts down the Yankees opposite Clemens with 12 strikeouts in seven innings. Take that, Zim!

9. **September 1, 2007:** Clay Buchholz becomes the first Sox rookie to throw a no-hitter against the lousy Baltimore Orioles.

10. **September 30, 1967:** Setting up the "Impossible" run, Carl Yastrzemski smacks his 44th home run as the Sox defeat the Twins to tie them for the lead in a four-team pennant race.

Fans must've known the 2007 campaign was going to be one to remember right from the start. On April 22, the Sox hit four consecutive homers for the first time in their history (Ramirez, Drew, Lowell, and Varitek) to chase the Yanks. The winning ways continued all season long.

The rookie triple-threat was matched with outstanding seasons by 20-game-winner Josh Beckett, an unswerving bullpen led by kilted closer Jonathan Papelbon, the power bats of standby slugger David Ortiz and a resurgent Mike Lowell, and a breakthrough year from Kevin Youkilis (Manny had a relatively good year, too). They all helped the Sox stay on top or close to it all season long. Eventually, the Sox would hold off "Judas" Damon and the Bombers and finish with a first-place record of 96–66. It was the first time in a dozen years the Sox placed atop the AL East.

When it came time for the playoffs, the Sox seemed to be the team to beat, but of course, as is their nature, they didn't make anything a cake walk. Like 2004 all over again, the Sox steamrolled through the first round of the playoffs only to hit a snag in Round 2. But, first things first…in the ALDS, the Sox dominated with impeccable pitching performances and timely hitting. Josh Beckett, a proven postseason juggernaut (just ask the Yankees, or Cubs, about 2003), continued his dominant ways by silencing Halo bats in Game 1 with a complete-game shutout. It was more of the same in Game 2 with the Sox bats coming to life and winning via a Manny Ramirez walk-off, three-run homer. Game 3 saw Curt Schilling, who had struggled to stay healthy and consistent all season long, turn back the clock without the use of a bloody sock, and shut the Angels down to propel the team to the ALCS.

After Game 1 of the ALCS, it seemed like the Sox would steam-roll by the Cleveland Indians, who had dominated the Yanks in the ALDS, 3–1. Josh Beckett once again pitched like, well, Josh Beckett with a six-inning, seven-strikeout effort. Just as pitching dominated Game 1 in the Sox's favor, it dominated Game 2, but for the Tribe. Game 2 was supposed to be a pitching duel, but like Clemens vs. Gooden 21 years prior, the battle between aces—in this case Schilling vs. Fausto Carmona—proved to be a slugfest. In the end, the Sox bullpen fell apart, and the team fell 13–6. With Dice-K on the mound (and pretty lackluster at that), the Sox stayed in it through Game 3, but ended up on the short-end of the stick despite a two-run jack from Jason Varitek in the seventh.

With their red-and-navy backs against the wall—right where they like it—the Sox were forced into a must-win situation for Game 5. In a 3–1 hole after a 7–3 Game 4 loss, Beckett (aka "Mr. Reliable") took the mound and rose to the occasion and then some. He struck out 11 over eight dominant innings, the

Sox won 7–1 (powered by Ramirez—although he stopped at first base at one point, thinking his ball went over the fence, but that's Manny), and the team was back in business.

The Sox played the next two games, but the Indians didn't. Games 6 and 7 were drubbings, and faster than the midges flung to Joba the Gut, the Sox were back in the Series. Game 6 was a 12–2 win powered by a J.D. Drew grand slam in the first inning and another solid outing from Schill. Game 7 was a rematch between Jake Westbrook and Dice-K, but the results were very different this time. The Sox sent the Indians home unhappy with a 13–2 laugher, highlighted by Pedroia and Youkilis bombs and a six-run eighth inning. The game was at one point close, but Indians third-base coach (and former Yankees backup backstop) Joel Skinner held up speedy veteran Kenny Lofton from scoring on a hit, and Casey Blake ended up killing any rally by hitting into a double play.

The World Series, against the NL-champion Colorado Rockies, played just like the last three games of the ALCS, and similar to 2004, it seemed pretty much in the bag for Boston. At Fenway, the Red Sox cruised to a blowout win in Game 1 behind ALCS MVP Josh Beckett, who struck out nine batters and earned his fourth win of the postseason. Offensively, Pedroia led off the game with a homer over the Green Monster, and two more runs scored later. The Sox scored seven in the fifth and ended up scoring 13 runs—the most ever for a Series Game 1. It was a different story in Game 2 with Schilling on the mound. Runs were hard to come by for both teams, but the veteran pitched into the sixth, and the combo of Okajima and Papelbon shut the Rox down, albeit narrowly with a 2–1 win.

Dustin Pedroia is about to connect on a home run in the first inning of Game 1 of the 2007 World Series vs. the Colorado Rockies. The Sox would go on to their second Series sweep and world title in three years. Photo courtesy of Getty Images

For Game 3, the Sox tapped the Rockies. Actually, they slapped the Rockies. From the get-go, the Sox gave Dice-K enough of a lead to protect with six runs in the third inning, knocking out perennial average pitcher Josh "the Dragon Slayer" Fogg. (Dice-K even had a pair of RBIs.) While the Rockies mounted a comeback—highlighted by a Matt Holliday smash, the Sox fought right back thanks notably to the theatrics of Pedroia and Ellsbury in the eighth. The team went on to win 10–5 and set the stage for their second World Series sweep in three years.

That's exactly what happened in Game 4 with Jon Lester on the mound in place of an ailing Tim Wakefield. Lester pitched well through six, and eventual Series MVP Lowell scored two runs while rally igniter Ellsbury did his part again. The Sox narrowly edged the Rox 4–3 for the win thanks to a Bobby Kielty home run (yes, we said Bobby "Fuckin'" Kielty), and Papelbon saved the game. Following the victory, Papelbon danced with a kilt on—becoming the first man since "Rowdy" Roddy Piper to pull one off.

2
WE LOVE RED SOX
PLAYERS AND LEGENDS

If a player hits, you're going to like him. If a player pitches well, you're going to like him. If a player makes fine plays, you're going to like him. If a player puts together a career worthy of Cooperstown, it's a no-brainer. But players don't have to be the best ever to become fan favorites. Just ask guys like Scott Podsednik, Edgar Renteria, Endy Chavez, or Dan Gladden.

Forget the Yankees dynasties of yesteryear, some of the best players to ever play the game did so in Boston. But that's not all who have called Fenway their home park. There are players who had a swagger to them whom we admired. They represented us on the field by wearing their hearts on their sleeves and feeding off the energy of the most passionate fans in any sport. In Boston, all you have to do is play hard, love the game (and the city you're playing for), and perform every now and then or, well, every time.

It doesn't matter if they were here for over a decade like Yaz or just a handful of seasons like impact "idiot" Millar, they were and are an integral part of our history. From little big guys like Johnny Pesky to the finest hitter of all-time, Ted Williams, there are so many players we fondly remember. Some might not be enshrined anywhere or have their numbers retired alongside Yawkey Way, but for us, they're just as monumental as the best and brightest bulbs to ever shine in Boston.

LEFT FIELDERS

Playing in the shadow of the Green Monster can be a daunting task for any left fielder. Since Duffy Lewis mastered the spot, three Hall of Famers, a tainted RBI machine, and an under-rated steady performer have turned left field into the glamour position of the Boston Red Sox. Carl Crawford has 142 million reasons to thank the Splendid Splinter, Yaz, Jim Rice, Mike Greenwell, and Manny. The Hall of Fame trio of Williams, Yastrzemski, and Rice combined for four MVPs and 39 All-Star Game appearances. Greenwell would've had an MVP if not for finishing second to the juiced-up Jose Canseco, but the 1988 slight pales in comparison to the four second-place finishes by Teddy Ballgame. In 1941 the voters determined that Joe D's hit streak and first-place finish by the Yankees should trump Williams and his .406 average for the MVP. But modern-day fans can only wonder what was in the water of the 1942 voters' cups as they selected Yankees second baseman Joe Gordon over Triple Crown–winner Williams. The Kid would go on to lose again to Joe D (in 1947, another Triple Crown year for Williams) and his replacement in center field, Mickey Mantle (1957, when Teddy hit .388). MVP awards aside, the left-field position has thrilled Red Sox Nation for the entirety of Fenway Park's existence. The Yankees lineup might revolve around center field, but we are sure you'll agree that the Red Sox left fielders can hold their own with any franchise at any position.

Duffy Lewis

Part of a million-dollar outfield that included Tris Speaker and Harry Hooper, Duffy Lewis played eight seasons in Boston, two with the Yankees, and one in Washington. Thanks, but we'll talk about the first eight. Lewis was a very productive hitter, but his fielding is the stuff of legend. As we know, there was a 10-foot-high mound and incline in front of the left-field wall from 1912 to 1933, and no one mastered it better than Lewis. Fittingly, the area that no longer exists (although some of it still did as late as 2004) is still referred to as "Duffy's Cliff."

Ted Williams

> *One of my best friends on earth and the greatest hitter I ever faced. And I faced a lot of guys, including Lou Gehrig. He was a great American.*
>
> —Bob Feller

If you remember Ted Williams as the lousy first manager of the Texas Rangers or as a punchline to any number of cryogenics jokes, you've come to the wrong book. Simply stated, Ted Williams was the greatest hitter of all-time, and it would be difficult to find any Red Sox or baseball fan to disagree. Simon and Garfunkel wrote no songs about "Teddy Ballgame," but his swing was a symphony of success. The man known as the "Splendid Splinter" was an outdoorsman, a military hero, and a brilliant, albeit surly, superstar of the diamond.

After purchasing his contract from the Pacific Coast League's San Diego Padres, the Red Sox did all they could to make Fenway Park as cozy as possible for the budding teen star. Boston

Ted Williams, seen here in 1941 when he batted .406, was probably the greatest hitter in baseball history. He finished his 19-year career with a .344 lifetime batting average, 521 home runs, 1,839 RBIs, 2,021 walks, a .482 on-base percentage, and a .634 slugging percentage.

A man has to have goals—for a day, for a lifetime—and that was mine, to have people say, "There goes Ted Williams, the greatest hitter who ever lived."

—Ted Williams, *My Turn at Bat*

If he'd just tip the cap once, he could be elected mayor of Boston in five minutes.

—Eddie Collins

RED SOX

even went so far as to create a bullpen area, soon to be known as "Williamsburg," in right field.

When Williams began his career with the Red Sox, it would be as a young man with dreams of becoming the greatest hitter of all-time. On his first Sunday at Fenway in 1939 the Kid went 4-for-5 on the day, including a home run. He was well on his way. By the time he reached his last at-bat in 1960 (a home run at Fenway), his star was on its way to mythic horizons.

In his third season (1941), Williams was matching Joe DiMaggio for the rights to the greatest hitting season of all-time (all this despite being late for spring training because he was hunting wolves). Joe D won the MVP in the season of his 56-game hitting streak, but Williams would become the last batter to hit .400 in either league. Slightly below the mark for the first time since July 25 at .3996, Williams refused to sit out the end-of-the-season doubleheader. He simply went 6-for-8 to raise his average to .406. The second game was called on account of darkness, so there is no telling if the Splinter could've taken the average even higher. For an encore in 1942, Williams would "slump" to batting .356, while winning his first of two American League Triple Crowns. Once again an MVP bridesmaid in '42, Thumper would miss the next three seasons admirably serving his country in World War II.

Despite his heroics on and off the field, Williams was not well liked by fellow ballplayers, the media, and even Red Sox fans. Jack Miley of the *New York Post* wrote, "When it comes to arrogant, ungrateful athletes, this one leads the league." Fellow Hall of Famer Al Simmons made a point to stop Williams on the baseline, as a coach in 1941, to point out he wouldn't hit .400. He alienated writers and confused Sox fans with his spits and spats. Worst of all, he refused to tip his cap to Red Sox Nation for the majority of his career. Thumper returned from the service and won his first of two overdue MVP trophies in 1946. This season would end in a disappointing seven-game World Series loss in which he would bat .200 against the St. Louis Cardinals. The 1948 and 1949 seasons would end disappointingly for Williams and the Sox as Boston finished second on the final day of each season. Lou Boudreau's Indians orchestrated the '48 downer. The Hall of Famer Boudreau would go on to manage Williams, but not before he instituted the "Williams Shift." Many baseball fans see this move to this day when three infielders are moved to the right side of the infield against a lefty. It was commonly believed that Teddy Ballgame could've batted .600 if he weren't so stubborn and decided to punch hits to the vacant left side of the field.

Despite winning six batting titles (one at the age of 38 while batting .388), Williams' legacy is one of unfinished business. In missing time due to injury and fighting in two wars, it's not inconceivable that Williams could have made a run at Babe

Ruth's 714 home runs. He played long enough to hit home runs off of a father-son combo (Don and Thornton Lee) and totaled 521 home runs to go with 525 doubles. The Kid did not reach 3,000 hits, but he is one of four major leaguers to reach 2,000 walks. With his legendary eyesight, he led the team in walks seven times (the last coming in 1954 when he played in only 117 games).

Williams' No. 9 uniform was the first to be retired by the Red Sox, but prior to that ceremony, he would leave Sox fans with one last flash of greatness. As the 1960 season came to an end, 10,454 fans, including author John Updike, came to Fenway Park for a last chance to see the Splendid Splinter. In his last at-bat, Williams did not disappoint. In his wonderful essay, "Hub Fans Bid Kid Adieu" in the *New Yorker*, Updike described the blast best, "It was in the books while it was still in the sky." While fans, teammates, and umpires urged him back on the field, Williams once again refused, as Updike wrote, "He never had and did not now. Gods do not answer letters." At this moment, with Williams deceased for nearly a

Ted [Williams] was the greatest hitter of our era. He won six batting titles and served his country for five years, so he would have won more. He loved talking about hitting, and he was a great student of hitting and pitchers.

—Stan Musial

Ted Williams is the classic ballplayer of the game on a hot August weekday, before a small crowd, when the only thing at stake is the tissue-thin difference between a thing done well and a thing done ill.

—John Updike

RED SOX

decade, he's truly transcended from man to mythology where he now rests *frozen in time*, revered in the hearts and minds of Red Sox Nation.

Carl Yastrzemski

Imagine what it must've been like for Conan O'Brien to replace David Letterman, and for Jay Fiedler to take over for Dan Marino, and multiply it by infinity. That's probably how it felt for Carl Yastrzemski to supplant Ted Williams in left field for the Red Sox after the beloved future Hall of Famer called it a career in 1960. With the largest feet to fill, the man who would eventually be dubbed "Captain Carl" not only rose to the challenge, he made it look easy. Yes, long before Jarrod Saltalamacchia tested the patience of announcers and fans with pronouncing his surname, there was "Yaz," and we don't mean the British duo that scored hit singles with their synthesizer sounds in the 1980s. Arguably the best player to ever wear a Red Sox uniform (and its most consistent) not dubbed the "Splendid Splinter," Yastrzemski met the challenges of replacing an icon and forged a Hall of Fame career himself. It seemed long before joining the Sox, Yaz was destined for greatness. At Bridgehampton High School, the New York native excelled in basketball, football, and baseball, and eventually scored a basketball and baseball scholarship from Notre Dame. Based on his play for the Fighting Irish, he signed an amateur free agent contract with the Sox. After spending two years tearing up the minor leagues, Yastrzemski arrived in Boston in 1961 and stayed there for a whopping 23 years. Throughout his entire career, the workhorse was an offensive and defensive dynamo. He also was a passionate man. (Who can forget a 1976 argument with an ump where he covered home plate with dirt in protest?) In the field, he

*Carl Yastrzemski takes a swing during the 1967 World Series against the
St. Louis Cardinals. He won the AL MVP award that year and hit .400 with three
homers and five RBIs during the seven-game Series.* Photo courtesy of Getty Images

flawlessly patrolled the Green Monster, and at the plate, he
was a hit machine, becoming batting champ in just his third
year. He may not have always hit for power, but one thing was
for sure, he always seemed to hit. While we could go on and
on about his accolades, and we will, one magical season arguably defines how much Yaz has meant to the Red Sox. During
the Sox's 1967 "Impossible Dream" campaign, in which they
won the pennant on the last day of the season, No. 8 feasted

on American League pitching like Sloth on a Baby Ruth. With 44 home runs and 121 runs batted in, Yastrzemski earned the American League Most Valuable Player Award. More hardware would follow Yaz throughout his career. The 18-time All-Star received seven Gold Glove awards and was the 1970 MLB All-Star Game MVP. (In the 1975 World Series, he batted .310 and hit over .400 in that year's ALCS.) But Yaz was more than heavy metal.

The first-ballot Hall of Famer stands as the all-time American League leader in games played with 3,308 and the only AL player to have more than 3,000 hits (3,419) and 400 dingers (452). Sorry, New York fans, contrary to your city's media, Derek Jeter isn't the only man to get 3,000 hits. Despite keeping a low profile since retiring in 1983, Yastrzemski has remained close to the organization. Watching his two final games sums up how much Yaz meant to us, and what we meant to him. On his second-to-last game, he took a victory lap around Fenway, shaking hands and high-fiving adoring fans. On his final day, he took off his jersey and gave it to a young fan. Yes, you'd be hard pressed to find a better left fielder who hit, fielded, and felt as well as Yaz.

Jim Rice

Rudy Ray Moore and Richard Roundtree. Dave Parker and Jim Rice. Each combo spent the better part of the 1970s smacking their opponents around. The former appeared on the silver screen as Dolemite and Shaft, respectively, while the latter appeared on the diamond as the Silver Sluggers known as the Cobra and Jim Ed. While Parker produced a World Series championship with Pops and the Family, Rice would suffer two seven-game disappointments (the first injured and

MOST 30-HOMER SEASONS
IN RED SOX HISTORY

Ted Williams	8
David Ortiz	6
Manny Ramirez	6
Jimmie Foxx	5
Jim Rice	4
Mo Vaughn	4

the second in stunned disbelief). However, it was Jim Rice who got the last laugh as he was elected into the National Baseball Hall of Fame in 2009. Jim Rice is one of four Hall of Famers who didn't get into Cooperstown until their last year on the ballot, but most people will tell you it's because the steroid era made his numbers look pedestrian. For a three-year span (1977–1979) Rice was the most fearless and feared hitter in the junior circuit. In his MVP season of 1978 he recorded 406 total bases and became the first and only AL batter to do so since Joe DiMaggio in 1937. During that bittersweet 99-win

SOX CAREER GRAND SLAMS

Ted Williams	17
Rico Petrocelli	9
David Ortiz	9
Bobby Doerr	8
Trot Nixon	8
Jim Rice	8

RED SOX CAREER HOME RUNS AT FENWAY

Ted Williams	248
Carl Yastrzemski	237
Jim Rice	208
Dwight Evans	199
David Ortiz	150
Bobby Doerr	145
Manny Ramirez	136
Rico Petrocelli	134
Jimmie Foxx	126
Mo Vaughn	118

season, 30 of his 46 tots either tied the game or gave the Sox the lead. He would lead the league in total bases four times in his career, and he is the only player in history with three straight 35-homer, 200-hit seasons. If that isn't enough Hall of Fame material, consider he was also the only major leaguer to outright lead the league in homers, RBIs, and triples. As a matter of fact, in 1977 and '78, Rice combined for 30 of his career total 79 triples. In the midst of his career, Red Sox fans voted him onto the all-time Red Sox second-team in 1982. Upon his retirement, Boston inducted Rice into their Hall in 1995 and formally retired his number in 2009.

Mike Greenwell

Try playing the same position as three consecutive Hall of Famers; it's enough to make a .303, 12-year career seem unspectacular. With a rich history of brilliant left fielders playing in front of the green monster at Fenway, it's easy to see why Mike Greenwell often gets lost in Red Sox history.

Greenwell's career spanned 1985 to 1996, and in that time, he saw service as a 23-year-old pinch-hitter in the 1986 World Series and started in left field in the 1988 and 1990 ALCS and 1996 ALDS. Unfortunately for Greenwell, the Sox, and Sox Nation, all four series ended in losses. Gator played well enough to make two All-Star performances, and he was a non-steroid user in a time when 'roids were beginning to be all the rage. In 2005 Greenwell explained he had a problem with his second-place finish in the 1988 MVP ballot to admitted steroid user Jose Canseco. Greenwell will have to settle for his well-earned Silver Slugger from that career year (.325, 22 homers, 119 RBIs). Throughout his career, spent entirely with the Red Sox and totaling in 1,400 hits, Greenwell was a portrait of reliability. Whether playing at Fenway (.312) or away (.294), in the day (.316) or at night (.296), against lefties (.293) or righties (.307), his numbers were rock solid. While Greenwell missed out on the recent renaissance of Red Sox fortune, his career should not be forgotten but appreciated as the Red Sox World Series count rises.

Manny Ramirez

When it came to RBIs and ADD, Manny Ramirez led the league. The lovable and often clueless baseball star is quite easily one of the best players to ever don a Sox uniform. When the "Man-Ram" stepped up to the plate, you got the impression that the opposing pitcher could throw anything, ranging from pocket lint to a cinderblock, and he would find a way to drive it into the outfield for an RBI. To think the pride of Washington Heights could've worn pinstripes had the Yankees selected him instead of pitching prospect (who ended up with no prospects) Brien Taylor No. 1 overall in the 1991 draft. The Bombers were among the dozen teams to pass on Ramirez until the Cleveland Indians stepped to the plate. After leaving the Tribe (and spurning the Yankees) in 2001, Ramirez made Boston his home and quickly feasted on American League East pitching like those midges did to Joba in 2007.

Whether it was hitting 11 postseason home runs for the Sawx, chilling in the Green Monster scoreboard during game time, leading the league in hitting (.349 in 2002) and homers (43 in 2004), or high-fiving fans after a catch, Manny was busy... being Manny.

In his seven-plus seasons with the Red Sox, the baby bull thrilled Red Sox Nation by hitting seven grand slams, earning six Silver Slugger awards, and driving in 868 runs. More importantly, he won two World Series titles with the team—earning a World Series MVP trophy in '04—and became the first outfielder ever to cut off a cutoff.

Sure, Ramirez wore out his welcome by not hustling and speaking his mind one too many times in his final days (and we won't get into his early retirement), but it's hard to argue Ramirez's stats and importance to the franchise. He trails only Hall of Famers Ted Williams (.634) and Jimmie Foxx (.605) for the Red Sox all-time slugging percentage mark with .588. Making his stats even sweeter? His performance was always enhanced against the Yankees: in two ALCSs against New York, Ramirez posted a .305 average with two homers; his lifetime Yankee Stadium line reads, .338, 18 home runs, 43 RBIs; and overall against the Bombers, he hit .346, with 36 homers, and 101 RBIs. Manny being Manny? Better than Kei Igawa being Kei Igawa.

DUSTIN PEDROIA, 2B

If you don't love Dustin Pedroia, you're either a Yankee fan,
a dumbass, or a dumbass Yankee fan.

—@SoxPinkPony (Twitter)

If you had Albert Pujols at first, Dustin Pedroia at second, Cal Ripken playing short, and Pete Rose at third, you'd have an incredible infield. If you added Thurman Munson or Johnny Bench behind the plate, you'd be pretty set at catcher. Add Willie Mays and Frank Robinson to the outfield, and the team would be deadly (even if you added Shane Spencer as the third outfielder). What does Pedroia have in common with the rest of the star-studded gallery? The answer is simple. Each major leaguer won the Rookie of the Year, MVP, a Gold Glove, and a World Series. What makes Pedroia's achievement incredible is that it took him just over two seasons to accomplish the feat. In his short career so far, Destroy-ah has won over Red Sox Nation by becoming the fifth player in club history to have 50 career home runs and 50 career steals by his fifth season. The *D* in Dustin has stood for doubles and defense, as well. Up until Pedey came to Boston, the only laser show worth seeing was probably some Pink Floyd light performance. In 2008 Dustin hit the third most doubles (54) in franchise history, and his 98 games without an error is a franchise record for second basemen. While he has yet to have a successful ALDS, Pedroia has hit .345 in two ALCS rounds. In his World Series–winning rookie season, he tied Derek Jeter's rookie record for most runs in a postseason (12). At 5'9", Terry Francona memorably placed Pedroia in the cleanup role during his MVP season of 2008. "The Muddy Chicken" proceeded to bat .667 with two homers and seven RBIs in five games in that gig.

RED SOX

TOPPS ALL-STAR ROOKIE TEAM

1959   Pumpsie Green (2B), first African American to play for Sox, 40 hits with 10 for extra bases

1961   Don Schwall (RHP), 15-game winner as a "rook," 15-game loser in second and final season with Sox

1964   Tony Conigliaro (OF), 24 of 162 injury-shortened career Red Sox homers hit in rookie season

1965   Rico Petrocelli (SS), modest .232 average with 13 HRs for future All-Star

1966   George Scott (1B), 27 HRs and 90 RBIs to go with league-leading 152 strikeouts and 25 double plays

1967   Reggie Smith (OF), Rookie of the Year runner-up with 15 HRs and 16 SBs

1969   Mike Nagy (RHP), 12–2 with seven CGs in 28 starts

1970   Billy Conigliaro (OF), .271 with 18 home runs

1971   Doug Griffin (2B), 118 hits and Gold Glove in season 2

1972   Carlton Fisk (C), the original "Pudge," and most likely the only Pudge to enter the Hall of Fame legally

1975   Fred Lynn (OF), greatest rookie season ever! MVP and ROY! .331, 47 doubles, 105 RBIs, 103 runs

1975   Jim Rice (OF), ROY runner-up to Lynn, third in MVP vote, Hall of Famer

1980   Glenn Hoffman (3B/SS), .285 rookie season and four seasons as Sox starter before becoming known as Trevor's older brother

1984   Jackie Gutierrez (SS), 118 unmemorable hits

continued

1987 Ellis Burks (OF), 20 HRs, 27 SBs

1987 Mike Greenwell (OF) .328 average with 56 extra base hits

1997 Scott Hatteberg (C), .277 with 10 home runs

1997 Nomar Garciaparra (SS), Rookie of the Year, Led AL with 209 hits and 30 game hitting streak

1999 Brian Daubach (1B), 21 home runs and 73 RBIs

2007 Dustin Pedroia (2B), ROY and World Series champ, '08 MVP follow-up

2007 Hideki Okajima (LHP), five saves and 2.22 ERA in middle relief

2011 Josh Reddick (OF), .280 with seven home runs

While the Red Sox came up short in the ALCS to the upstart Rays that season, Pedroia was well on his way to being first in the hearts of many Red Sox fans. Not bad for a team that started the decade with Jose Offerman at second.

FRANK MALZONE, 3B

Let's be clear: he was great in Boston, but we remember Wade Boggs as a horse-riding "chicken man" in the Bronx. Speaking of steeds, Frank Malzone wasn't a one-trick pony. Frank Malzone didn't become a Red Sox full-timer until the age of 27, but his Boston career was significant enough to warrant induction into the franchise's Hall of Fame in 1995. Starting in 1957, Malzone began an eight-year run (six All-Star seasons) as Boston's starting third basemen. He remains the only Red Sox regular born in the Bronx. The BoSox could count on Malzone for 15 HRs and 80 RBIs per season, but more importantly, he won the first three American League Gold Gloves at the hot corner before Brooks Robinson's 16-year strangle-hold on the award took place. In a career that was more Chris Sabo than Mike Schmidt, Malzone ranks ninth in hits (1,454) and 11th all-time in games played (1,359) in franchise history. Unfortunately, like many Red Sox of his era, he did not appear in a postseason game. But his lengthy stay as a player was turned into a gig as a Red Sox advisor. Not bad for a ballplayer born in the heart of Yankees territory.

JASON VARITEK, C

Leading by example—that's what a captain is all about. Sure, Jeter gets praise for doing just that, and that's well and good, but he's a Yankee, so who cares? Now, Jason Varitek, the 18th captain in Red Sox franchise history, let's talk about him. Little League World Series. Check. Florida High School State Championship. Check. College World Series Finals. Check. MLB World Series. Check. If you don't get the picture, Tek is associated with win-ning for a reason. Let's not forget he has represented the United States in the Olympics and the World Baseball Classic. Vari-tek has been the glue to the recent Red Sox golden age while catching a record four no-hitters and smashing 11 postseason home runs. On the tail end of a borderline Hall of Fame career, it is the opinion of most that a managerial career will not be far behind when Tek finally hangs up his cleats. Varitek was acquired with Derek Lowe from Seattle in 1997 in a deadline deal that most assuredly haunted the Mariners throughout the 2000s. The three-time All-Star is one of five catchers to spend at least 1,500 games behind the plate with one franchise, join-ing the Yankees' Jorge Posada and Bill Dickey, the Tigers' Bill Freehan, and the Reds' Johnny Bench. The Silver Slugger and Gold Glover owns the franchise record for most home runs by

SOX POSTSEASON HOME RUN LEADERS

David Ortiz	12
Manny Ramirez	11
Jason Varitek	11
Nomar Garciaparra	7
Kevin Youkilis	6

a catcher, as well as most postseason games and at-bats. He was the Red Sox rookie of the year in 1998 and team MVP in 2003, but he was never more valuable than when he face-mashed Alex Rodriguez in the summer of '04. This incident (along with Bill Mueller's eventual walk-off against Mariano Rivera) turned the tides of the BoSox season and attitude. While Varitek has rarely caught for knuckler Tim Wakefield, nobody in the history of the game has caught more no-hitters. Tek has guided the no-hit gems of Jon Lester, Clay Buchholz, Derek Lowe, and Hideo Nomo. In contrast, how many did Jim Leyritz catch?

PEDRO MARTINEZ, P

> *I don't believe in damn curses. Wake up the damn Bambino and have me face him. Maybe I'll drill him in the ass.*
> —Pedro Martinez

Throughout history, the world's greatest heroes have had to overcome the odds and combat the evil forces of a heinous archrival. For instance, Batman continues to keep Gotham streets safe from that pesky Joker, while He-Man protects citizens of Eternia as well as the secrets of Castle Grayskull from the evil clutches of Skeletor.

For every Godzilla flick, there is a Mothra waiting in the wings, and for every Smurf there is a Gargamel ready to smurf Smurfs up. In the case of the New York Yankees, heroes to many in the baseball world, there is only one true archrival worth noting. For the better part of the 21st century—and with all due respect to the great Chuck D.—Pedro Martinez has been public enemy No. 1 in the eyes of a Yankees Universe that has been witness to one of the greatest clutch performing pitchers of our time.

From his days as the brother of Ramon Martinez to becoming an eight-time All-Star, Pedro and greatness have gone hand in hand. From his early days as a near-perfect pitcher in the not-so-friendly confines of Montreal's Olympic Stadium, Pedro became an instant hit in the American League East when he was acquired by Boston for Tony Armas Jr. and Carl Pavano. His second season in New England alone is the stuff of legend, finishing 23–4 with a 2.07 ERA and 313 strikeouts. Of course, in typical Pedro fashion, he came back the next season even stronger when he posted the lowest American League ERA since 1978 at 1.74.

Martinez is not only a three-time Cy Young Award winner but is the fourth pitcher to reach 3,000 Ks with fewer than 1,000 walks as well as the third 3,000-strikeout pitcher to have more strikeouts than innings pitched. In fact, Pedro is the first Latin American pitcher to reach the 3,000-K plateau, in a career that includes stints with the Dodgers, Expos, Sox, Mets, and Phillies.

Although he once threatened to drill the ghost of Babe Ruth in the ass, as well as parading around with his diminutive

If the Lord were a pitcher, he would pitch like Pedro.
—**David Segui, 1999 Seattle Mariners**

sidekick, Nelson de la Rosa, during the 2004 championship run, the surefire Hall of Famer finished his storied Sox career with a 117–37 record, the highest winning percentage by a pitcher with any team in history, which of course begs the question in regards to our favorite Yankees archrival: who's your daddy now?

BILL "SPACEMAN" LEE, P

I was watching the intro to a game last week, and they showed a montage of all the Yankee/Red Sox fights. The first shot was Bill Lee going after Graig Nettles. Bill's skirmish with the Yankees in 1976 was as nasty as it gets. Bill played the game for the Red Sox the same way he plays it now. He's a gamer. I don't see Yaz or Fisk going out and playing at 64. He played a doubleheader two Sundays ago—he hit a home run and pitched 12 innings in the two games. He lives to play.

—Brett Rapkin, director of *Spaceman: A Baseball Odyssey*

While the Yankees have the Church of Yogi, the Red Sox have the galaxy-spanning thoughts of Bill "Spaceman" Lee. Bill Lee came to Boston from a solid baseball family and a successful college career with the USC Trojans. Once his time in the U.S. Army reserves was completed, his Red Sox career was sent into full orbit. The ever-quotable iconoclast spent

Bill "Spaceman" Lee stares in to get the signal from his catcher during a game against the Baltimore Orioles on June 25, 1978, at Fenway Park.

four seasons coming out of the pen and then reeled off three straight seasons of 17 wins. Teamed with Luis Tiant to form a potent front of the rotation, the eccentric lefty relied on his arsenal of pitches (fastball, curve, slider, screwball, eephus pitch, and any other piece of junk that could get a hitter out). Lee made many claims (among them that he had a super power…being left-handed) and he despised the Yankees, so he was a reliable source of entertainment to Boston writers and Red Sox Nation. A fan of Kurt Vonnegut and dadaism, Lee was no fan of the New York Yankees.

In the excellent 2006 documentary, *Spaceman: A Baseball Odyssey*, Lee is shown on his farm with a rifle, as he states, "I'd like to get a weather vane with Yankee players and shoot one every day." During his playing days he explained, "You take a team with 25 assholes, and I'll show you the pennant. I'll show you the New York Yankees." *Boston Globe* writer Dan Shaughnessy was quoted in the film, stating that Lee was "never afraid of the Yankees, even after they tore his arm off." This is supported by a 12–5 career record against the Bombers pre– and post–1976 brawl. From 1973 to pennant-winning 1975, Lee completed 51 of his 104 starts. The Spaceman didn't appear in the 1975 sweep of the Oakland A's, but he started Game 2 of the World Series against the Reds. A brilliant effort against the Big Red Machine was wasted when Dick Drago coughed up the lead and the game. No. 37 returned for Game 7, where he pitched well until he gave up a home run to Hall of Famer Tony Perez. In becoming a member of the Buffalo Head Gang with Bernie Carbo, Fergie Jenkins, and Jim Willoughby, he did not endear himself to Red Sox manager Don Zimmer (whom he referred to as a designated gerbil) or baseball commissioner Bowie Kuhn. He explained to the commish that he sprinkled pot on his pancakes. Inevitably, he was traded to the Expos for backup infielder Stan Papi in a move that seemed out of spite to most (Papi would bat .188 in 50 forgettable games for the Sox).

While Montreal lacked a chance to taunt the Yankees, Lee would be reunited with former manager Dick Williams and teamed with future Hall of Famers Gary Carter and Andre Dawson before being "blackballed" from baseball. Immortalized in song by Warren Zevon in "The Ballad of Bill Lee," Spaceman is currently a modern-day baseball barnstormer.

Never at a loss for words or a chance to talk politics or the plight of the world, Lee once ran for president of the United States. He only accepted 25¢ in campaign funds, claiming the job was a "two-bit office." In the *Spaceman* film, which details his career and recent playing trip to Cuba, Lee explains, "I'm invited to throw out the first pitch, but I won't unless I get to throw out the rest." Proving that he does not do just first pitches in his sixties, in 2010 Lee became the oldest pitcher to win a professional game at the age of 63, when he won for the Brockton Rox.

TONY CONIGLIARO, RF

Nothing in life is a guarantee—except when Red Auerbach would seal a Celtic win and light a victory cigar. Sadly, the rule applied in the case of beloved Sox slugger Tony Conigliaro. Tony C, as fans affectionately knew him, realized his impossible dream when he signed with his hometown team in September of 1962 at the age of 17. He became an instant hit when he smashed the first pitch he saw over the Green Monster and onto Lansdowne Street. In 1965, just his sophomore season with the big club, Conigliaro topped the league in home runs on his way to becoming the youngest home-run champion in American League history at 20 years old.

The sky was the limit for this bright Boston star as Sox fans were elated when, at the age of 22, Tony C became the youngest player to reach 100 home runs. Tragically, on August 18, 1967, during a home game against the Angels, Conigliaro was struck by a pitch on his left cheekbone. After leaving the field via stretcher, the slugger (not yet 23) had sustained a linear fracture of the cheekbone and a dislocated jaw, as well as

SOX SIBLINGS*

2B **Marty Barrett** (1982–1990) and 2B **Tommy Barrett** (1992)

OF **Roy Carlyle** (1925–1926) and OF **Cleo Carlyle** (1927)

OF **Tony Conigliaro** (1964–1967, 1969–1970, 1975) and OF **Billy Conigliaro** (1969–1971)

C **Rick Ferrell** (1933–1937) and RHP **Wes Ferrell** (1934–1937)

C **Alex Gaston** (1926, 1929) and RHP **Milt Gaston** (1929–1931)

C **Johnnie Heving** (1924–1925, 1928–1930) and RHP **Joe Heving** (1938–1940)

RHP **Long Tom Hughes** (1902–1903) and RHP **Ed Hughes** (1905–1906)

OF **Roy Johnson** (1932–1935) and OF **Bob Johnson** (1944–1945)

RHP **Pedro Martinez** (1998–2004) and RHP **Ramon Martinez** (1999–2000)

C **Ed Sadowski** (1960) and RHP **Bob Sadowski** (1966)

*Courtesy Red Sox Media Guide

RED SOX

severe damage to his left retina. Adding insult to injury was a nation of Red Sox fans who were left with broken hearts.

A year and a half later, in 1969, his return to the Sox was capped with a Comeback Player of the Year award, along with a career-best 36 HRs and 116 RBIs in 1970. However, while the back of his baseball card was reaching new heights, Tony C continued to deal with eyesight issues that lingered like a *Lord of the Rings* flick.

The one-time All-Star was forced to hang up the cleats for good in 1975 due to permanent damage from the horrific event. It was clear that the once-remarkable slugger's fast-rising career was sadly over forever.

The courageous and multitalented Conigliaro (he once performed his hit "Little Red Scooter" on *The Merv Griffin Show*) will remain among the most popular figures among the annals of New England sports teams. Sadly, Fenway's favorite son left us all way too soon at the age of 45, but he is remembered each year when a member of major league baseball is honored for overcoming obstacles and adversity through determination and courage, much like Tony C had to endure during his comeback. One of the most notable honorees in recent years is pitcher Jon Lester who, one year after being diagnosed with lymphoma, returned to the Sox rotation, where he remains to this day. In recognition of his hard work on the road to recovery, he was given the Tony Conigliaro Award in 2007.

Tony C's career may have been crushed, but his spirit will live forever.

OIL CAN BOYD, P

The '80s will always be remembered for being a breeding ground for outlandish personalities that exhibit behavior beyond the extreme. Morton Downey Jr. took trash television by storm, Jackée Harry gave new meaning to the term "sexy neighbor," and New Coke pitchman Max Headroom told all of us to "catch the wave." But of course none of these three charismatic characters can hold a candle to the astonishing journey of one Dennis Ray Boyd. Better known as "Oil Can" due in part to his beer guzzling days in his hometown of Mississippi, the Can was a mainstay in the Boston rotation throughout a decade that also introduced us to *Alf*, *Flashdance*, and the Cobra Kai. So, while most of us were toying with the Rubik's Cube, Boyd had a few above-average seasons during a solid

10-year run with the Red Sox. His 1985 season was among his best, when he posted personal highs in games started (35), complete games (13), and innings pitched (272$^1/_3$). During the Sox run to the World Series in 1986, Boyd won 16 games, also a career high.

Despite his decent stay in Fenway, it is his often-noted and highly publicized personality that he will be remembered for. After being left off the '86 All-Star team, Oil Can went off the deep end, earning both a suspension and a trip to the psych ward. It's safe to say that, during an era in which being a Donruss Diamond King was the be-all and end-all, the All-Star Game was actually taken seriously. Boyd was also slated to start Game 7 of the World Series, but a soggy Shea prevented him from making the start. When Sox manager John McNamara went with Bruce Hurst instead of Boyd, the outspoken Oil Can cried when he learned of the decision. Despite pit stops in Montreal and Texas, respectively, the Oil Can's career

TOP 10 FAVORITE RED SOX NICKNAMES

1. **Dennis Boyd: "Oil Can"**
2. **David Ortiz: "Big Papi"**
3. **Ted Williams: "The Splendid Splinter"**
4. **Bill Lee: "Spaceman"**
5. **Luis Tiant: "El Tiante"**
6. **Jimmie Foxx: "Beast"**
7. **Rich Garces: "El Guapo"**
8. **Carlton Fisk: "Pudge"**
9. **Carl Yastrzemski: "Yaz"**
10. **Mike Greenwell: "Gator"**

RED SOX

faded into the sunset in the summer of 1991. Two years later, Boyd made headlines when he threatened to sue the Sox for not inviting him to spring training. He never did make it back to the big leagues, but the odyssey of Oil Can Boyd's baseball adventures reached an all-time high when he announced in 2009 that he was attempting a major league comeback. Finishing with a 78–77 record, a 4.04 ERA, and a few fries short of a Happy Meal, the righty was always capable of throwing a gem. However, it was his colorful personality that will shine for many years to come.

DWIGHT EVANS, RF

I'd say my favorite player was Dwight Evans. I just loved watching him play, he was so amazing defensively and he possessed one of the strongest throwing arms I had ever seen. Most importantly, though, he's a quality human being and he played the game the right way.

—Mark Gangone, Boston Red Sox fan

Johnny Pesky says that Dwight Evans is the best Red Sox right fielder he ever saw, so that's good enough for us. The popular MLB Network show *Prime Nine* agrees, naming him the right fielder on their all-1980s squad and ranking him as one of the nine best outfield arms in baseball history. Add eight Gold Gloves, three All-Star appearances, two Silver Slugger awards, and it's easy to see why Dewey was inducted in the Red Sox Hall of Fame in 2000. His 385 career home runs ranks 10th all-time for American League right-handed hitters. His 2,505 appearances in a Red Sox uniform ranks second only to Yaz, and he played in two World Series losses (1975 and 1986), batting .300 with three home runs. Evans set the stage for

Carlton Fisk's 12th-inning 1975 World Series walk-off homer by robbing Joe Morgan near the Pesky Pole, then doubling up Ken Griffey Sr. off first in the 11th inning. Always known as a defensive specialist and the third wheel of the Rice-Lynn outfield, his career renaissance came when Ralph Houk moved him into the second spot in the lineup (up from the bottom where Don Zimmer was batting him). Evans exploded into the league-leading home-run hitter (22) in the strike-shortened season of 1981. Dewey would follow that season with three 30-plus-homer and four 100-plus-RBI seasons. While a few others have worn Evans' No. 24 since his retirement, the Fenway Faithful will most likely remember him to be the best to roam the spacious right field at the home ballpark.

DAVID ORTIZ, DH

Kirk Gibson doing his best Roy Hobbs impression, Joe Carter taking "Wild Thing" deep in a pivotal Game 6. These major league moments are the epitome of clutch performances. These are the moments that live with us forever, all while conjuring up a posthumous "how 'bout that?" from Mel Allen. MLB is never without its share of clutch performers, and when the dust finally clears in the Sox-Yanks battle royale, no star shines brighter than Boston slugger David Ortiz. Before becoming the game's greatest designated hitter, David Ortiz looked more like a flash in the pan than a diamond in the rough. Signed originally by the Seattle Mariners in 1992, Ortiz was eventually "the player to be named later" in a deal that landed him with the Minnesota Twins four years later. Ortiz showed some signs of brilliance during his stint in the Twin Cities, but it was not until he signed with the Sox in 2003 that the former David Arias was transformed into a full-

David Ortiz hits a two-run, walk-off homer in the 12ᵗʰ inning of Game 4 of the 2004 ALCS against the Yankees to win it 6–4 and propel the Sox to the greatest comeback in baseball postseason history. Photo courtesy of Getty Images

fledged "Big Papi." The Twins' recent losers of twelve straight playoff games are surely kicking themselves in the backside for giving up on the well-known Yankees killer.

In 2004 Papi played a pivotal role in leading Boston to the world championship. Making his first All-Star appearance, Ortiz would go on to hit .400 with five Tater Tots and 19 RBIs in a postseason that Sox fans had been dreaming of for decades. Ortiz became the first player in history with two walk-off homers in the same postseason. First a walk-off to win the ALDS against Jarrod Washburn and the Angels, then an encore in Game 4 of the ALCS, where he took pitcher Paul Quantrill deep for his second historic walk-off. Not done, just 16 hours after his Game 4–winning moon shot landed the previous night, it was Ortiz again who won Game 5 with a

14th-inning, walk-off single to score Johnny Damon and reignite a Fenway frenzy that had begun the night before.

In 2006 Big Papi became the Red Sox single-season home-run leader when he blasted 54 out of the park. A year later he helped the team win another pennant, leading the American League in extra-base hits. In the postseason he batted a blazing .370 with three home runs and 10 RBIs. In 1919 the Red Sox traded the Bambino to the Bronx, leading to an 86-year journey filled with plenty of heartache and disappointment. Thanks to the power of Big Papi, the curse is now an afterthought and the Red Sox are once again world champions.

A DOZEN WALK-OFF HOME RUN HITTERS*

David Ortiz—11: 9/23/03, 4/11/04, 10/8/04 (2004 ALDS), 10/17/04 (2004 ALCS), 6/2/05, 9/6/05, 6/11/06, 6/24/06, 7/31/06, 9/12/07, and 8/26/09

Jimmie Foxx—8: 5/14/38, 8/23/38, 4/25/39, 6/2/40, 6/6/40, 7/3/40, 8/16/40, and 8/4/41

Jackie Jensen—6: 4/18/54, 5/14/55, 5/30/57, 6/8/58, 9/26/59, and 8/24/61

Jim Rice—5: 5/28/78, 8/30/80, 5/21/81, 7/4/84, and 6/10/85

Vern Stephens—5: 5/5/48, 8/24/48, 8/13/49, 8/24/50, and 5/30/51

Bobby Doerr—4: 7/11/40, 5/6/42, 5/12/48, and 8/18/5

Dwight Evans—4: 5/6/78, 7/4/79, 6/28/84, and 6/23/90

Ted Williams—4: 7/8/41 (All-Star Game), 5/2/46, 5/19/47, and 7/19/58

Carl Yastrzemski—4: 9/15/61, 9/14/65, 5/9/79, and 5/27/80

Carlton Fisk—3: 10/21/75 (1975 WS), 9/27/79, and 4/17/80

Nomar Garciaparra—3: 8/11/98, 9/2/98, and 4/20/03

Sammy White—3: 6/11/52, 7/13/52. and 6/30/53

*from sonsofsamhorn.net

RED SOX

JOSH BECKETT, P

While Dan Marino and LeBron James found it hard to win titles in Miami, Josh Beckett did not have that problem as a member of the Florida Marlins. So, when the Red Sox came calling after the Marlins second post-championship fire sale, Beckett parted ways with South Beach. The 6'5" Texan built a reputation as a Yankees Killer with his career-defining 2003 World Series Game 6, MVP performance. In the regular season, Beckett is just 14–7 with a 5.36 ERA against the Bombers, however, he didn't need to face them in winning the 2007 ALCS en route to winning his second World Series. While regular-season consistency has eluded him (a modest three All-Star appearances and just one 20-win season), Beckett has been masterful in playoff situations. Comparisons to Bob Gibson and Sandy Koufax would be ridiculous when looking at regular season results, but would not be off-base when analyzing Beckett's playoff dominance as a Marlin and Red Sox. Beckett is built in the Big Texan mold, à la Pettitte and Clemens but minus the performance enhancement. In 2011, like many other hurlers, Beckett added Mariano Rivera's cutter to his repertoire. Well into a solid career, Beckett looks to add more postseason hardware to his already full trophy case.

"EL GUAPO" RICH GARCES, P

You don't have to pitch like Pedro Martinez or Cy Young to be embraced at Fenway. Rich Garces was a relatively successful relief pitcher for the Red Sox from 1996 to 2002 who never won a World Series with the team and finished with a somewhat high ERA with the team (3.78). Still, the chubby Venezuelan is—to this day—a fan favorite at Fenway. You can walk along Yawkey Way tomorrow, and chances are, you'll spot

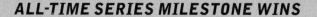

RED SOX

ALL-TIME SERIES MILESTONE WINS

The Yankees lead the all-time series 1,132–954 (including an 11–8 edge in playoffs). However, the Sox once led the series (last holding a 269–268 lead). Ted Wingfield won the 269th Sox victory over the Yankees. Listed below are other milestone victories:

250th win: Jack Quinn (6/26/23)
300th win: Wilcy Moore (4/19/32)
400th win: Tex Hughson (6/18/43)
500th win: Mel Parnell (9/19/53)
600th win: Dick Radatz (9/5/65)
700th win: Bill Lee (7/27/75)
800th win: Roger Clemens (5/28/91)
900th win: Mike Timlin (5/1/06)
954th win: Franklin Morales (9/25/11)

someone with an "El Guapo" T-shirt. The right-handed pitcher was nicknamed "El Guapo" by former teammate Greg Maddux, who gave him the namesake after watching *The Three Amigos*, which featured that—we'll say it—*legendary* cinematic villain of the same name.

"The handsome one" was a presence on the mound and became a cult classic just as that Steve Martin–Chevy Chase–Martin Short film would eventually become. The guy was simply hard not to love, as evidenced by the crowd of cheers that erupted every time he came out of the bullpen. The pitcher's best year was 1999, when he posted a 1.55 ERA and shut AL offenses down. But who are we kidding? What we remember most about Garces isn't his stats, it's Garces himself.

JON LESTER, P

Reggie Cleveland was the Red Sox Game 5 loser in the 1975 World Series against the Cincinnati Reds. While Boston's Reggie was no "Mr. October" against a Big Red Machine lineup that included three Hall of Famers and the all-time Hit King, Cleveland did enjoy much success against the Bronx Bombers during his days with the Red Sox. It's too bad the Sox sold him to the Texas Rangers just days into the ill-fated 1978 season because Reggie's 8–3 record and 3.35 ERA against the Yankees while in Boston would have been helpful. Until 2011, Cleveland was the last Red Sox pitcher to defeat the Yankees five consecutive times. Jon Lester added to his recent résumé by duplicating Cleveland's five consecutive wins against the Yankees. Lester has not only endeared himself to Red Sox Nation because of overcoming opponents on the field, but he won the deciding game of the 2007 World Series and threw a 2008 no-hitter just two years after being diagnosed with lymphoma. He was honored with the Tony Conigliaro Award and

RED SOX

TOP 10 SOX WHO WEREN'T ONLY SOX

1. Lefty Grove
2. Jimmie Foxx
3. Carlton Fisk
4. Fred Lynn
5. Luis Tiant
6. Dave Henderson
7. Curt Schilling
8. Manny Ramirez
9. Adrian Gonzalez
10. Josh Beckett

the Hutch Award for battling adversity in the early stages of his career. Lester has earned two All-Star berths while posting a career record of 76–34, including starting his career 50–18. In the past 30 years, only Dwight Gooden (50–16) and Tim Hudson (50–17) have gotten off to better starts. Lester has twice won Red Sox Pitcher of the Year (2008 and 2010). In 2010 he shared the award with Clay Buchholz. They became the first BoSox pair to share the trophy since Bill Lee and Luis Tiant in 1973. With eight career wins against the Yankees and 15 career September wins, Jon Lester (signed with an option through 2014) should be playing a major role in the Red Sox's success and Yankees rivalry for years to come.

CURT SCHILLING, P

Turkey. Stuffing. Schilling shillings. That was probably the order of business at the Schilling family dinner table on Thanksgiving in 2003 when Theo Epstein was a guest. In an off-season dominated by will they/won't they acquire Miami-bred metrosexual Alex Rodriguez for dreadlocked hometown hero Manny Ramirez, the Red Sox GM's courting of Curt during turkey day proved to be the final piece the team needed to win their first championship since 1918.

Two years removed from a World Series title, the Diamondbacks were looking to dump salary and made ace pitcher Curt Schilling available. The young dynamo Red Sox GM pounced on him faster than you can say Carlos Quintana. Spending Thanksgiving at the 2001 World Series MVP's Arizona home proved to be a stroke of genius on the part of Epstein, considering the pitcher had declared publicly he'd only accept a trade back to Philadelphia or to the dreaded Yankees.

After a few days of negotiating, Schilling waived his no-trade clause and waved good-bye to Cy Young hog/counterpart Randy Johnson, and Boston bid adieu to a wad of cash and a quartet of prospects who never would've gotten them to the Promised Land, anyway. Right from the start, the starting pitcher seemed focused on bringing a championship to long-suffering Boston. His contract featured incentives that were built around his rising to the occasion during the regular season and postseason, but also were catered to the Sox staying in the thick of it each October.

A true fan of the game, Schilling told the media before putting on his first pair of red socks that he was intrigued by the chance to make history in Boston and promised he'd try his hardest to win not just one title but a few in the city. One wonders if Schilling caught up with Biff Tannen from *Back to the Future* and read the almanac that predicted the future in that franchise's lackluster sequel.

Matched with new manager Terry Francona, whom he endorsed from years playing for him in Philly, Schilling delivered on his promises. He won 21 games for the Sox in 2004 (he lost only six), and brought some of that old Arizona magic with him in the postseason. You know how it all played out, but we'll tell you again because it never gets old. Following a mediocre Game 1 performance due to an injured ankle, Schilling sucked it up on October 19, 2004, and pitched flawlessly in a must-win Game 6 against the Yankees. With his white sock soaked in blood (captured on TV forevermore), Schilling shut the Yankees down and forced a Game 7, which the Sox handily won to complete the "Choke of the Century."

Schilling's heroics didn't stop there. Stabilizing his right ankle once again with similar bloody good results, he pitched nicely in Game 2 of the 2004 World Series and helped honor Sox players of old as he hoisted the trophy when they won. (Who can forget his declaring the team the greatest Sox of all-time, and unloading some bubbly on top of Johnny Pesky's head?)

Schill continued to, when healthy, come up big in the years to come. Memorable outings included tossing seven shutout innings in Game 3 of the 2007 ALDS against the Angels and earning the win in Game 6 of the ALCS against Cleveland to force yet another Game 7. Schilling won Game 2 of the 2007 World Series against the Colorado Rockies as the team prevailed to another title. In a sport where promises are broken (insert Johnny Damon reference here) and rarely translate on the field, Schilling is that grand exception. He came. He saw. He won. *Twice.*

NOMAR GARCIAPARRA, SS

Most remember his oddball batting stance and his quirky near-OCD routines or how it all ended in Boston, but we choose to reflect on all those hits, flashy plays, and how it all began for *No*-Mah. The Sox picked Garciaparra first in the 1994 draft, and in just over two years, he was a fixture on the team. By 1997 he was a star, slamming 30 dingers, driving in 98 runs, and hitting in 30-straight games. He followed up his Rookie of the Year season with even bigger numbers, and his stock continued to rise until chronic injuries got in the way. By 2002 new ownership wasn't feeling the love anymore, and in the off-season of 2003, they tried to trade Manny Ramirez to the Rangers for A-Rod to displace him as their shortstop. When

Nomar Garciaparra rips a base hit off of the Yankees' Roger Clemens on May 26, 2003, at Yankee Stadium to extend his hitting streak to 26 games. It would be Nomar's last full season in Boston.

the trade fell through, bridges were burned, and "Spider-Man" was traded away. That bold move, which split devotees to No. 5, proved to be the final piece the Sox would need to become champions. He left on bad terms, but there's no mistaking the six-time All-Star's importance to the franchise.

JOHNNY PESKY, IF

From the Splendid Splinter to Pudge to Big Papi, some of the finest ballplayers with equally memorable monikers have taken the field in Boston. Only one player, however, holds the distinction of being called "Mr. Red Sox," and that's Johnny Pesky. More beloved than the Ted Williams' red seat and any Frank Malzone–turned double play, the man they called "Needle" has been a beloved fixture in Beantown for eight decades. In contrast, Jose Offerman was for eight days.

Pesky joined the Red Sox in 1942, and quickly became a sure-fire tough-out who pounded out more than 200 hits in each of his first three seasons. A hero well beyond the Fenway great wall, the infielder actually left the team after the first two years to serve his country during World War II. After three years abroad, he returned to Boston and instantly put up similar numbers with similar fanfare.

While he went on to play for other teams and coached for different minor league systems, Pesky always came back to Boston. As a matter of fact, he should be called the "Beantown Boomerang" because each time he left the organization, a return was never far behind. Even when he wasn't affiliated with the team, he was often welcomed in the dugout with a smile (sorry, Dusty Baker's kid). For all his accolades with the team as a player (he was a key member of the 1946 AL champs), hitting or first-base coach (he helped lead the 1975 AL East champs), or as a color commentator on television and radio, Pesky's lasting legacy may actually be having the right-field foul pole at Fenway named after him. While power alluded him throughout his career, the "Pesky Pole" will always be synonymous with players who go yard. There are various stories behind the pole position, but most involve teammate Mel Parnell's tale of Pesky smashing a dinger in that spot and winning a game for him.

10 BEST THINGS YOU CAN GET AT FENWAY PARK THAT YOU CAN'T GET AT YANKEE STADIUM

1. Green Monster
2. Fenway Frank
3. Wooden seats
4. Manual scoreboard
5. "Sweet Caroline" played
6. Pesky Pole
7. Cubano sandwich
8. Yawkey Way bar crawl
9. Ted Williams' red seat
10. Respect

More popular in Boston than Johnny Depp is in the Magic Kingdom, the love for Pesky goes well beyond a pole. Case in point: the 2004 world champs included him in their on-field celebration after defeating the Cardinals, and he was awarded a championship ring, as well. The following season, he (along with Yaz) raised the championship banner, and he did again in 2007. In addition, his number was retired in 2008 even though, at the time, Boston only retired numbers of players who entered the Hall of Fame. With Pesky, rules were meant to be broken. If ever there was a face of the organization, it's his.

CARLTON FISK, C

The Yankees and Red Sox were sort of like Rock 'Em Sock 'Em Robots in the 1970s, and no player personified the feud more than Carlton Fisk. Whether it was rebelling against a Thurman Munson body blow in an epic bench-clearing brawl in

1973 or shoving a pre-cool Lou Piniella three years later after a play at the plate, Pudge always seemed to be in the thick of an altercation between the Pinstripes and the Olde Towne Team. He was also in the thick of a rally.

Jim Fregosi once said no one played the game as hard as Fisk did, and if you watch the videotapes (or YouTube), that statement is still easy to back up. Apologies to Lou Gehrig and Cal Ripken Jr., but Fisk may actually be the real Iron Horse of baseball history. Those guys didn't have to squat for nine innings, and for a whopping 2,226 games Pudge did just that behind the plate. That's a record broken only by Ivan Rodriguez. Altogether, Fisk played 24 years—a record for catchers that still stands—playing for both the Red and White Sox. But Fisk didn't just show up to play ball. He crushed it. The New Hampshire native, who was drafted by the Sox in 1967, became the first player to be unanimously named Rookie of the Year in 1972, and picked up a Gold Glove award that year, too. From then on, Fisk was money in the lineup and was one tough SOB. Case in point: in 1974 a knee injury at the plate threatened to cut his career short. It didn't. Fisk battled back a year later and continued his dominance.

He ended up winning three Silver Slugger awards, set a record for most dingers by a catcher (he's currently second only to Mike Piazza), and was voted to the All-Star team 11 times. He also was the first catcher in history to tag out two players— Dale Berra and Bobby Meacham—on the same play.

Easily elected to the Hall of Fame in 2000, Fisk always played the game right and was a model teammate who was ready for battle on any given night. Having said all of that, let's be

CAREER EXTRA-INNING HOME RUN LEADERS

Ted Williams	13
Jackie Jensen	8
Jim Rice	8
Carl Yastrzemski	8
Dwight Evans	7
David Ortiz	7

honest—Fisk is most remembered in Boston and arguably major league baseball history for jumping, waving his arms, and almost willing a ball he hit off Cincinnati Reds reliever Pat Darcy in Game 6 of the 1975 World Series to stay fair. As we know, it did, and the Sox, who had been down to the Big Red Machine three games to two, forced a Game 7. The homer is one of the most legendary of all-time, and even if Fisk went on to trade in his red socks for a pair of white, he'll always be a member of the Fenway faithful.

JIMMIE FOXX, 1B

Jimmie Foxx is a Hall of Famer who smashed more than 500 home runs and received the MVP award three times in his career. There's no question "the Beast" was one of the best. That said, his years in Boston somehow fly under the radar because he became a star and won two titles with the Philadelphia Athletics over a 10-year span. But look closer and you'll find some pretty spectacular numbers with "Double X" in a Sox uniform. In a Boston playing career of six-plus years, he feasted on AL pitching and likely bought a thousand rounds of gin at the local watering hole. Latter comment aside, let's look at the facts: in 1938 alone, in which he won his third MVP, Foxx slammed 50 home runs, batted .349, and knocked in 175 runs for the team. A year later, he batted .360. Before and during his career with the Sox, Foxx seemed to hit everything that came his way. No Cecil Fielder, Foxx made stellar numbers a habit throughout his entire career and truly flourished in his time in Boston.

CY YOUNG, P

Can you imagine how many Cy Young Awards Cy Young would have won if they had Cy Young Awards when Cy Young played? Setting the standard of excellence on the mound, the name Cy Young has been synonymous with great pitching since the 1800s. In honor of his achievements Major League Baseball created the Cy Young Award in 1956 to honor the year's greatest pitching performers. Sure, many consider the Joe D 56-game hit streak to be the game's most untouchable record, but it is hard to imagine that Denton True Young's record of 511 wins will ever be touched, and his 749 complete games is a dead certainty to remain the all-time mark.

With three no-hitters, including a perfect game, to go along with five 30-win and 10 20-win seasons, respectively, it's hard to argue Young's spot among the legends of the game. After a nine-year run with the Spiders of Cleveland and a two-year stop in St. Louis, Young jumped ship and joined the newly created American League, where he began his career with Boston. In his second year alone, he logged $384^2/_3$ innings. Clearly, there were no Joba rules during the Cyclone's days.

Even before Fenway Park's Green Monster was built, it was Young who stood tall and led Boston to victory against the Pittsburgh Pirates in the first modern World Series played back in 1903. Young finished with a 2–1 record and an even more impressive 1.85 ERA in the best-of-nine series, in which he started in four of the eight games played. It's only fitting that Young threw the first pitch in modern World Series history.

Some 70 years before Thurman dubbed Jackson "Mr. October," and every prepubescent kid in the tri-state area was clamoring over Reggie Bars, Young, the most prolific pitching hero, outshined them all during the game's first-ever Fall Classic.

Sadly, Young is tied for most career Red Sox victories with "the Rocket." However, although both pitchers share the lead with 192 Boston wins, you can almost guarantee that we won't ever see today's best pitchers win anything called the Roger Clemens Award.

TIM WAKEFIELD, P

Truly an unselfish player, Tim Wakefield is graciously approaching many of Boston's all-time pitching records. Already the team leader in innings pitched (3,000 and counting), the mighty knuckleballer is also closing in on most Red Sox career wins, as well as most wins at Fenway Park. Before his historic rise in Boston, Wakefield was drafted in 1988 by the Pittsburgh Pirates to play first base. However, after he was told he would never play above Double A, Wakefield made the transition to pitcher. He made an immediate impact in his first-ever start in the majors in 1992 striking out 10 St. Louis Cardinals for a complete-game victory. He went 8–1 with a

2.15 ERA during a solid rookie campaign that culminated in a National League East Pirates Pennant. The rookie righty was on his way to an NLCS MVP after throwing a complete game in Game 3 and another complete game in Game 6 on just three days rest, all until Braves scrub Francisco Cabrera singled in Sid Bream who, even though he looked as if he were running with a piano on his back, somehow beat the throw from left fielder Barry Bonds to score the winning run from second. Unfortunately for the Pirates, they have not sniffed the playoffs since. Sadly for Wakefield, he lost his spot in the starting rotation a year later and was sent up and down between the minors, becoming an obvious victim of the fabled sophomore jinx. Wakefield was released on April 20, 1995, but thanks to two former major league knuckleballers, the Pirates' loss turned out to be an enormous Red Sox win (186 Ws and counting).

Just days after his pink slip from Pittsburgh, the right-hander signed with the Red Sox, and under the watchful eye of the brothers Niekro, the inspired Wakefield went 2–1 with a 2.52 ERA for Triple A Pawtucket. With a Boston rotation in flux due to injury, Wakefield proved he belonged back with the big boys as he began the season 14–1 with a 1.65 ERA in his first 17 games. The return was capped off with an American League East title and both a third-place Cy Young finish and an American League Comeback Player of the Year award in 1995.

Always a sure thing, Wakefield was used in and out of the Boston rotation over the next few seasons, even spending a brief time as the team's closer. In the 2003 ALCS, despite winning Games 1 and 4 against Mike Mussina and the Yankees, it was the first pitch of the 11th inning of Game 7 that most fans will remember. Wakefield is such a reliable part of the Red Sox resurgence that the Nation was able to forgive him for the extra-inning meatball he tossed to Aaron "Freakin'" Boone. In 2004 Wakefield pitched Game 1 of the World Series and helped the team to an unforgettable championship run. Wakefield's historic pitching career is not slowing down anytime soon, despite his becoming the oldest Red Sox pitcher ever to win a game (at 45). Like a fine wine, he just gets better with age. Speaking of wine, in 2007 Wakefield's Caber-Knuckle helped raise more than $100,000 for charity. Three years later, he was awarded the highest honor given to players who best reflect the spirit of giving back to the community when he was chosen as the winner of the 2010 Roberto Clemente Award (we will certainly toast to that).

TRIS SPEAKER, CF
WHEN "THE GREY EAGLE" LANDED

Who names their kid Tristram? That's a good question, but you won't find the answer here. Instead, you'll read about the greatest baseball player who ever lived with that name or arguably any other one. Tris Speaker was the most complete ballplayer, consistent hitter, and fielder the Red Sox ever had. Plain and simple. As big a threat to rob you of an extra-base hit as he was to smash a double down the line or steal a base, "the Grey Eagle" soared for the Sox and eventually the Indians in a 22-year career. How good was Speaker? He hit a record 792 doubles. How good was Speaker? He stole 436 bases. How good was Speaker? He struck out just 283 times in 10,195 at-bats. How good was Speaker? He hit .296 in a down year, and compiled a career batting average just slightly higher than Ted Williams' (.3447 to Ted's .3444). Focusing on his

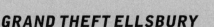

R E D   S O X

GRAND THEFT ELLSBURY

Jacoby Ellsbury hasn't played a decade yet, but he continues to amaze—especially his MVP-worthy 2011 campaign. Here are his and other Sox achievements on the base paths:

Most Steals

Career: 300—**Harry Hooper**

Season: 70—**Jacoby Ellsbury** (2009)

Game: 4—**Jacoby Ellsbury** (August 9, 2010, at New York Yankees) and **Jerry Remy** (June 14, 1980, at California Angels)

Rookie Season: 50—**Jacoby Ellsbury** (2008)

Consecutive: 20—**Julio Lugo** (2007)

Playoffs: 8—**Johnny Damon**

Red Sox Stolen Bases by **Rickey Henderson**: 8

Red Sox Stolen Bases by **Babe Ruth**: 13

Career Steals by **Jacoby Ellsbury** vs. Yankees: 25

Red Sox 30-30 Club: **Jacoby Ellsbury**—32 HRs, 39 SBs (2011)

Sox years, "Spoke" was as good as you could get. Purchased from a Texas League team for about the cost of a flat-screen TV today, Speaker battled to get in the everyday Sox lineup for a few years before breaking through in 1909. Part of the "Million-Dollar Outfield" with Duffy Lewis and Harry Hooper a year later (and through 1915), Speaker became a household name in Beantown and helped put the team in the 1910 pennant hunt. Two years later, he led them to their second World Series title. That year, he batted .383, led the league with 53 doubles, and stole 52 bases, winning his only MVP award (then called the Chalmers Award) of his career. He was in form in the 1912 Series win over the New York Giants, as well—knocking nine hits in the contest. Three years later, Speaker, along with a newbie named Babe Ruth helped the Sox got their third title in a win against the Phillies. After a falling out with the organization, Speaker was traded to the

Cleveland Indians for the 1916 season and continued to play like a bad mother—shut your mouth. He stayed in the Forest City for a total of 11 seasons, breaking more records and winning the team's first Series title in 1920 as a player/manager. What's in a name, anyway?

BOBBY DOERR, 2B

Decades before the Pedroia laser shows, it was the consistency of Bobby Doerr that sparked the potent Red Sox lineup, which included the likes of Joe Cronin, Jimmie Fox, and Dom DiMaggio. Right out of the gates, Doerr had made an impact, going 3-for-5 in his first game for Boston in 1937. Two years later, which was Ted Williams' rookie campaign, Doerr began a streak of 12 straight seasons with 10 or more home runs and 73 or more runs batted in. In fact, the always-reliable second baseman's six seasons of more than 100 RBIs at that position would not be matched for another 25 years, when Cincinnati's Joe Morgan repeated the feat. He was an offensive machine who helped lead the Sox to the World Series in 1946 and a third-place finish in MVP voting that same season. "The silent captain of the Red Sox," as he was referred to by the Splendid Splinter, batted .409 during the Fall Classic, compared to Williams' .200 and Stan Musial's .222 average. The Sox lost the Series to the Cards, but the accolades hit an all-time high when Babe Ruth said, "Doerr, and not Ted Williams, is the No. 1 player on the team. He rates the Most Valuable Player in the American League." He is the only Red Sox player to hit for the cycle twice in his career, and on June 8, 1950, he hit three home runs in a 29–4 slaughter of the St. Louis Browns (what were they hitting off, a tee?). He did it with his bat and his glove, as well. Doerr is regarded as one of the top defensive second basemen of his time. Churning out 1,507 double plays in his career and 132 in 1943 alone, his .980 fielding percentage was second only to Jackie Robinson when he retired. Doerr hung up the cleats for good at the age of 33 due to a back injury, leaving behind one of the greatest Red Sox careers of all-time. His No. 1 uniform was retired in 1988, two years after he was enshrined into Cooperstown. He was a true Red Sox in every aspect, hitting .315 with 145 home runs at Fenway, compared to his .261 and 78 home runs on the road. More importantly, Doerr was not only an offensive threat and defensive game changer, but he was an even greater teammate. He played his entire 14-year career with the Red Sox and never wore out his welcome, much like Jorge Posada has done in New York.

KEVIN YOUKILIS, 1B/3B

The best thing to happen to Boston since Sam Adams started brewing beer in 1984, Kevin Youkilis has been a main cog in the Red Sox dominance for the better part of the 21st century. Sure, he may look more suited for crushing long balls and throwing back cold ones on your local softball team, but since 2004 "Youk" has become one of major league baseball's top stars. This scrappy sock is known best for getting on base, playing hard, and of course being a constant pain in the behind of the entire Yankees Universe.

Thought to be thick and pudgy by some during his minor league days, this fan favorite made waves by going yard in his first game ever with the Sox. After a few stints between the minors and majors, Youkilis has become a fixture in the everyday operations of Red Sox Nation with several All-Star appearances under his belt as well as a Gold Glove to go along with his World Series rings. You can bet (not in the Pete Rose sense, of course) that this big righty is destined to be a card-carrying member of Cooperstown somewhere down the road. The ultimate gamer, he has often made the move to third to make room for Big Papi during interleague games, as well as for the 2011 arrival of first baseman Adrian Gonzalez. With his unmatched intensity and grittiness, Youk is one of the hardest-working SOBs in the game.

FRED LYNN, CF

For new major leaguers, it's not uncommon for broadcasters or media to mispronounce or screw up their names, just ask any Mets fans about Ralph Kiner. So, when Fred Lynn became the first player to win the AL Rookie of the Year and MVP in the same season (1975), it should have been no surprise to the Red Sox newcomer to see his name misspelled on the trophy. We agree spelling Fred Lynn wrong is pretty weak (for the record, Fredric Lynn was spelled "Frederic"). Speak and Spell hadn't been invented yet, so we'll give the engravers a pass and get to the facts. Fred Lynn was actually drafted in the third round by the New York Yankees out of El Monte High School (California) in 1970. He opted to attend and play ball for USC, where he won three NCAA baseball championships. In 1973 the Red Sox used a second-rounder on Lynn and quickly moved him through stops at Bristol and Pawtucket. After 15 games with the Sox in '74, Lynn enjoyed one of the most successful rookie seasons in the history of baseball, forming one-half of the Gold Dust Twins with fellow sensation Jim Rice. The only player to duplicate winning both awards in one season was Ichiro, and that was after nine seasons of pro ball in Japan. In his rookie

Fred Lynn, the first player ever to win MVP and Rookie of the Year honors in the same season (1975), strokes a line drive against the Yankees during a regular season game in 1976. Photo courtesy of Getty Images

campaign, Lynn led the AL with 103 runs, 47 doubles (29 at Fenway), and a .566 slugging percentage. Not only did he play a Gold Glove center field, but he helped sweep the Reggie Jackson–led, three-time defending champ Oakland A's by batting .364 in the ALCS. Lynn and the Red Sox were the underdogs to the Big Red Machine in what would become one of the greatest World Series ever played. During the series, Fenway fell silent as the eventual four-time Gold Glover slammed into the outfield wall. He would play all seven games, batting

.280 in the epic losing effort. After the season, Fenway would upgrade to padded walls, and Lynn would once again pad his BoSox legacy in 1979, leading the league in batting (.333) and hitting a career high in home runs (39). After being traded by the Red Sox in the winter of 1980, Lynn's career contained more unique achievements. He remains the only player in history to hit a grand slam in an All-Star Game. For serving up this slam, Atlee Hammaker has a place in baseball history. While the Iron Horse might be the all-time grand slam leader and A-Rod is a close second, neither can say they hit one in the All-Star Game. Freddie Lynn can. The only ALCS MVP on a losing team when the Gene Autry–owned Angels lost to the Harvey's Wallbangers (the 1982 Milwaukee Brewers). In 2002 Fred Lynn entered the Boston Red Sox Hall of Fame with a .308 lifetime Red Sox average (.348 at Fenway). His name was spelled correctly on the plaque this time.

KEVIN MILLAR, 1B/OF

Don't awaken a sleeping giant. That's the mantra Kevin Millar essentially repeated moments before the start of Game 4 of the 2004 ALCS. With the Sox down three games to nil, the scrappy and lovably quirky outfielder told the press if the team won the game, they'd essentially go on to win the rest. Boy, was he right—the team won in 12 innings that night, and well, we know how the rest turned out. A pivotal member of the 2004 world championship team, Millar is among the most beloved stars in the team's 100-plus-year history. And to think his Sox tenure may never have happened.

Following the 2002 season, the Marlins sold their star to the Chunichi Dragons of the Japanese Central League. In a rare event, the Sox blocked the deal with a waiver claim on the player. That bold move paved the way for Millar to "Cowboy Up" in Boston. With a winning mentality and personality, Millar instantly became a fan favorite in Boston. Knocking in runs and slamming home runs didn't hurt—neither did catch-phrases. In 2003 he coined the phrase "Cowboy Up" to rally his teammates, and the following year, he kept his teammates invigorated by referring to them lovingly as a merry band of "idiots."

Although he began and ended his baseball journey away from the friendly confines of Fenway Park and only played for the team for three seasons, Millar will always be a member of Red Sox Nation. Thanks to clutch hitting, hard work, and that bold prediction, Millar was just as integral a part of the recent Beantown dynasty as Pedro, Papi, and Schilling's bloody sock. He may not be the biggest, the baddest, or the fastest—or have a foul pole named in his honor—but thanks to his moves and his mouth, Boston faithful will always love their cowboy.

LUIS TIANT, P

Simply known as "El Tiante," the Cuban-born pitcher left his mark in Fenway Park, and to this day he has become one of the most beloved Red Sox in history. With his signature 'stache and cigar, Luis Tiant also had no problem in smoking the opposition. After a rough start in 1971, he bounced back with an impressive 15–6 and led Boston with a 1.91 ERA. Winning 20 games in 1973 and 22 in 1974, Tiant would win 18 games for the 1975 AL champions, despite being slowed down with back issues, and thankfully saved his best for the postseason. The popular pitcher would go on to pitch a

RED SOX

BEYOND RED SOX NATION

(RED SOX BORN IN OTHER COUNTRIES)

Victor Martinez (C), Venezuela
Tony Perez (1B), Cuba
Jose Offerman (2B), Dominican Republic
Luis Aparicio (SS), Venezuela
Mike Lowell (3B), Puerto Rico
Manny Ramirez (OF), Dominican Republic
Tony Armas (OF), Venezuela
Jason Bay (OF), Canada
David Ortiz (DH), Dominican Republic
Dave Roberts (PR), Japan
Julio Lugo (UTIL), Dominican Republic
Luis Tiant (P), Cuba
Fergie Jenkins (P), Canada
Pedro Martinez (P), Dominican Republic
Daisuke Matsuzaka (P), Japan
Ugueth Urbina (REL), Venezuela
Byung-Hyun Kim (REL), South Korea
Hideki Okajima (REL), Japan

complete-game, one-run, three-hitter against the defending champion Oakland Athletics, as well as shining bright in what many call the greatest World Series of all-time. Tiant pitched a complete-game win in Game 4, in which he threw 163 pitches, and a no-decision in Game 6. But the defining moment of his career was his five-hit shutout in the Series opener at Fenway, a game attended by his father, Luis Taint Sr., a former Negro Leagues pitcher for the New York Cubans who, along with Tiant's mother, was allowed to visit from Cuba under a special visa. Even a brief two-year rub with the Yankees—or in *Star*

Wars terms, Anakin Skywalker turning to the dark side—Luis Tiant remains beloved and admired by his adopted hometown of Boston.

MIKE LOWELL, 3B

Mike Lowell began his career as a Yankees castoff and finished as one of the most beloved Red Sox of the last 25 years. After appearing in eight games for the 1998 world champion Yankees, the third baseman was sent to the Florida Marlins in a trade that would come back to haunt New York. When the '03 Yanks faced the Marlins in the World Series, Lowell was in the midst of a career year. (In contrast, Ed Yarnall, one of the crappy prospects the Yankees got in return from the Fish, pitched in seven games with the Yanks and never had much of a career.)

While Lowell batted just .217 in the Series, it was better than the Yanks' hot-corner, one-homer wonder Aaron Boone (.143), and the Marlins took the title in six. After a few All-Star appearances, Lowell suffered his worst full season of his career with the Fish, and in November 2005 he was essentially a throw-in in the trade that would net the Red Sox noted Yankees killer Josh Beckett. Reenergized, Lowell would respond with a solid bounce-back year in '06 and an even better '07. The Puerto Rican–born star would finish in the top five in the voting for AL MVP with a .324 average and 120 RBIs (a Red Sox record at 3B), kicked ass in the playoffs, and picked up World Series MVP hardware. While there would be a few attempts to trade him in his final seasons, Lowell eventually retired as a Red Sox. The Marlins still have the young stars they received for Lowell and Beckett in Hanley Ramirez and Anibal Sanchez, but Red Sox Nation can revel in a second championship in three years thanks to Lowell's heroics. It should be noted that Lowell is linked to another popular Red Sox. In 1999 Lowell was awarded the Tony Conigliaro Award as he underwent surgery for testicular cancer.

RICO PETROCILLI, SS

Some people say that history has a tendency to repeat itself. Jason Varitek's 2004 Brawl with the Yankees' A-Rod was a motivational tool that Red Sox Nation had seen the likes of before. In 1967 at Yankee Stadium, the benches cleared when bean balls were exchanged. Even Brooklyn childhood friends Rico Petrocelli and the Yankees Joe Pepitone went at it in the all-out battle. Security pulled the opponents apart, but the event pulled the Red Sox together. They went on a 60–39 run, including a 10-game July win streak. Jim Lonborg won the Cy Young Award, Yaz won the Triple Crown, and Rico Petrocelli won back the hearts of Red Sox Nation. Petrocelli even contributed by making the catch on the last out of the regular season against the Twins on Rich Rollins' pop-up. Despite the league hardware won by Lonborg and Yaz in the pennant-winning season of '67, Rico was the inaugural winner of the BoSox Club Man of the Year for contributions to the success of the Red Sox and in community endeavors. Extremely popular in Boston, the native New Yorker wore No. 6 during a 13-year career spent entirely with the Red Sox. He had a tailor-made "Fenway Stroke" and hit 134 of his 210 home runs in New England. A rare power-hitting shortstop during his time, he produced nine career grand slams in the middle of the BoSox lineup. In 1969 he was the Red Sox MVP when he slugged a then single-season shortstop record 40 home runs (one more than Boston's own SS Vern Stephens in 1949). Petrocelli started in two All-Star Games at shortstop and played in two World Series losses for Boston. Displaying incredible unselfishness, Rico moved to third in 1971 when the Sox had the opportunity to bring in Hall of Famer Luis Aparicio. Injuries led to an early retirement at 33, but he stayed active with the organization by working as a writer for the *Boston Herald*, being an early pioneer in sports talk radio, working with the Jimmy Fund, and managing the Triple A Pawtucket Red Sox. A Red Sox lifer, Petrocelli was elected into the team's Hall of Fame in 1997.

JOHNNY DAMON, CF

Apologies to Lady Gaga but we're not in love with Judas. We loved Johnny Damon before the ultimate betrayal…when he was our Jesus. We'd love to remember the outfielder for his shaggy and fuzzy days in Beantown, but it's pretty hard, considering he went Boggs and bolted for the Bronx in 2005.

While it still stings to think of Damon as a member of those "Damn Yankees," Sox fans remember all that the player did for the city, the fans, and the team. He was an integral part of the 2004 squad that buried the "Curse of the Bambino" for good and sent the Yankees packing in the pivotal ALCS Game 7 of what would be known as "the Choke of the Century."

Damon was beloved in Boston for his scrappiness, solid play, and charismatic, low-key Joe Cool demeanor. The long-time Kansas City Royals outfielder joined the Sox in 2002 following a halfway decent run in Oakland and quickly earned Yawkey Way street cred by stealing bases, scoring runs, pounding

RED SOX

10 OTHER MEMORABLE RED SOX WHO WORE PINSTRIPES

1. Jose Canseco
2. Don Baylor
3. Roger Clemens
4. Wade Boggs
5. Jack Clark
6. Steve Farr
7. Tom Gordon
8. Frank Gilhooley
9. Babe Ruth
10. Lee Smith

out extra-base hit after hit, and providing more "True Grit" than that Hollywood actor with the same last name. No Ricky Ledee or Rich Monteleone, he performed consistently each year thereafter.

In his four-year career with the Red Sox, Damon played in 597 games, scored 461 runs, smashed 730 hits, did 487 naked pull-ups, and probably drank a lot of beer with Millar. He also earned All-Star selections twice for the American League in this span, providing what we thought would be the only time he and Derek Jeter would be in the same lineup together. Boy, were we off. Despite telling the press that he'd never play for the Yankees, and the strong bond he created with the Fenway faithful, Damon left the idiots of Boston for the suits of New York in 2005. One wonders if he really left Boston because he wanted a guaranteed fourth year or if it was just another example of a client listening too much to agent Scott Boras (aka "Bor-Ass"). Whatever the reason, Damon's departing our team for the dreaded Yankees still hurts more than any morning after a night of drinking during any of the final four 2004 ALCS games. It almost negates all of what he accomplished in his long hair and furry fury days in Boston. Almost.

THE TEAM OF FORGOTTEN SOX

Who doesn't love Ted, Pesky, or Big Papi? No one in Boston, that's for sure. Double negatives aside, the Red Sox franchise has had a bevy (isn't that a fun word to say?—*bevy*) of stars who somehow have flown under the radar over the past few seasons or decades. Some are prominent stars who simply get left off everyone's "top Sox" list because they played in a pre-NESN era, while others have been somewhat forgotten because their final days in the red and navy weren't exactly spectacular. In this segment, we'd like to celebrate the best Sox who—in our opinion—don't get as much said or written about them as they should. Let's go around the diamond, position by position, as we pay homage to the Sox we forgot.

Sammy White, C

Jason Varitek holds the MLB record for calling four no-hitters, but before he was even a twinkle in his parents' eyes, Sammy White was doing the same—catching a no-no for Mel Parnell. On July 14, 1956, the backstop called a hitless game, and throughout his entire career, he was considered a top defensive catcher who had a strong arm and made a habit of expanding the strike zone. The one-time All-Star was also a capable bat in the lineup and held the pitching staff together. In later years, he became a professional bowler, and we're betting he never pulled a Munson.

George Scott, 1B

Before David Wells wobbled his way to Beantown, there was a credible Sox player nicknamed "Boomer." An offensive and defensive threat (he has more Gold Gloves than Knoblauch, that's for sure), Scott slammed 27 home runs in his rookie year and was a two-time All-Star for the Sox. He was also known as a jokester—wearing his batting helmet on the field before John Olerud made it cool.

Pumpsie Green, 2B

"I hope someday Satchel Paige and Josh Gibson will be voted into the Hall of Fame as symbols of the great Negro players who are not here only because they weren't given the chance." With those words in his Hall of Fame induction speech on July 25, 1966, Ted Williams very likely opened the doors for the greats of the Negro Leagues to be elected to Cooperstown. While the effects of Jackie Robinson, a Hall of Famer and Negro Leagues veteran himself, had impacted every team,

MOST SEASONS WITH THE RED SOX

23 **Carl Yastrzemski** (1961–1983)
19 **Dwight Evans** (1972–1990)
19 **Ted Williams** (1939–1942, 1946–1960)
17 **Tim Wakefield** (1995–2011)
16 **Jim Rice** (1974–1989)
15 **Jason Varitek** (1997–2011)
14 **Bobby Doerr** (1937–1944, 1946–1951)
13 **Rico Petrocelli** (1963–1976)
13 **Bob Stanley** (1977–1989)
13 **Roger Clemens** (1984–1996)

the Boston Red Sox were the last to introduce an African American player to their ranks. Unfortunately, this did not transpire until William's second-to-last season, when the Sox promoted middle infielder Pumpsie Green from the minor leagues. Green occasionally batted leadoff or pinch ran while contributing 12 homers and 12 steals in four seasons with Boston. In the past decade under the new ownership of John Henry, Tom Werner, and Larry Lucchino, Boston has stressed "Five Commitments to Excellence." They have also done their part in addressing the team's earlier history of discrimination. On April 17, 2009, the 50th anniversary of his debut season, Pumpsie Green appropriately threw out the first pitch.

Rick Burleson, SS

Back in the '70s and '80s, when shortstops were known for being skinny, defensive wizards with no stick, Rick Burleson was one of the best. The fiery player known as "the Rooster" was a .273 hitter who averaged about five home runs per season in seven years (three of which were as an All-Star) with the Sox. The fifth overall pick in 1970, the intense Burleson batted .333 in 10 games of the epic 1975 postseason. He batted leadoff in 1977, and his 663 at-bats that season ranks fourth in Red Sox franchise history. In 1979 Burleson scooped up his first and only Gold Glove award and won his first of back-to-back Thomas A. Yawkey Red Sox MVP awards. By the winter of 1980, contract hassles with the Sox led to his being dealt to the California Angels in a five-player trade that brought 1981 AL batting champ Carney Lansford to Boston.

Bill Mueller, 3B

While he played mostly third base, we could slide him in at any number of positions because he could play everywhere.

Sure, he could field, but Mueller could hit the ball on a regular basis. He played for the Giants and Cubs beforehand and finished his career with the Dodgers, but to us, this switch-hitting infielder is legend in Boston even though he played just three seasons here. Known for his clutch hits throughout the 2004 regular season and postseason (who could forget his walk-off homer against Mariano Rivera following the Tek/A-Rod brawl July 24? or his RBI single to score Dave Roberts in Game 4 of the ALCS?), there would be no World Series trophy without the bat of the 2003 hitting champ.

Harry Hooper, OF

Harry Hooper is a Hall of Famer and a former captain of the Sox, but he played so long ago some of the newer Fenway faithful might need a Cliffs Notes recap of one of the best Sox players ever. As solid as a professional baseball player could be in the field, the plate, and on the base paths, Hooper did it all in Boston. Among his many accomplishments were becoming the first AL player to hit a leadoff home run in a each game of a doubleheader and holding the team record for most triples (130) and steals (300). The sparkling leadoff hitter also won four World Series rings with the team. How many Sawx players can say that? No one. Certainly not Johnny Damon.

Reggie Smith, OF

The Yankees' outfielder named Reggie had a bad attitude and terrible-tasting candy bars named after him. The Sox's Reggie, however, had everything going for him. A switch-hitter who broke out with a huge rookie campaign (15 homers, 16 steals), Smith proved to be an integral part of the 1967 pennant-winning team. A two-time All-Star with the Sox, Smith found a lot more success on other major league teams—notably the

RED SOX

SEVEN LOSSES: GOTTA GO TO MO's

With 603 regular season saves and an ironic 42 postseason saves, a 75–57 career record plus an 8–1 postseason record, Mariano Rivera is generally considered the greatest closer of all-time and a first-ballot Hall of Famer. Yet he has earned seven of his 57 career losses against the Boston Red Sox:

No. 1 (April 13, 2001). In the 10th game of the year in the bottom of the 10th, Manny Ramirez hit a ground-ball single to center on a 2–0 count off of the Great Mariano. The knock was good for two runs and a 3–2 Red Sox walk-off win.

No. 2 (April 13, 2002). The Sandman enters in the bottom of the eighth but is greeted with a blown save by giving up a home run to Shea Hillenbrand. Mo coughs up a 6–4 lead, while Ugie Urbina earns the save for the Sox.

No. 3 (July 24, 2004). A sign of '04 magic to come. Mo' ninth-inning blues for Mo. Double by Nomar, Millar single, Bill Mueller home run! 11–10 Red Sox. Rivera, blown save and a loss!

No. 4 (September 17, 2004). At Yankee Stadium, we see a rare unraveling by the stoic closer: a walk, a hit by pitch, two singles from Orlando Cabrera and Johnny Damon. Boston wins 3–2 as the ALCS rematch draws closer.

No. 5 (April 6, 2005). With the Yankees up 3–2 and Mariano facing the bottom of the order, you can usually book the save. Not on this day. Rivera loads the bases immediately. He never escapes the inning, giving up five runs on three walks, three singles, and an error. Enter Felix Rodriguez. Red Sox 7–3.

continued

> **No. 6 (April 20, 2007).** Rivera enters in the bottom of the eighth with a 6–3 lead. A single by 'Tek, triple by Coco Crisp, and single by Alex Cora, and you've got a 7–6 BoSox victory.
> **No. 7 (May 18, 2010).** Metallica blasts at the top of the ninth in a tie game, but Red Sox Jeremy Hermida does the head-banging with a two-run double for the lead. Jonathan Papelbon survives his own scare in the bottom half to preserve the 7–6 victory.

Dodgers, with whom he won a Series in 1981—but he was an invaluable member of the Sox with his power, speed, and cannon of an arm.

Jackie Jensen, OF

All-America fullback. Olympic medalist wife. New York Yankee. Sounds like a movie script, except that the Yankees part just didn't work out for Jackie Jensen. In parts of three seasons with the Bombers, Jensen hit a dismal nine home runs. He was shipped to the Washington Senators shortly into the 1952 season. After two decent seasons with the Sens, he was traded to Boston. However, his fear of flying would rear its ugly head and almost prevent him from reporting to Boston. Once he made it to Boston, Jensen jumped to the top of the AL leader boards, ranking first in triples, steals, RBIs, and sacrifice flies at various points in his seven Sox seasons. After winning the AL MVP in 1958 and a Gold Glove in 1959, the "Golden Boy" sat out the 1960 season because of his intense fear of flying. The California native returned for the 1961 season, but as baseball continued to move westward, no hypnotist could get him onto a plane. In a season's worth of appearances against the Yankees in his career (659 at-bats), Jensen belted 26 home runs and knocked in 122 runs. He was inducted into the Red Sox Hall of Fame in 2000.

Trot Nixon, OF

The 2004 Boston Red Sox were such a complete team that it's hard to single out just one player. That said, some do, anyway, and immediately think of stars like Curt Schilling, Manny Ramirez, and David Ortiz or role players like "Cowboy" Kevin Millar or even Dave Roberts as the main catalysts for the World Series win. Arguably, fans often overlook one player and his overall contribution to the franchise. With a swagger like no other and a uniform dirtier than Peanuts' Pig Pen (as if he had just stolen second at a sandlot), Trot Nixon wore his heart on his sleeve and played the game as hard as he could no matter how banged up he was. The scrappy right fielder dubbed "Dirtdog" was drafted by the Sox in the first round of the 1993 MLB Draft and broke through in 1999 with decent numbers. In the should've-been-historic 2003 season, he charged the team up with a .306 batting average and 28 homers in the regular season and dazzled in the ALDS, on his way to leading them to the ALCS. Plagued by injuries throughout the epic 2004 season, Nixon persevered throughout the regular season, playing 48 games, and stayed healthy to help ensure a World Series victory. In the World Series, he drove in three runs, including an RBI double, which gave the team an early lead that remained in the deciding Game 4 at Busch Stadium. Nixon didn't always have spectacular numbers, but he led by example and was beloved in Fenway for nearly a decade. A throwback to players of old, he always hustled, didn't take himself too seriously (check out his hair styles), and fought for his team by any means necessary. Heck, he's the only player we can remember who got tossed out of a game for arguing a call while on the disabled list sitting on the bench.

Rich Gedman, C

Rich Gedman's first at-bat with the Red Sox was pinch-hitting for Carl Yastrzemski. The following year, he replaced Carlton Fisk as catcher along with Gary Allenson. Replacing two Sox legends in under two seasons? Talk about baptism by fire and intense pressure. No matter—he was up to the challenge. After sharing catching duties for his first few years, the backstop became a two-time All-Star with the Sox, shining especially in 1984, when he slammed 24 home runs, and in 1985, when he batted .295 and hit for the cycle (with seven RBIs) in a game against the Blue Jays. Arguably, Gedman's biggest contribution in a Sox uniform came in Game 5 of the 1986 ALCS, where he smashed a two-run home run and scored on the über-memorable Dave Henderson's two-out dinger off of Donnie Moore. But Gedman wasn't known primarily as a threat in the lineup. He was a solid defender behind the plate, throwing out almost half of those who dared to steal on him, and setting an American League record for putouts in a game (20) in 1986. Injuries forced an early retirement for Gedman, but he's remembered fondly, as well he should be. In recent years, he has coached independent and minor league ball—most recently serving as hitting coach for the Sox affiliate Lowell Spinners.

Dave Henderson, OF

Hendu was a clutch-hitting outfielder who played 14 seasons in the big leagues. The one-time All-Star slugger helped his teams reach the World Series four times, reaching the Promised Land with the 1989 Oakland Athletics. His best statistical season was in 1988, when he set several career highs (.304

BEST SUPPORTING ACTOR?
FIVE FLICKS THAT FEATURE FENWAY

1. *The Town*
2. *Field of Dreams*
3. *Good Will Hunting*
4. *Moneyball*
5. *Fever Pitch*

batting average, 100 runs, 154 hits, .525 slugging, and 38 doubles). Henderson was a solid bat that bridged the gap between Hall of Famer Rickey Henderson and the Bash Brothers (Jose Canseco and Mark McGwire). During this career year, the powerhouse Athletics were 23–1 in games that Henderson went yard. Always a threat during a big game, Henderson hit .298 with seven roundtrippers, 20 RBIs, 24 runs, and a .570 slugging average in eight postseason series. Perhaps his greatest contribution was during the 1986 ALCS as a member of the Boston Red Sox. With his team one out and one strike away from elimination and continued Sox misfortune, Henderson, who was primed to become the game's goat after a Bobby Grich fly ball bounced off of his glove and over the wall for an Angels home run, took a 2–2 Donnie Moore pitch and planted it into the left-field seats. After a signature pivot hop and dance around the bases in celebration of a Boston lead, it would be his bases-loaded blast in the 11th inning of that game to score Don Baylor that would stand up as the game's winning run. The Red Sox would go on to win the series, setting up a memorable match-up against the New York Mets, also assuring Henderson's place in the game as a postseason hitting threat for years to come.

Jim Lonborg, P

> *No player in the history of the World Series, before or since, did what Jim Lonborg did in 1967. Lonborg still holds the record for the fewest hits given up in back-to-back starts, when he was simply brilliant in Games 2 and 5 in the great Series with the St. Louis Cardinals that year.*
>
> —Boston Globe

Jim Lonborg was a pitcher, not a belly-itcher. As *Swingers'* Vince Vaughn might say, "Gentleman Jim" was "money" for the Sox, rising to the occasion when the Sox needed him most in 1967. That year, he helped lead the team to their "Impossible Dream" run by winning 22 games and striking out 246. One win, in particular, helped give the Red Sox their first pennant in 31 years. On the last day of the season in the midst of a three-team fight for first place, Lonborg tossed a complete game against the Twins to take the Sox to the Series. As if that big win weren't enough, Gentleman Jim brought his A-game to the postseason. In a duel between the Sox and the Cardinals (sound familiar?), the All-Star pitched like the ace he became, throwing a one-hitter against the Cards in Game 2 (losing a no-hitter in the eighth) and three-hit them over six innings in Game 5. The Sox ended up losing the Series (Lonborg couldn't be Lonborg in Game 7), but he got some gold following the Fall Classic—earning the Cy Young Award (the first Sox to do so).

Lonborg is sometimes forgotten because his magic didn't expand to future years (an injury following the 1967 campaign altered his career), but in a 15-year career, he compiled a 157–137 overall record with 15 shutouts and 1,475 strikeouts. After he retired, Lonborg shifted gears, went to dental school, and became a professional dentist in Massachusetts. For years of drilling the strike zone, he was inducted into the Sox Hall of Fame in 2002. Don't forget to floss, kids.

Mel Parnell, P

When you had a lineup that included the greatest hitter who ever lived (Ted Williams) and a bunch of trustworthy bats like Dom DiMaggio and Bobby Doerr, all a pitcher really needed to do on the Red Sox in the late 1940s to mid-1950s was keep his team in the game. Mel Parnell did that, and then some. A lefty who was often lights-out, the pitcher enjoyed a decade-long career with the Sox, putting up two 20-game-winning seasons and tossing a no-hitter against the White Sox in his very last year, 1956. A leader on the mound, a poised Parnell helped keep the Sox in the pennant race in 1949 against the Yankees with a 25–7 record and 2.77 earned run average. True, Parnell is beloved in Sox Nation, but he often gets passed over when talking about the best pitchers in team history. He shouldn't be. Next to Wakefield, Clemens, and Young, he has the most wins for the BoSox with 123. Who knows how many more he could have had? His career was cut short due to arm damage. Still, he boasted a career line of 123–75, a 3.50 earned run average, and 113 complete games.

A two-time All-Star, he was also one of the most successful starting pitchers to throw at Fenway Park and was selected to the team Hall of Fame in 1997. He's also immortalized in the terribly catchy "Talking Baseball" tune ("Willie, Mickey, and The Duke") by Terry Cashman, who thankfully is no relation to Brian Cashman.

Dennis Eckersley, P

Before he revolutionized the closer position in Oakland, playing for the Athletics from 1987 to 1995, Dennis Eckersley was a starting pitcher predominantly with the Red Sox from 1978 to 1984. Elected to Cooperstown in his first year of eligibility, Eck is one of only two pitchers—the other being John Smoltz—to have both a 20-win season and a 50-save season in a career. His Boston tenure was highlighted by a career-high 20-win season in 1978 as well as being part of a trade to the Chicago Cubs in 1984 for Bill Buckner. Certainly without the first-ballot Hall of Famer, Mookie Wilson's grass stain never would have gone through the Red Sox first baseman's legs. In 1992 the six-time All-Star and member of the Red Sox Hall of Fame captured both the American League Most Valuable Player and Cy Young Award for the A's, which is something that the great Mariano Rivera has not done during his entire 17-plus-year career.

Tom Gordon, P

Tom Gordon spent his hard-throwing career with eight different major league clubs, earning three All-Star appearances and one world championship as a part of the 2008 Philadelphia Phillies. His best years were spent in Fenway as a member of the Red Sox between 1996 and 1999. Boston converted Gordon from a starting pitcher to a closer, where he set the club's single-season record with 46 saves in 1998. With his career reignited, the pitcher known as "Flash" would spend another 10 years in the big leagues with stops in Houston, both Chicago clubs, Philadelphia, the Diamondbacks, and even a stint as a set-up man to Bombers immortal Mariano Rivera and the greed-infested New York Yankees. Despite his dabble on the dark side, the right-handed Flash was never more popular in Boston when he appeared as the object of infatuation in Stephen King's 1999 novel *The Girl Who Loved Tom Gordon.*

Joe Cronin, Manager

With his 744 wins as Red Sox manager, Terry Francona is (and will remain) second by more 300 wins to the club record holder, Joe Cronin. What makes Cronin's 1,071 Hall of Fame wins unique is that the majority of them came in the role of player/manager. For 11 seasons, Cronin wrote the lineup (often batting anywhere from third to fifth before using himself as a pinch-hitter in his final seasons) played an All-Star level shortstop but failed to get the Red Sox to the World Series. When he finally hung up the cleats—*voilà*—the 1946 Sox were pennant winners. Cronin was a .301 career hitter and an extra-base-hit machine for the Sox (270 doubles, 44 triples, and 119 home runs), so it's easy to see why he batted himself in the heart of the lineup. By the end of his playing days, he was noted for strategically using himself in pinch-hitting situations. As Dennis Purdy points out in *The Team-by-Team Encyclopedia of Major League Baseball*, "Cronin would occasionally put himself in to pinch-hit, especially when the wind was blowing out. In 1943 he hit five pinch-hit home runs, including two grand slams." A Hall of Famer in 1956 and AL president from 1959 to 1974, Cronin's No. 4 was retired by the Sox in 1984.

Ellis Burks, CF

There's a reason why players gave Ellis Burks the trophy to carry off the plane coming back from St. Louis after the Red Sox won their first World Series in 86 years. He's Sox royalty, was beloved by fans, played flawless center field, and knocked nearly 100 homers in his seven years with the team. Rather than write about our love for the Sox icon, we'd rather have him talk about his love for the team:

On the Dominant Red Sox Teams He Played On: We definitely had a lot of talent. From the Jim Rices to Wade Boggses, Roger Clemenses, and Marty Barretts. There were a slew of great players and a great pitching staff of Clemens, Bruce Hurst, Al Nipper, and Oil Can Boyd—great pitchers who had their own personalities and were pretty dominant from that era. When you combine the talent we had and the desire that was in Boston to win, we had some pretty good teams.

On Playing at Fenway: I liked the whole aspect of playing at Fenway. Growing up through the minor league systems of Winter Haven and Double A New Britain, I always pictured myself playing at Fenway one day and always wanted to make impact. When I got an opportunity, I wanted to be the best I could be. Sometimes the injuries kept me back—I'm sure I would have had a much better career there—but it was a wonderful thing. And, the fans were so supportive.

On Yankees Fans: My experience with Yankees fans was, like you said, [different.] We were playing each other and the rivalry was there, but they didn't have great teams and were very competitive—not like the Yankees of the 1990s who just dominated. But they had history just like we had history and a

Ellis Burks greets Mike Greenwell and Wade Boggs at home plate after belting a two-run home run against the Yankees in New York on September 21, 1990.

winning tradition. [The fans] had arrogance, of course. Fans in the outfield would just heckle you. Some fans sometimes would even throw things at you. You knew they were there and they'd stay on you from the first through the ninth inning.

It was a rivalry throughout my minor and major league career with Red Sox. It was pretty much a learning process not to like the Yankees even in the minor leagues. Any time we played the Yankees—even in A ball, it was the same thing: even at the minor league level, it was intense.

On Why People Hate the Yankees: It's sort of like the Lakers or any winning organization—you're either going to be loved or hated. The Yankees have such an air about themselves—that whole Yankees empire and the history of them dominating free agency. It's a great organization, but I always said as minor leaguer I'd hate to be in the Yankees system because you wouldn't get a fair shot to move up in the system because they'd go out and get free agents who would put you on hold.

On Being on the 2004 World Champions: Let me tell you something—it was one of the most gratifying moments of my career just being a part of that team. I was not 100 percent healthy—there were two knee surgeries I had—but I was there every day. I felt nothing but inspiration from those guys: Pedro Martinez, Tim Wakefield, Jason Varitek, and all the veteran guys looked at me somewhat as a leader. I was a bit surprised. I didn't contribute as much as I wanted to, but they acknowledged my presence. That really made me feel good, and it was very touching.

On Where the Rivalry Will Go: The Yankees–Red Sox rivalry will go on for years to come. You don't see it slowing down at all. Last year early on, the Red Sox had the Yankees' number. Then, later on, the Yankees had the Red Sox's number. This year, it's back to the Red Sox owning the Yankees again. It'll continue to do that. Through free agency, they'll bid against each other and sometimes go after the same player just so the other team doesn't get him.

On Whether He Still Considers Himself a Red Sox: I always will. I came through the trenches in the organization, I left and came back. It's one of those things—I always will consider myself a Red Sox. I still find myself watching games.

3
WE LOVE RED SOX NATION

You hear so many negative things about the fans in Boston, but it's so not true. They love and respect the game, and if players love and respect it as much and you play hard, you're going to earn their respect. A lot of people have misconceptions of the fans.

—Ellis Burks
Gold Glove outfielder, Boston Red Sox

There are absolute truths in life. You live. You die. And if you live in Boston—you live and die with the Red Sox. Unlike the Bronx dynasty, whose fandom seems to come out in droves with each free agent splash, being a Red Sox fan means you root for your team whether it's a bag of balls playing for the team or a bunch of All-Stars.

Long before Theo and Tito gave Sox fans reason to celebrate in 2004 and 2007, fans supported the Sox even when the team gave them every reason to jump ship. Buckner balls and Dent homers couldn't dampen the spirits of the most passionate fans in the game—nothing could and nothing will. Red Sox Nation is a proud group who can get behind underdogs like the 1967 team or the group of idiots who ran wild on the AL East in 2004. So much has been said and written on

The citizens of Red Sox Nation come from six New England states and parts of Canada. They are old, young, male, female, rich, and poor. The Sox fan base crosses into every group. Poets, farmers, school kids, and shut-ins are Red Sox fans. Horror man Stephen King is a Sox fan, as were the last two baseball commissioners, Fay Vincent and the late Bart Giamatti. All those folks have one thing in common: they break out in a rash at the very mention of Bucky Dent.

—Dan Shaughnessy, *At Fenway: Dispatches from Red Sox Nation*

the rivalry between the Sox and the Yankees, and rightfully so. Both teams compete for the top of their division each year, and there's a playoff vibe any time they meet no matter what month it is. Beyond the obvious, the Sox are the working-class heroes, while the Yankees are the corporate suits. Rick Reilly once said rooting for the Yankees was like rooting for Brad Pitt to get the girl. Rooting for the Sox, however, is like rooting for the infinite underdog. Yes, no matter how many All-Stars the Sox sign from here on out, they'll always play second fiddle to an organization that has so much history and mystique it's nauseating.

It's easy to root for the Yankees. They're always built to win and are the most celebrated team in sports history. Being a Red Sox fan takes balls (especially if you're an in-betweener in Connecticut)—and we say that knowing full well their payroll is close to the Bronx Bombers these days. The Sox can be the top dog, the mid-carder, or down and out, and you love them the same. Like any great franchise, they can lift you up, they can bring you down, and above all—no matter the outcome of September—they're the most reliable thing you can count on in life. Whether it's Youk or Yaz or Young or any other player with a surname sans *Y*, the Sox are the Sox because they're the Sox. We love the Red Sox and hate the Yankees because we are one with the team. Like them, we might get beat, but we'll get right back up. You count us out, we'll prove you wrong. You tell us we're not as good as the Yankees, and we'll tell you to kiss our Pesky-loving asses.

ORTIZ JERSEY

Less than four years after the Red Sox shook their supposed "curse" and won their first championship since Woodrow Wilson was in the Oval Office, the Yankees were faced with a rare position of giving in to superstitions. On April 13, 2008, after days of speculation, it was discovered that a construction worker had indeed buried a Sox jersey of David Ortiz in the concrete of the new Yankee Stadium. Gino Castignoli, a future Hall of Famer in our book, had hoped implanting the Big Papi shirt in the depths of the new stadium, which turned out to be essentially a bloated version of the older one when it opened in 2009, would cast a spell against the ballpark. But it wasn't to be. With rumors swirling in the New York media, the Yankees decided to dig down deep, and stop the hex before it started. The team ended up donating the shirt to the Jimmy Fund, which showed class. But we'll focus on burying the shirt in the hopes of creating a "Curse of Big Papi" for the next century, because it showed balls.

LARRY LUCCHINO

In a lot of ways, the New York Yankees and their fan base are Jay, while the Red Sox and their Nation are arguably Silent Bob. Throughout their history, the Bombers and especially

their arrogant fans talk big (yes, we know you've won 27 championships—thanks for the reminder), while the Sox and Fenway followers are reserved, making smaller, more poignant
statements. Driving that snootchie bootchies point even further—George Steinbrenner made a career of opening his
mouth about everything and anyone since taking the reins in
1973. Rarely, however, did it seem that a Red Sox exec would
do the same or at least stand up and take a stand against the
Bronx bank. That was, until December of 2002, when Red Sox
team president and CEO Larry Lucchino decided to say what
everyone else was thinking. Following their failed pursuit of
Cuban pitching ace Jose Contreras, Lucchino referred to the
Yankees as "the Evil Empire," and noted how even in Latin
America, they can "extend its tentacles" to acquire a player
no matter how much money it cost. Hearing one of our own
stand up for his team and take on the monopoly that is the
New York Yankees was more refreshing than smoking the finest cigar from Fidel-town. The "Empire" namesake has stuck
ever since, and Lucchino has remained vocal and honest in
the media every time the AL East rivals come up. Making the
comment even sweeter was the fact that Contreras never lived
up to his contract, and was jettisoned out of town after less
than two mediocre seasons for the lackluster Esteban Loaiza.

THEO EPSTEIN

On November 25, 2002, while wunderkind Mark Zuckerberg was enjoying the first few months of his freshman year
at Harvard by plotting world dominance, the Red Sox hired
the youngest general manager in baseball history in 28-year-
old Theo Epstein. Yes, Zuckerberg would go on to change
the world we live in with his revolutionary social media giant

Their passion is the thing that makes [Red Sox fans] so unique, and so challenging, to play in front of. They accept nothing but the best, and as a player I never took issue with that.... There is still a deep, abiding love and passion, or hatred, for anyone wearing that sacred red-and-white home jersey.

—**Curt Schilling**

Facebook, but Epstein would forever change the lives of Red Sox Nation by extinguishing years of suffering with a world series championship in 2004. Before Epstein took over, our most likeable Theo was Malcolm-Jamal Warner on *The Cosby Show*. Epstein, plucked from the Padres organization, made an immediate impact on the Sox in the winter of '02. Sure, Twitter wasn't around then for everyone to tweet about the acquisition of David Ortiz, Bill Mueller, Kevin Millar, and Mike Timlin, but that's all right because that squad finished five outs away from the World Series. One can only imagine the tweets that would've been fired during and after Grady Little's Game 7 performance. Epstein got the message, anyway, and fired Little, replacing him with Terry Francona. But he didn't stop there, he would spend the rest of the winter burning up the hot stove and reshaping his pitching corps by adding Curt Schilling and Keith Foulke without the aid of Craigslist.

As the 2004 season played out, Theo stunned the baseball world and the Garciaparra family by shipping Nomar out at the trade deadline. The Sox then stunned the rest of the league into submission, ending the season on a 42–18 tear and winning their final eight postseason games. With a World Series under his belt, Epstein guided the Sox to another playoff appearance only to briefly resign after the 2005 season. This departure lasted slightly shorter than Friendster. Injuries wrecked the team's chances in 2006, but the picks from Epstein's first draft (Jonathan Papelbon and Dustin Pedroia) would help the team to their second championship of the decade. Old Media Publications (we're talking about you, *Sporting News* and *Sports Illustrated*) would name Theo Epstein Executive of the Decade.

If you Google "Youngest Baseball GM" nowadays, you'll see that Texas' Jon Daniels has broken Epstein's record. The Tampa Bay Rays have played copycat in hiring under-30 Andrew Friedman who, like Epstein, never played major league baseball. In 2011 with rumors of a move to the Chicago Cubs buzzing, both Daniel's Rangers and the Friedman's Rays reached the playoffs for the second season in a row. Sensing the time was right for a new challenge after a collapse for the ages, Epstein accepted a job as president of baseball operations with the Cubbies. In his classy sendoff to Red Sox Nation in a *Boston Globe* ad, Epstein summed it up best "Ten Years, Two Championships, Countless Memories." Next up for Epstein? Dinner with Steve Bartman to plan an end to yet another curse.

TERRY FRANCONA

On some parallel Earth, the 2011 Red Sox played .500 baseball in September and easily held onto the American League wildcard. At season's end, Terry Francona's option was picked up and his quest to overtake Joe Cronin as the winningest manager in Red Sox history continued. But alas, parallel worlds are the stuff of comic books and *Lost* subplots. The 2011 Red Sox collapse was a real and painful reminder of Red Sox seasons past. In the weeks that followed the Sox's most recent "Epic Fail," Francona was painted as the scapegoat who oversaw a

BOSTON RED SOX FIVE COMMITMENTS
TO **EXCELLENCE (DECEMBER 21, 2001)***

No. 1: To Field a Team Worthy of the Fans' Support

No. 2: To Preserve All That's Good about Fenway Park and Take That Experience to a Higher Level

No. 3: To Market Aggressively to a New, Broad Region

No. 4: To Be Active Participants in the Community

No. 5: To End the Curse of the Bambino and Win World Championships for Boston, New England, and Red Sox Nation

*Source: Red Sox Media Guide

RED SOX

dysfunctional clubhouse. However, it is most likely Tito will be remembered more for his two world championships than final two tumultuous seasons.

Francona's managerial career was preceded by modest playing days in Montreal, Chicago, and Milwaukee. His journeyman days followed the footsteps of his All-Star father, Tito Francona. Nobody could have expected so much success (a Rocky Marciano–like undefeated 8–0 World Series record) from a manager who produced four sub-.500 seasons with the Philadelphia Phillies. Francona signed on with Sox shortly after his former Phils ace Curt Schilling accepted a trade to the Sox. Soon afterward, 86 years of misery was put to an end. The man who once managed six-time NBA champion Michael Jordan with the Birmingham Barons became the 20th manager in baseball history to win multiple World Series titles in 2004 and 2007. (The oldest members of Red Sox Nation were born when Bill Carrigan also accomplished this for the 1915–1916 Red Sox.)

While Francona's exit was marred by allegations and blame—most of which involved chicken and beer in a frat party locker room—he freed the team of its curse and will be a tough act to follow, even for Bobby Valentine.

THE JIMMY FUND

The Boston Red Sox have had a few winning double-play combinations, but their best tandem comes off the field. Since 1948, the Jimmy Fund has changed and saved the lives of countless children and adults worldwide by fighting cancer at the Dana-Farber Cancer Institute in Boston. Since 1953, the entire Red Sox organization has been behind the cause and has literally put its money where its mouth is. The team and the charity have been inseparable for more than 50 years, and they represent the best of what Boston can bring.

"TESSIE" AND THE ROYAL ROOTERS

Team-specific sports anthems often provide more embarrassment than enthusiasm and more misses than hits. Who can forget (if only we could) recent themes like those arrogantly annoying "How ya doin'?" ditties produced during the Yankees late 1990s run, or the awkward Chicago Bears "Super Bowl Shuffle" in 1985 in which each player sang off key and danced like Eugene Levy in *Best in Show*? There are more painful examples of that, but we digress. And we're not even referencing "Who Let the Dogs Out?" thank you very much.

Thankfully, in Boston we've been spared the embarrassment with a flagship song that has become our own battle cry thanks, in particular, to Fenway's favorite sons—the Dropkick Murphys. More on those fellas later.

The song "Tessie" wasn't actually written about the Sox. Back when Teddy Roosevelt was eating beef jerky in the Oval Office, the tune was part of the Broadway musical *The Silver Slipper.* Titled "Tessie (You Are the Only, Only, Only)," the catchy ditty was written about a woman singing to her parakeet of the same name. A little song about some serious fowl love soon evolved into an anthem for a band of righteously devoted fans called the "Royal Rooters," who sang the song to motivate the then–Boston Americans and traveled to opposing parks to annoy the home team.

"Tessie" became the unofficial MVP of the 1903 World Series when it was reportedly played in Pittsburgh with the Pirates up three games to one in a best-of-nine series. The Rooters sang the tune repeatedly, and even Pittsburgh outfielder Tommy Leach was quoted as saying it helped propel the Americans over the Bucs in the next four games. After a long and fruitful run, the Rooters phased "Tessie" out in 1918. The song wasn't the only thing that ended—the winning did as well. That was, until 86 years later. Mass bagpipin' rockers Dropkick Murphys resurrected it with updated, team-appropriate lyrics.

The band recorded the song in June 2004, and according to their album liner notes, guaranteed a Series win if it was played. They would eventually, and the team, down to their last three outs from elimination in the ALCS Game 4, rebounded and trumped the Yankees and eventually the Cardinals in the 2004 World Series.

> We debuted "Tessie" the day of the A-Rod brawl/Bill Mueller walk off, and multiple playoff games including Game 1 of the World Series and Game 7 of the 2007 ALCS. It was the original good luck charm for early incarnations of the team here in Boston. It went away after 1918 and so did the championship for the next 86 years. The year we bring it back, they won. And the two years we actually played the song on the field, they won both times.
>
> —Ken Casey (bassist/vocalist/founder, Dropkick Murphys)

Since then, the song—which features several prominent ex-Sox players on backup—has once again become a staple at Fenway and throughout Boston as are many of Dropkick Murphy's park-thumping tracks.

JERRY REMY

If owning a hot dog stand on Yawkey Way, making the All-Star team in your first season with the Sox, writing books about Wally the Green Monster, and being the first president of Red Sox Nation sounds like the ultimate Red Sox life, then welcome to the World of the "Rem Dawg," Jerry Remy. While Derek Jeter was busy closing in on 3,000 hits, Remy was approaching 100,000 Twitter followers in the summer of 2011. The Massachusetts-born Rem Dawg arrived back in Red Sox Nation in the winter of '77 from the Angels for Don Aase (of Don Aase fame). Remy made his only All-Star Game in his first Sox season, batting at the top of the order in the heartbreaking season of 1978. During his seven seasons with the BoSox, Remy hit two home runs (so few that we can name the opposing pitchers—the A's Matt Keough and the Brewers Eduardo Rodriguez). In his tenure, he played with six Sox

Cooperstown members (Dennis Eckersley, Carlton Fisk, Jim Rice, Carl Yastrzemski, Tony Perez, and Wade Boggs). After his retirement, Remy joined NESN, was named the 100th best second baseman by Bill James in 2002, and was inducted into the Red Sox Hall of Fame in 2006.

FENWAY PARK

> *You can't go to Fenway Park and not be a Red Sox fan when you're there. It's like Wrigley...you go there, and you're like, "Yeah, I get it."*
>
> —John Slattery, actor, *Mad Men*

> *It's my home. You feel mystique here, like the energy of history.*
>
> —Jason Varitek on Fenway (*USA Today Sports Weekly*)

On April 15, 1912, a passenger liner destined for New York City struck an iceberg and sank, resulting in one of the most tragic incidents of the 20th century. The horrific crash also spawned an awful Celine Dion soundtrack some 85 years later, but enough about the *Titanic* because this book is not about sappy Leonardo DiCaprio flicks. Five days after the ship sank and far removed from the great tragedy, a new era was rising in Boston. On April 20 the first official game was played in the team's new home, Fenway Park. The game, which was witnessed by 27,000 baseball fans, saw the hometown Red Sox beat the New York Highlanders 7–6 after Tris Speaker drove in the winning run in the bottom of the 11th inning. Of course, the Highlanders would later become the hated Yankees, and thus a rivalry was born. Dubbed "America's Most Beloved Ballpark," Fenway Park is the oldest ballpark in the major leagues.

Complete with its many unique nuances, including "Pesky's Pole," "the Triangle," and the world-famous Green Monster, the park has been home to the Red Sox for the past century.

On February 26, 1911, General Charles H. Taylor purchased land for the park during an auction, and although the record books show the Highlanders loss as the first official game, it was in fact a Red Sox exhibition win on April 9, 1912, against Harvard that ushered in the Fenway era despite snow flurries and a small crowd of only 3,000 people. Like every baseball masterpiece, the park that sits between Isbeth and Lansdowne has several firsts that should be mentioned. The first home run was hit by first baseman Hugh Bradley on April 26, 1912, during a game against Philadelphia. It was the second and last home run of his major league career before he traded in his red socks for a stint with the Brooklyn Tip-Tops of the long-since-forgotten Federal League. On June 21, 1916, right-hander Rube Foster threw the first no-no by a Red Sox pitcher at Fenway Park, leading Boston to a 2–0 win over the fourth-place Bronx Bombers and the infamous Wally Pipp of "I'm the guy who lost my starting job that began Lou Gehrig's streak" fame.

On September 11, 1918, the Red Sox clinched the World Series with a 2–1 Game 6 win over the Cubs, which remains as the last championship clincher won by the Sox at Fenway Park. Among the early highlights, Fenway Park had its share of close calls, including a five-alarm blaze on January 5, 1934. Destroying construction that was underway by then new owner Thomas A. Yawkey, the shrine was fitted with a new left-field grandstand, bleachers, and a new left-field wall. The new Fenway Park was christened on April 17, 1934, by a Washington Senators victory—but, more importantly, Duffy's

Fenway Park, the oldest stadium in the major leagues, was opened on April 9, 1912, for an exhibition game against Harvard. The 37-foot Green Monster in left field was installed during renovations after a fire in 1934. Photo courtesy of Getty Images

Cliff in left field, which had been a 10-foot incline mastered and named after outfielder Duffy Lewis, was replaced by a monumental 37-foot-high wall. The first Sunday game ever at Fenway Park was played on July 3, 1932. The game is noted not for its 13–2 shellacking by the visiting Yankees but for the end of the law that prohibited Sunday baseball due to Fenway's proximity to a church.

Speaking of proximity, it was a 502-foot moon shot by Teddy Ballgame on June 9, 1946, off of Detroit's Fred Hutchinson that landed on top of the straw hat of New Yorker Joseph A. Boucher. The unforgettable blast that landed in Section 42, Row 37, Seat 21, is the only seat in the house that, despite the surrounding green mass of seats, is forever painted Red Sox red.

Speaking of green, in 1947 green paint replaced advertisements covering the left-field wall. Standing at a very modest 315 feet from home plate, the wall has been an attractive target for decades, especially from those sluggers who bat from the right side. To this day, the Green Monster, originally just known as "the Wall," remains one of the most recognized structures in baseball. In 2003 seats were added to the top of the Monster, making this priceless view one of the best seats in the house.

Two of the more notable victories in Sox history were won on the home field. October 1, 1967, during the final day of the regular season, the "Impossible Dream" Red Sox clinched the American League pennant with a 5–3 victory over Minnesota. Game 6 between the visiting Reds and hometown Red Sox on October 21, 1975—which just so happened to be the first World Series game played at night—also turned into an instant classic. The memorable match-up was a battle for the ages, still talked about and replayed to this day. We may always overlook Bernie Carbo's pinch-hit, three-run, game-tying homer with two outs, but we never forget the Carlton Fisk home run off Pat Darcy leading off the last of the 12th.

Almost three years later, after finishing the season with identical records, the Red Sox and New York Yankees played a one-game playoff at Fenway Park. Thanks to Bucky Dent and that three-run, seventh-inning homer, the Yankees defeated Boston 5–4 to capture the AL East division crown. April 29, 1986, Roger Clemens struck out a major league, single-game record 20 batters in a 3–1 victory over the Seattle Mariners. Clemens earned AL MVP and Cy Young honors, leading the Red Sox to the 1986 World Series, where they lost to the New York Mets in seven games. Speaking of '86, can you imagine if that Mookie dribbler went between Buckner's legs under the Fenway lights? Selling out every home game since May 15, 2003, no Red Sox moment may have shined brighter than on October 17, 2004, with the team down to their last three outs in the 2004 ALCS. Pinch-runner Dave Roberts stole second base off Yankees immortal Mariano Rivera, setting up a game-tying RBI by third baseman Bill Mueller. The game would enter extra innings, when "Big Papi" David Ortiz ended the game on a walk-off home run and eventually ended that damn dopey curse. Thanks to current ownership led by John Henry and Larry Lucchino, the greatest stadium in pro sports is here to stay, and as the Red Sox blow out the 100 candles on the 2012 opener, the memories past, present, and future will always be an integral part of the legendary Fenway Park.

NATION TESTIMONIALS

Red Sox fans live and breathe the team. Here are a few stories that embody that notion…

> I live in Missouri now, but my mom's from Concord, New Hampshire. She was also a school teacher, so we'd spend our summers "back home" in New England. We'd spend a few weeks in Concord with my grandparents. During those

RED SOX

15 FAVORITE FAMOUS SOX FANS

1. *Matt Damon*
2. *Stephen King*
3. *Denis Leary*
4. *Ben Affleck*
5. *Mark Wahlberg*
6. *Jake Gyllenhaal*
7. *John Krasinski*
8. *Jimmy Fallon*
9. *Laurie Cabot (the official witch of Salem)*
10. *Mike Barnicle*
11. *Rachel Dratch*
12. *NKOTB*
13. *Seth Meyers*
14. *Dane Cook*
15. *Steven Tyler*

days, nights would usually be spent on the floor while my Grampa Steve parked himself in the "loungah" with a Molson in one hand and the "clickah" in the other, screaming at the Sox. The late '80s and early '90s weren't always the best years to be a Red Sox fan, so most of the screaming wasn't good. I would be 20 years old before I realized that "Goddammit" wasn't Mo Vaughn's actual first name. From Concord, we'd leave to go to York, Maine, where we'd camp in an RV without electricity. Our lone entertainment at night was Joe Castiglione's dulcet tones and the roar of the crowd competing in volume with the crackle of a campfire and the crash of waves against the beach. You could pick worse ways to grow up. And, hey, all those sad years brought me 2004 and 2007, and I wouldn't trade those memories. Hell,

I still have the bottles from the beers I was drinking when each of those titles was won.

I have a Red Sox basement. I've got a Varitek jersey in a case, a ton of wall art, a Kevin Youkilis (who else?) Fathead, and, best of all, an accent wall. A Monster green accent wall, complete with disks representing the retired numbers in right field. I…well, I'm 30 and with disposable income. Why not, right? (I've also got a Celtics bathroom. I may have a problem.) You can also see my Fenway Park dirt coasters there in the front, themselves a gift from Jamie Brooks, one of two of my closest friends…Red Sox fans I met through Twitter and who now are so interwoven into my life (and my spring training plans) that I can't remember life before I knew them.

My family, not unlike a lot of other families with ties to the Sox, always considered itself to be "long odds" sort of people. The perpetual underdogs, so to speak. As a result, it was no surprise that our family's "lucky number" was 13. We can trace that back to our father, the man who's the reason why we love baseball at all. When dad was growing up, he happened to be a part of a ballclub with a limited number of jerseys, and he was last to pick. It stuck. Each of his three sons would grow up to one day proudly wear the No. 13 on Little League teams and the like. That number became a source of strength for us, a symbol of rising over long odds. Dad underscored it for us by beating a rare brain tumor when we were 12. It was no surprise then that, on the 2004 Sox team, our favorite player was Doug Mientkie-wicz, No. 13. His number was appealing, but he also suited a family of long-odds folks: he was a journeyman picked up as a defensive replacement to help "lock down" games. He did the dirty work. I bought a No. 13 home Red Sox jersey that season and was wearing it when the Sox won the 2004 title. It's gotten a lot of use in the intervening years.

Four years ago, when my first niece was born, she was a breach birth and an emergency C-section. I lived three hours away. As I packed an overnight bag, I tucked "the family jersey" into the bag. When I walked into the waiting room, I chucked it at my brother. I didn't have to tell him why it was there. He hung it over a chair in the corner, number facing the family as a reminder that we had faced long odds before and come out on top. Three years ago, my father was diagnosed with small-cell carcinoma, a particularly lethal brand of lung cancer. The family jersey hung in dad's house all the way through treatment. Three years on, dad's cancer is still in our rearview mirror. When my sister-in-law had another difficult pregnancy with my two-month-old nephew, John, the first thing I did when I heard there were issues was overnight him the jersey. It's currently hanging in John's nursery, itself also Boston-themed. (Fun story: when my niece was told she was going to have a little brother, her parents asked what they should name him. "Boston Red Sox," the then-three-year-old replied in a tone that made it sound like someone had asked her what color the sky was. To her, it was the only logical choice. To this day, my nephew, who was named after my father, is "Boston John" to the family.)

—Kevin Meyers, Springfield, Missouri

In 2004, when I found out the Sox were advancing to play the Yankees in the ALCS, I took a week off from work so I could watch it. I remember telling my older brother (an Orioles fan) that I absolutely wanted the Sox to play the Yankees. I figured, if there was anyway to break the 86-year-old curse, it had to be by going through those damn Yankees, ya know? Well, including weekend days, I got, like, 10 days off. Obviously, the series started horribly as the Yanks won the first three games. My friend Pete and I were always going out somewhere to watch. We really liked our chances before the Series started, but after the Game 3 drubbing, we couldn't show our faces anymore. Sadly, this was an all-too-familiar feeling for us Sox fans. We were used to the constant tease that was the Boston Red Sox. It was a perpetual feeling of dating that hot girl from school, only to never be able to close the deal with her. Then, you split, and the first thing she does is put out. What does this say about you? You beat yourself up over what you might have done wrong…how things could have been better if you had done something differently. Well, that's what being a Sox fan before 2004 was for me. Too embarrassed, we decided to watch Game 4 in seclusion. Toward the end of Game 4, we went back to his apartment (the only safe place we knew to watch the *Titanic* finally sink) and were completely pre-pared for the Sox to get swept. We sat down to watch. He on his couch, and me on his mini couch (love seat). Then came up Kevin Millar, who promptly was walked by Mariano Rivera. Kevin Millar runs about as fast as you or I would… only if we had a dump truck tied to our waist. Seriously, molasses moves faster than this man. So the Sox pinch ran Dave Roberts for Millar. You want an unsung hero? Dave Roberts. Everyone at Fenway. Everyone watching on TV. Everyone listening on the radio. We all knew what was coming. Roberts was going to try and steal second. Seri-ously, it was basically as if someone had put one of those neon signs you see by strip joints (so I hear) advertising, "Hey! Hey, you! Dave is going to steal second. Just sayin'!"

And you know what? He took off! The lives of Red Sox fans everywhere were in slow motion. It was the longest stolen base in the history of baseball. But he made it! Next thing you know, he scored.

Later in the game, Ortiz won it with a homer. From there on, we watched every game from Pete's apartment.... Sitting in the same spots.... Wearing the same shirts and hats. There is a slight—okay, maybe more than slight—chance that I wore the same jeans too. I do know that I remembered to shower and change underwear. Other than that, all bets are off. I was in such a trance that, looking back on it now, I think I was in some sort of alternate dimension. All I did for the rest of the series was sleep at my place, get up, and then walk to Pete's place to hang before the game, and then we'd watch the game. We lived in the city, so I passed Subway every time I walked to Pete's, so all I ate for 10 days was Subway...pre–$5 footlongs. Once I got to his place, I'd claim the same spot (love seat). He had his same spot on the couch. Some nights, our friends would come over to join, but they had to find their own seats. No one was allowed to touch or even look at our seats. It was beyond surreal, because for those 10 vacation days, I was completely detached from the real world. Thankfully, nothing monumental was happening in the world because it would have completely blown right past my radar. I was about six months away from meeting my wife for the first time, so luckily I was not in a relationship. If I was, there is no way any girl would have put up with me.

Needless to say, the Sox became the first team in the over 100 years of baseball to come back from a 3–0 deficit in a seven-game series in the playoffs. Even as I tell you this story, I am not sure I believe it. I mean, what are the odds that I had the vacation time to spend at the exact time in life when the Sox would come back in historical fashion versus their archrival Yankees?

To this day, I always look back on that time as one of the best moments in my life (aside from meeting and marrying my wife). You couldn't write a better script even if you tried. And there is no way, not one single decimal point of a percentage that the Sox would have won without Dave Roberts stealing second. Ninety feet. Let me say that again: *90 feet.* One man has to run 90 feet before the pitcher can throw to the plate and the catcher fires a bullet to second base. Oh, and have I mentioned yet that everyone on Earth knew it was coming? The perfect steal at the perfect moment in what became the perfect series to lead into the perfect way to win a World Series. Did that really happen? I hope so. If not, that must mean I'm still dreaming, and if that's the case.... Don't wake me up. Ever. These moments may come across as generic, but to me they are priceless. The 2004 title changed the landscape of being a Sox fan, both in good and bad ways. My life is completely different than it would have been if the Sox never won. While I will

Red Sox Nation is so intense it makes it very difficult for visiting ballclubs to close the game down from the seventh, eighth, and ninth innings. For guys to come in and think they are going to get nine outs against a ballclub when they are only two runs up—it just makes it very difficult. So you have a huge advantage playing there and also understanding the Green Monster in left—some of your outfielders being able to play the ricochet balls easier than visiting teams make it a little easier to have an advantage.

—Bronson Arroyo

RED SOX

forever be superstitious, I am not going to lie; my superstition has toned down significantly as I watch the Sox. I can say that I have seen something that many people lived and died with a span of 86 years without seeing. You cannot put a price on that. People often ask why sports fans invest so much time rooting for something beyond their control. My answer is always simple. We want to believe in something beyond our control. We want to put our faith out into the world with no guarantees of fulfillment so that when the day comes, and we are rewarded, the happiness we feel is a state of euphoria that cannot be described through words, yet can completely be described through emotions…sweet, triumphant, ecstatic emotions.

—Steven Houseman, English teacher/lifelong fan

I'm a 15-year-old male who has spent all of his young life living 15 minutes away from Yankee Stadium. Since my family is close to the stadium, my mom or dad and I will often go and see a Yankees game. One time, when my Dad and I went to see a Yankees game and the Yankees went into the bottom of the fourth inning down 3–0, every Yankees fan around us was dead silent, all confidence was lost. In the bottom of the seventh inning, the Yankees took the lead on a Jorge Posada two-run homer. The crowd out of nowhere became extremely interested in the game. On the other hand, you have the Red Sox fans, who have an unconditional love for their team. The Red Sox didn't win a championship for 86 years, but the fans stayed passionate. The Yankees fans turn their back on the team when they don't win the championship in any given year. I was fortunate enough to be able to go to Game 5 of the 2008 ALCS against the Rays. The Red Sox were down 7–0 in

the bottom of the seventh with two outs. Dustin Pedroia
hit an RBI and the crowd erupted like Pedroia had just hit
a walk-off home run. The fans stayed more than interested
but also involved by being extremely loud the entire game!
—Brett Dymek, White Plains, New York

Growing up in Boston in the 1970s, I was able to witness
some of the greatest events in Red Sox history. The players on the Red Sox during that decade were a colorful mix
of characters; there was Yaz, El Tiante, Dewey, Jim Rice,
the Spaceman, Freddy Lynn, the Rem Dawg, the Rooster,
and of course Pudge. During this time period, the rivalry
between the Red Sox and Yankees reached full boil. From
the Fisk-Munson fight in 1973 to the one-game playoff in
1978, this was war, and to a 10-year-old kid living in the
Boston suburb of Needham, the Yankees were clearly the
bad guys. It was in this atmosphere that I attended my first
Red Sox–Yankees game at Fenway Park on September 11,
1979. Earlier that day, my friend had called and said that
his dad had an extra ticket to the game that night and either
my brother or I could have it. I won the coin toss and, with
my parents' permission, headed to Fenway with my friend
and his dad for what might be a historic night.

Red Sox legend Carl Yastrzemski was sitting on 2,999
hits, he had been hitless in the previous game, so it seemed
very likely that we would witness the first Red Sox player to
reach 3,000 career hits. (Ted Williams would have reached
the milestone if he had not missed four-plus seasons due to
military service.) We had seats in the lower bleachers and
got to the sold-out Fens in time to see the first pitch. John
Tudor was on the hill for the Sox, and he quickly retired
the first three batters in Billy Martin's lineup. Tiant was

the starting pitcher for the Yankees. He had joined them as a free agent in the off-season after Red Sox GM Haywood Sullivan only offered a one-year deal, whereas the Yanks offered an additional year. This was my first experience with the Yankees taking a local hero away, although it had been happening since the days of Babe Ruth. Most Red Sox fans still respected El Tiante, and he did not draw the ire that players like Boggs, Clemens, and Damon would in the future for joining the Evil Empire. He did, however, rile some Sox fans when he made the commercial endorsing Yankee Franks and said the line, "It's great to be with a wiener." Jerry Remy led off the game for the Sox and ripped a single to center, making it likely that Yaz would bat that inning. Yastrzemski was batting fifth in the order and playing first. He had been battling a nagging injury to his Achilles tendon most of the season. Burleson was up next and hit a fly ball to right near the bleachers where I was sitting. Reggie Jackson caught the ball for the first out of the inning. Fans around me immediately started yelling, "Reggie Sucks! Reggie Sucks!" causing the Yankees slugger to turn and glare at the crowd, which only made the chanting louder. Fred Lynn then flew out to bring up my childhood hero, Jim Rice. I had a Stop & Shop poster of the power-hitting future Hall of Famer on the wall in my bedroom. Rice had hit 46 homers in the previous season and was one of the most feared hitters in the American League. With Rice at the plate and Yaz walking into the on-deck circle, the crowd rose to its feet and got louder. El Tiante struck out his former teammate, so Yaz and the fans would have to wait until the second for a chance at No. 3,000. Tudor again went through the Yankees in order in the top of the second and struck out the last two batters.

With Yaz leading off the bottom of the second inning, the crowd had extra time to cheer—35,689 fans at Fenway erupted into a huge cheer as Carl Yastrzemski made his way to the batter's box. It was the loudest and most exciting thing I had ever seen in my life. You couldn't hear the person next to you, it was just constant noise throughout his entire at-bat. The cheers turned to boos when Luis Tiant threw ball four, giving Yaz his first walk in 24 games to the disappointment of all. Yaz got to third on a single by Dewey Evans but was left stranded there. Scott led off the third with a single for the Yankees, bringing up Bucky Fuckin' Dent. Less than a year after Dent's improbable homer in the 1978 playoff game, he was not getting much love from the Fenway Faithful. Tudor then got Gulden to hit into a 6-4-3 double play.

The Red Sox failed to score in the bottom of the inning, and the Yankees took a one-run lead in the top of the fourth. Yaz would once again lead off for the Red Sox in the bottom of the fourth inning. The crowd was just as loud as it was during Yaz's first at-bat. He had not got a hit the night before and he walked his first time up, so he was due. Everyone was on the edge of their seat as he faced Tiant for the second time. This time he got under a pitch and hit a pop fly to second base. But it was only the fourth, and we knew he would have more at-bats. The game stayed close with the Yankees holding a one-run lead until the bottom of the sixth. Rick Burleson singled and Fred Lynn then belted a two-run homer to put the Red Sox in the lead. Jim Rice then hit a deep fly ball to right but it was caught by Reggie Jackson. Billy Martin had seen enough of Tiant and signaled to the bullpen for the righty Ron Davis. As Davis warmed up, the crowd once again had extra time to go into a frenzy in anticipation of Yaz's coming to the plate. If the Red Sox held on to the lead, this might be Yaz's final at-bat of the game, so there was a lot of finger-crossing in the stands. This time Yastrzemski made solid contact of off Davis' pitch. The already loud Fenway Park grew decibels louder as the ball sailed into the outfield, but Reggie Jackson tracked down the ball and caught it. The disappointment in the crowd disappeared quickly when Carlton Fisk singled after Yaz's fly-out. Butch Hobson then hit a double to plate Fisk and give the Red Sox a 3–1 lead before Davis got out of the inning. The Yankees would come back to win the game in the eighth inning and Yaz would foul out to the catcher in his last at-bat, but I still went home happy. The game was one of the most exciting things I had ever seen in my life. The excitement in the bleachers and the heat of the Red Sox–Yankees rivalry instilled a passion for baseball and for the Red Sox that has stayed with me to this day. I learned it was sometimes tough to be a Red Sox fan and the Yankees often came out on top, but if you were patient, revenge would come. The next night I watched the Red Sox beat the Yankees on 9–2 on TV.

When Yaz hit a single for his 3,000th hit in the bottom of the eighth, I felt as if I were standing in the stands cheering with the rest of the Fenway Faithful. It was my first time understanding what it truly meant to be a member of Red Sox Nation. The win allowed the Red Sox to end the season ahead of the Yankees and in third place in the American League East. Finishing ahead of the Yankees in 1979 would not be enough revenge for Bucky Dent's homer in the 1978 playoff game, that would come in later. I moved to New Jersey for high school and attended many Red Sox–Yankees games at Yankee Stadium. I sat through countless

"1918" chants and watched Yankees fans set fire to a Red Sox hat in the bleachers. This only made me love the Red Sox more and also made 2004 so much sweeter. The New York Yankees chose Bucky Fuckin' Dent to throw out the first pitch for Game 7 of the 2004 ALCS. When the game was over, the Red Sox had won 10–3 and completed the biggest comeback in professional sports history. This is why I love the Red Sox and hate the Yankees.

—Matt O'Donnell, owner, FenwayWest.com

I'll never forget attending the after-party following the New York City premiere of the acclaimed, eventual Oscar-winning film *Sideways* in October 2004. But it's not for what you think. Yes, I drank way too much fine wine and brushed elbows with many of the film's cast members and the director, Alexander Payne, but what was more memorable was crowding around the TV at the swanky spot's bar and watching Game 4 of the ALCS with a few special new friends. Down three games to zip, everyone in New York had thought it was a forgone conclusion that the Yankees would head to the World Series that night. Well, that was except for *Sideways* star Paul Giamatti, who watched a couple innings with me, and a nice Boston-bred couple who insisted the Sox would win not just that night but the next three games. Clearly drunk from the free-flowing spirits (I actually asked Giamatti, whose father was once Major League Baseball commissioner, if he followed the Red Sox—duh!) and ever the pessimist (as always when it comes to baseball and life), I gave the couple my number after David Ortiz homered off Paul Quantrill to force Game 5 and insisted they call if that happened. Zoom forward to Game 7 with the Sox on the verge of completing the biggest comeback in sports history. I got into my car to Allie Tarantino's apartment to watch the final three innings of the game with his brother Rich. I was called upon to "close out" the victory, and to celebrate with some champagne Al had purchased for the occasion. Moments after the final out was recorded and the biggest choke of the century was clinched, Allie, Rich, and I cheered, hugged, and probably dropped our pants with excitement. Then, my wife called. She wasn't cheering—far from it. She called to ask me why "some girl" I met at the *Sideways* after-party called asking for me. I quickly put my wife's mind at ease, hung up the phone, and popped open the champagne. The couple was right, and I toasted them along with the Sox with this book's coauthors on that delightful night.

—Jon Chattman, author

I grew up much closer to Yankee Stadium than Fenway Park, therefore any chance of seeing the Red Sox was relegated to a view from the Bronx. At the height of Lou Piniella's playing-day popularity, my dad kindly bought one of those killer red Red Sox hats for me, at Yankee Stadium no less. In those days you could still get other team hats (more on that later). With my Sox hat on, I joined a chorus of kids and ladies hollering for "Sweet Lou" to grace us with his presence and maybe sign an autograph. After most people walked away, my mom and I still continued to scream for Piniella, but he never came over. Yet we would still leave the stadium with a cherished signature. Hall of Famer Jim Rice walked over and signed my scorecard. I'm sure I rooted hard for the Sox that night; I'm also sure I lost my new Red Sox hat on the Cross Bronx Expressway. While holding it out the window in excitement, my young mind didn't realize it would get swept away.

The next day my dad made sure to have a new Red Sox hat for me. My baseball cap collection hasn't stopped growing since. When the Sox weren't in town, I made it a point to root, root, root for the Yankees opponent. In my teens I was showered with pretzels for standing up to cheer after a Bo Jackson home run. In 1993, while defending their championship in a not-too-crowded Yankee Stadium, I bought a Toronto Blue Jays pennant and helmet (can't do that anymore). When I returned to my seat, Bronx fans chanted "Off with his head!" and heckled me to go back to Canada. In actuality, my home was only 25 minutes away, where I now follow the Sox via the MLB Extra Inning package or on a trek up to Fenway.

—Allie Tarantino, author

It felt like hours, days even. For the first time in my life I was about to be face to face with greatness, I was about to be among an immortal, yes a true legend. I remember waking up that morning like it was Christmas, except it wasn't Christmas, it was in the middle of the summer—a time reserved for everything and anything baseball. It was a typical day in my life back then: eat breakfast, watch some television, head out, probably spend hours riding the blocks on my dirt bike, and after lunch at the pizzeria, I would play Wiffle ball and spend the afternoon trading cards. Except this wasn't any normal day for a 14-year-old kid who was usually more concerned with his Bo Jackson sneakers and his awkward but effective jump shot. The ride up the parkway felt like an eternity, and time spent on the line felt like ages. Finally, after a treacherous 45-minute wait, the time had arrived, and I made my way up and finally was eye to eye with a baseball icon. I guess at this point it would have been okay to tell you I was shaking hands with the Mick himself, or perhaps sharing pleasantries with the Clipper, or talking postseason round-trippers with Reg, but oh, no, it was much more intimate and memorable than that. With one quick stroke of the pen and one even quicker hand-shake, top it off with my patented half-assed half-cheese smile I can one day tell my children's children, who can one day tell their children's children, that good old Great, Great, Great Grandpa met and shared a Polaroid moment with the greatest Yankee legend himself: Mr. Kevin Maas—wait, hold on, quick, somebody cue the belly-flop, SPLASH!

—Rich Tarantino, author

My grandfather would frequently sit with me and listen to the game—in truth, he didn't understand the rules of the game—it was more about spending time with his grand-son. "Gramps" was an extremely quiet and unassuming man who generally kept his opinions to himself, so when he determined something was important enough to talk about, those of us within earshot listened intently. He was not an especially religious man, but he often spoke with me about the importance of faith. He taught me one of the great lessons of life—and faith—on the evening of October 21, 1975. I had been certain the Red Sox would win the 1975 World Series. In my mind, it was a matter of fate that the Olde Towne Team would prevail over the Big Red Machine; however, through the first five games of the series, things had not gone as I had foreseen. After the Red Sox prevailed in Game 1, things went awry. Reliever Dick Drago imploded in the ninth inning of the second game as

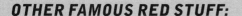

OTHER FAMOUS RED STUFF:

Red Lobster
The Big Red Machine
Red Velvet Cake
The Red Cross
Red Buttons
New York Red Bulls
Little Red Riding Hood
Red Auerbach
Redd Foxx
Red Panda
Red from Fraggle Rock

RED SOX

the Reds evened the series, and then home-plate umpire Larry Barnett handed the bad guys the third game when he failed to call interference on pinch-hitter Ed Armbrister in the 10th inning. The Red Sox won Game 4, and the Reds prevailed in Game 5, so the teams returned to Boston with Cincinnati leading the series 3–2. And then the rains came.… For three days, the baseball world watched and waited as rain soaked New England. Finally, on the morning of Tuesday, October 21, the clouds cleared and the sun shone, and I went to school certain that baseball would finally be played that evening. After school, I went to the local playground to play Wiffle ball. As children often do, we played that evening's game—pretending to be the Red Sox and Reds. Portraying Freddy Lynn, I hit the game-winning home run and forced the series to Game 7. Gramps and I took our places in front of the TV as the NBC broadcast began, not knowing that we were about to witness one of the greatest games in baseball history. It didn't take long for the Red Sox to jump out to a 3–0 lead, courtesy of a three-run home run by my hero, Freddy Lynn…but that excitement was tempered a few innings later when Lynn ran into the wall in left-center field trying to catch a long drive off the bat of Ken Griffey Sr. He crumpled to the ground in a heap as two runs scored. Fenway Park fell silent as the trainer and medical personnel tended to our fallen hero.

The earlier excitement dissipated. After several anxious minutes, Lynn rose to his feet and (surprisingly) stayed in the game. But the circumstances had seemingly taken the air out of the Red Sox balloon—moments later the Reds tied the game, and by the middle of the eighth inning, they had jumped out to a 6–3 lead. After Cesar Geronimo's solo home run in the top of the eighth, I became despondent. For the first time, I lost faith, and at the end of the frame I headed to bed. The game seemed lost. My grandfather encouraged me to hold on to a glimmer of hope, but I was inconsolable… I could not be convinced to continue watching the demise of my beloved Red Sox. But the truth of the matter is that I never really quit listening to the game. The spare bedroom was adjacent to the living room, and when I laid my head on my pillow, I was no more than 10 feet from the television. While Gramps had little interest in the outcome of the contest, he knew I was intensely interested and intently listening to the game as it continued. He never moved.

The television stayed on as I listened to Joe Garagiola, Tony Kubek, and Dick Stockton call the game…it was just like listening to the radio. My excitement rose when Lynn lined a single off the leg of Reds reliever Pedro Borbon and increased again when third baseman Rico Petrocelli worked an eight-pitch walk off the Reds righty. But it was quickly quelled when Reds manager Sparky Anderson turned to tough right-hander Rawly Eastwick to face right fielder Dwight Evans. I turned onto my right-hand side and moved to the edge of the bed as Eastwick went to a full count on Evans, determining I would get out of bed if Evans got on base…but Dewey whiffed on a 3–2 pitch, and I settled back toward the middle of the bed. Hope dwindled even further when shortstop Rick Burleson lined out to left field. As pinch-hitter Bernie Carbo walked to home plate, tears began falling onto my cheeks. Carbo worked the count to 2–2, and I rolled over onto my back. I crossed all of my fingers on both of my hands and held them to my face. I listened as Carbo fouled off a pitch and Dick Stockton declared that it looked like he had fouled the ball right out of the catcher's glove. Then I heard the sound of the bat strike the ball and the crowd start to roar…as I hit the edge of the bed, I heard Garagiola exclaim, "Deep center field… way back, way back…" By the time he proclaimed, "We're tied up!" I was already in front of the television. The tears poured down my face as I turned to my grandfather. He said simply, "Never lose faith."

Flash forward to 2004. The Yankees clobbered the Red Sox 19–8 in Game 3 of the ALCS. I sat on the couch in my home and tears rolled down my face. My wife came over and rubbed my back, and said, "There's always next year." I told her about Game 6 of the 1975 Series and the lesson my grandfather taught me those many years earlier. She said, "But no one has ever come back from being down 3–0," and I replied, "It ain't over until the fat lady sings!" Thanks, Gramps.

—Jeffrey Brown, sox1fan.com

The intensity. From Game 1 in spring training to Game 7 in October of the ALCS, this rivalry gives you a head start on playing in "big games." The fans bring it, and the teams are usually so evenly matched that you can carve a niche by performing in one game of one series, forever.

—Curt Schilling
(on what makes the Red Sox–Yankees rivalry so great)

My then-nine-year-old son and I started a tour of major league ballparks a little over six years ago. We have had the pleasure of enjoying 31 different parks on our tour. It is my opinion that there is no other ballpark in America that compares to Boston's Fenway Park. It is my feeling that a trip to the ballpark should offer a complete escape from one's everyday life and allow them to experience the childlike joy of being at a game. Fenway Park not only offers that feeling to children and adults alike—it creates a virtual alternate universe for those ready to immerse themselves in the game they love. From the moment you cross over Interstate 90 and approach the corner of Landsdowne Street and Yawkey Way, you are in baseball heaven. A place where everything else ceases to exist outside of the baseball world. All conversation turns to double switches, lefty/righty match-ups, and possible lineup changes. Food choices change to only baseball appropriate fare as you approach the Cask n' Flagon nestled in behind the "Green Monstah" bristling with baseball anticipation. No other place creates its own baseball sanctuary quite the way Fenway does. No other park presents batting practice as a salute to its own heroes more than a pursuit of souvenirs. No other crowd analyzes every aspect of their own players with less regard for the opponent. Fans could rarely care less about any opposing player besides the fact that they don't play for the Sox. No other ballpark celebrates the singing of "Take Me Out to the Ballgame" as simply a warm-up to their own unique eighth-inning anthem "Sweet Caroline."

As all Sox fans unite and join Neil Diamond in the singing of their song in their ballpark, you almost feel a sense of nearly 40,000 people joining together to celebrate the opportunity to have the privilege to root for their team. No matter the score—it is always a special moment when Sox Nation unites to celebrate their undying unity. As the game ends, you get an immediate sense that no one wants to leave. When you exit the stadium and look around, you wonder if anyone has. After a big win, there is truly nothing in the world like the streets surrounding Fenway Park. The emotion of the moment seems to carry you in the direction of your next generation. You find yourself cheering and chanting along with the euphoric crowd whether you are 14 or 41. Your exit is often sad, but you leave knowing that you have visited baseball heaven and that your next visit will not be far off as you continue to seek refuge in the joy of America's pastime. I have visited many of America's most beautiful cities and nearly every American ballpark, and I can honestly say that there is no place on earth quite like Boston's Fenway Park.

—Andy Dymek, White Plains, New York

4

RED SOX GAMES WE LOVE

Red Sox and Yankees is the single greatest rivalry in sports. It's the only rivalry where you don't have to say another single word and people understand. It's just Yankees–Red Sox period. Red Sox–Yankees period.

—Craig Carton
The Boomer and Carton Show, WFAN Radio, New York

You hear players saying once the Yankee series is over that it's time to get back to the regular grind. It's like coming off a playoff series when the two teams meet. It's so intense and it's not just brought on by the fans, it's by the media, as well. It's terrific. I think rooting for the Yankees is like rooting for US Steel. Now they're in the same ballpark—no pun intended. They both have great resources available to them.

—Jerry Trupiano

Pudge vs. Munson. Petey vs. Popeye. Ankle vs. Schilling. There are so many infamous games that have taken place between the Yankees and the Red Sox, it's hard to select just five that are our favorites—yet here we are. Anytime the Sox and Yankees get together for a series, it's like gearing up for a heavyweight fight or getting served a filet after a slew of appetizers—and it doesn't have to be October baseball.

Both teams are often so evenly matched and nipping at each other's heels in the standings all season long that even an opening series in April can bring a playoff vibe at either Fenway or Yankee Stadium. That said, the standings don't matter much to fill seats. The Sox could be down eight games, but the best of Boston will come out in droves to support their team to either Fenway or Yankee Stadium. Similarly, if the standings are not in the Yankees' favor, a strong Bronx contingent will travel to Boston to fill Fenway.

In the storied rivalry between the teams, five games in particular stand out for us as favorites. The games epitomize who the Sox are, and what the Yankees stand for.

MONDAY, OCTOBER 10, 1904
@ NEW YORK HIGHLANDERS

In 1903 the Boston Red Sox (then known as the Boston Americans) finished in first place in the American League and captured the inaugural World Series behind the play of Patsy Dougherty, Buck Freeman, and player/manager Jimmy Collins, to name just a few. One of the more notable stats of that vintage '03 season was the fourth-place finish of the New York Highlanders. Of course the Highlanders were to become the Yankees, and for the sake of a good stiff jab at the New York franchise, we take pride in noting that while the Sox were celebrating baseball's first-ever World Series championship, the Highlanders finished 17 games behind. A year later, the two teams would be in a position that seems all-too-familiar these days: slap dab in the middle of a heated pennant race, which saw the two teams separated by no more than $2^{1}/_{2}$ games since late July. Though known as the Americans and Highlanders, the 1904 season would be the first time ever that the Red Sox–Yankees war for the American League crown was settled in a head-to-head showdown. With their lead up to 1¹/₂ games, the Sox were guaranteed a second straight American League title with at least one win during the October 10 doubleheader played at New York's Hilltop Park. Despite finishing the 1904 season with the all-time Yankees and major league single-season pitching record of 41 wins, it was Jack Chesbro's wild pitch that sailed over the catcher's head, allowing Boston to take the 3–2 lead and eventual American League championship win. It would be the last time the Red Sox would beat the Yankees in a league-championship-deciding game in 100 years, but it's always great to know that it was Boston who drew first blood in the greatest rivalry in the history of sports.

WEDNESDAY, JUNE 6, 1990
vs. NEW YORK YANKEES

This was an unforgettable game not because of a rare Mike Boddicker complete game, but because finally the Red Sox would gain retribution on one of the most hated men to don the pinstripes, Bucky Dent. As the Yankees lay limp like a dead-fish handshake, the last-place cellar-dwellers posted an 18–31 record, the worst in baseball. Of course, this did not sit so well with the Boss, and because the Yankees were knee deep in their Steinbrennian ways, it was Bucky who was going to take the fall. Thankfully for Boston fans, Dent was given the hook in the same town where he reached the pinnacle of his career. It was at Fenway Park where he hit a three-run home run that carried the Bombers to a 5–4 victory in 1978 for the American League East title. However, before the 4–1 Red Sox victory, Dent was shown the door, making

Fenway the backdrop of his worst day as a major league manager. Red Sox fans were elated that Dent was tossed on their turf, despite getting swept away by the Bash Brothers and the rest of the Oakland Athletics in that year's ALCS. Legendary Boston sportswriter Dan Shaughnessy would later say that the "firing was only special because…it's the first time a Yankee manager—who was also a Red Sox demon—was purged on the ancient Indian burial grounds of the Back Bay." A wonderful day indeed for Red Sox Nation and a disappointing one for Bucky "La-Dee-Freakin'-Da" Dent.

FRIDAY, SEPTEMBER 10, 1999
@ NEW YORK YANKEES

Battling for the American League East division crown in the midst of the team's longest road trip of the season, Pedro Martinez took his familiar position on the mound at Yankee Stadium under the Friday night lights, ready to go to war with his most hated rivals. Much like He-Man conquering Skeletor on Snake Mountain, Pedro was ready to conquer the evil horde, better known as the New York Yankees. In one of the best non-no-hitter pitching performances of all-time, Pedro pitched one of the greatest games of his storied career. How's this for dominance? Petey threw a complete-game one-hitter, facing only one batter over the minimum all while striking out the side in the fifth, seventh, and ninth innings. He struck out every Bomber who came to bat at least once and clearly dominated a team that was on its way to becoming a dynasty. Pedro finished with a career high 17 Ks that night— the first time that any pitcher had ever struck out that many Yanks in a game. Allowing only two base runners the entire night, a home run by Chili Davis and a hit-by-pitch to Chuck

Knoblauch (who got caught stealing), the Yankees managed to hit only one fair ball after the fourth inning. Led by Pedro's pitching gem as well as some timely hitting by first baseman Mike Stanley (4-for-5, HR, two RBIs), the Sox beat the Yanks 3–1 in front of a packed Bronx crowd of more than 55,000. Pedro Martinez was at the top of his game in 1999. With a stat line of nine innings pitched, one hit, one earned run, no bases on balls, and 17 strikeouts, the Boston ace finished the year with a 23–4 record and a 2.07 ERA, striking out a team-record 313 and walking just 37. A strikeout ratio per nine innings pitched of 13.20, along with a strikeout-to-walk ratio of 8.46, helped win his second Cy Young Award of his masterful career. Among other highlights of the award-winning season was the honor of starting the All-Star Game, which was played that year at Fenway Park. In typical Pedro fashion, he responded by becoming the first pitcher to ever start the midsummer classic by striking out the side, earning All-Star Game MVP honors in the process. Taking over a playoff series was also part of Pedro's résumé in 1999. Forced out of Game 1 in the ALDS against the Cleveland Indians (minus Ricky Vaughn and Willie Mays Hayes) due to a strained back, Pedro exited the game after four brilliant shutout innings.

The Sox eventually lost the opener and dropped the second game, and sadly it appeared as though Pedro had thrown his last pitch and that the Sox's season was coming to an end. With a never-say-die performance in the works, Boston won the next two games, tying the series for a deciding fifth-game showdown. Still too injured to make the start, Pedro watched as the game became a hitter-friendly slugfest knotted at 8 after only 3¹/₂ innings of play. Entering the game as emergency relief, Pedro willed his way through the Cleveland lineup with

RED SOX

PEDRO 17K DAY!

On September 10, 1999, Pedro Martinez earned his 21st win of the season while setting a record for most strikeouts for the Red Sox against the Yankees. Pedro needed less than three hours and exactly 120 pitches to claim the victory at Yankee Stadium. Former Yankees 1B Mike Stanley provided four hits (one home run), which were more than enough for Pedro.

Batter	Result
Chuck Knoblauch	HBP, caught stealing
Derek Jeter	Strikeout swinging
Paul O'Neill	Groundout to 1B
Bernie Williams	Strikeout looking
Tino Martinez	Fly-out to CF
Chili Davis	Home run
Ricky Ledee	Strikeout looking
Scott Brosius	Strikeout swinging
Joe Girardi	Strikeout looking
Chuck Knoblauch	Pop-out to 3B
Derek Jeter	Fly-out RF
Paul O'Neill	Groundout to 1B
Bernie Williams	Groundout to 3B
Tino Martinez	Strikeout swinging
Chili Davis	Strikeout looking
Ricky Ledee	Strikeout swinging
Scott Brosius	Lineout to LF

continued

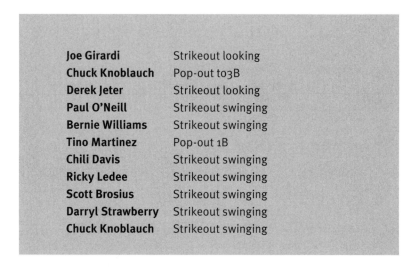

Joe Girardi	Strikeout looking
Chuck Knoblauch	Pop-out to3B
Derek Jeter	Strikeout looking
Paul O'Neill	Strikeout swinging
Bernie Williams	Strikeout swinging
Tino Martinez	Pop-out 1B
Chili Davis	Strikeout swinging
Ricky Ledee	Strikeout swinging
Scott Brosius	Strikeout swinging
Darryl Strawberry	Strikeout swinging
Chuck Knoblauch	Strikeout swinging

six no-hit innings and a win for the ages. Next up for the Sox was a date in the ALCS with the Yankees. Boston lost the series, but in a performance much like his unforgettable game on September 10, Pedro pitched seven shutout innings to beat Roger Clemens and the Bombers in Game 3, handing the eventual world champions their only loss of the 1999 postseason.

WEDNESDAY, OCTOBER 20, 2004
@ *NEW YORK YANKEES*

Game 7, American League Championship Series

"All empires fall sooner or later" said a gleaming Boston president Larry Lucchino, and with that said, the Red Sox were on their way to the 2004 World Series after overcoming a 3–0 postseason hole. It's amazing that just three nights earlier the down-and-out Red Sox were just three outs away from getting swept by the Evil Empire. With already two historic walk-offs in the series, David Ortiz started the Game 7 rout with a two-run rocket in the first off of Joe Torre's hand-picked starter, Kevin Brown. Brown, who lasted only an inning and a third, left the game after loading the bases in the second. Not to be outdone, Javier Vazquez's first pitch of the game landed in the right-field seats for a grand slam that was heard all the way from the South Bronx to Faneuil Hall. Adding insult to injury and thankfully a nail in the "Curse of the Bambino" coffin, Johnny Damon, who entered the game 3-for-29 (.103), got his third hit of the night, an upper-deck, two-run blast in the fourth inning. Inspired by the "Miracle on Ice," the visiting Sox slugged 10 runs in the decisive Game 7 spanking. Firing on all cylinders, Boston's offense was not the only highlight during the Yankees' monumental collapse. In fact, it was Sox pitcher Derek Lowe, pitching on just two days' rest, who allowed only one hit in six innings. Bomber bats were quiet for the most part, and so were the shocked fans that assumed a seventh World Series appearance in nine years was in the books. History was rewritten at one minute past midnight on October 21 when Ruben Sierra hit a grounder to second baseman Pokey Reese for the final out of the greatest comeback in sports history. Riding the emotional high of the series, the Sox swept away any lingering memories of the Curse in a non-competitive four-game drubbing of the St. Louis Cardinals. Owner John Henry summed up the championship victory best when he told the *Boston Herald*, "This is like an alternate reality. All of our fans waited their entire lives for this…. We won't even need the airplane to fly home." Indeed, the Sox were flying high and on top of the world, and it was Derek Lowe who summed it up best in regard to the rivalry between the Red Sox and Yankees: "I wish we could get our rings tomorrow. Unbelievable—no more going to Yankee Stadium and having to listen to '1918.'"

SUNDAY, APRIL 22, 2007
vs. NEW YORK YANKEES AT FENWAY PARK

In a clear sign of things to come in the 2007 season, this particular game is one we will not soon forget. Trailing the Yankees and rookie lefty Chase Wright 3–0, the Red Sox were about to briefly turn the game into batting practice. Thankfully for BoSox fans, Wright would be on the wrong side of history as he was the victim of some serious baseball whiplash in the form of back-to-back-to-back-to-back jacks. With two outs and the bases empty, Manny Ramirez sent a 2–1 pitch deep over the left-center-field wall. J.D. Drew was the next to go deep, sending a 1–2 pitch over the Red Sox bullpen, followed by a moon shot from Mike Lowell that cleared the wall and landed onto Lansdowne Street, tying the game 3–3. The excited Fenway crowd must have felt like they were watching one of those old 1960 *Home Run Derby* shows that featured Wally Post and Rocky Colavito, among others. It was finally Jason Varitek's turn to join the Boston Tee-off Party. The captain, who was swinging a hot bat already (5-for-8 in the last two games), wasted little time and sent the second pitch from the Yankees freshman clear over the Green Monster. Only seven times has a team gone and smacked four straight home runs. The other six teams to hit four consecutive home runs were the 1961 Braves (Eddie Mathews, Hank Aaron, Joe Adcock, and Frank Thomas); the 1963 Indians (Woodie Held, Pedro Ramos, Tito Francona, and Larry Brown); the 1964 Twins (Tony Oliva, Bob Allison, Jimmie Hall, and Harmon Killebrew); the 2006 Dodgers (Jeff Kent, J.D. Drew, Russell Martin, and Marlon Anderson); the 2008 White Sox (Jim Thome, Paul Konerko, Alexei Ramirez, and Juan Uribe); and the 2010 Diamondbacks (Adam LaRoche, Miguel Montero, Mark Reynolds, and J.D. Drew's brother Stephen). The Red

RED SOX

GONG SHOW (TOP 10 LOPSIDED RED SOX WINS AGAINST THE YANKEES)

1. **May 28, 2005 (17–1):** SS Edgar Renteria drives in five on three hits and one home run. In a rare Yankees start, Carl Pavano gives up 11 hits and five runs before being yanked in the fourth.
2. **July 15, 2005 (17–1):** What's better than a 17–1 victory over the Yankees? A second 17–1 victory over the Yankees less than two months later! A Big Papi grand slam and five RBIs from Trot Nixon drops New York's Tim Redding to 0–6. The Yankees starter gave up six in less than two innings.
3. **September 1, 1990 (15–1):** Stump Merrill didn't last two seasons with the Yanks, but he managed two of these lopsided Bronx Bombs. Andy Hawkins records just one out in allowing five Red Sox runs. Ellis Burks (two HRs) and Mike Greenwell (HR) combine for nine RBIs.
4. **August 22, 2009 (14–1):** A.J. Burnett (1–9 lifetime in August as a Yank) drops another summer bomb, giving up nine earned runs on three homers in five innings pitched. Kevin Youkilis smacks two tots with six RBIs.
5. **August 31, 1933 (15–2):** Sox 3B Billy Werber knocks in five runs from the lead-off spot, with a double and a triple. Relief pitcher George Uhle gives up eight runs in just over one inning pitched.

continued

6. **May 30, 1941 (13–0):** Mickey Harris holds the Yanks to two hits in the complete-game shutout. On the other hand, every Sox starter gets a hit. They are led by 3B Jim Tabor, who has the only homer among his three hits.

7. **July 9, 1959 (14–3):** Bob Turley starts for the Yankees and gives up seven runs. He is replaced by Jim Coates, who also gives up seven runs. Bobby Avila hits two homers, and Ted Williams places a frozen rope in the bleachers. The 1959 Red Sox score 10-plus off the Yanks six times!

8. **May 9, 2006 (14–3):** 2003 Marlins cast-offs lead the Sox to victory. SS Alex Gonzalez scores three runs and adds three RBIs. Josh Beckett strikes out seven Yanks in seven innings. The Big Unit doesn't last four, and A-Rod commits two errors.

9. **September 21, 1991 (12–1):** The second Stump Dump. Merrill's Yankees are no match for Phil Plantier (two HRs) and Jack Clark (25th homer of the season). Sox starter Joe Hesketh holds the Yankees 3-4-5 of Don Mattingly, Roberto Kelly, and "Bam Bam" Muelens hitless.

10. **September 6, 2003 (11–0):** Kevin Millar hits his 23rd home run of the season off of the Roger Clemens. The Rocket gives up seven runs in $3^1/_3$ innings during his "final season."

Sox edged the former Highlanders by the score of 7–6, led by Mike Lowell (2-for-4, two tater tots, four RBIs) and four homers that set the pace for another exciting and record-breaking Red Sox season.

AFTERWORD

It was the best of times, it was the worst of times. That's how *A Tale of Two Cities* starts. Dickens had it right, he always had it right! The Yankees are Scrooge, the Red Sox are Tiny Tim!

In *A Tale of Two Cities*, a man gives up his life for love. In our modern world, we love the Red Sox and we would give up our life to defeat the Yankees. Over the years, I have learned I don't hate the Yankees. Whenever I meet a Yankees fan, I tell them I love the Yankees, too. I love it when they show up. I beat them 12 times, I beat them like a red-headed stepchild, kind of like you!

In this book, I am reminded of the Jack Webb story of *Dragnet* and the drill instructor, "the facts ma'am, just the facts," and this book delivers the facts. What I can tell you is that Yankee Stadium was a dump. The outfield was like a rolling pasture, more suitable for grazing by just-bred content heifers. In Boston, Joe Mooney, the greenskeeper, would never let that happen, in fact you could hear him howl from his office in the left-field corner, "Get off my fucking grass." He loved me 'cuz I used to take off my spikes and roll around in his grass, hit fly balls to myself. It is sacred ground. Yankee Stadium no longer exists, it is a parking lot, it is a playground. In the new Yankee Stadium, the Babe spilt no DNA, yet he did in Fenway

Park. He christened the rivalry, he was stolen from Fenway. Fenway remains a lyric little bandbox. Duffy's Cliff became the 37-foot Green Monster, stopping line drives from killing commuters on the Mass Pike.

I will give you this, the fact the Yankees won 27 world championships—but they did not win until four years after they got the Babe. On that championship team, 81 victories were by ex–Red Sox pitchers, the Yankees bought most of their championships, we earn ours!

Did the Yankees have players like George "the Boomer" Scott, who hit tater after tater, no they had Danny Cater, who they sold for Sparky Lyle. Lyle gave them two more championships. Cater was nadir. We had Oil Can Boyd, whose grandmother said of Dennis at the age of five, "I think that boy has gotten into the 40-weight." And it was Dennis who said on a cold foggy day in Cleveland, "What do they expect, when they build a ballpark on the ocean?" Yes, the Yankees have Gehrig, who ruined Wally Pipps' career and did say, "Today, I feel like the luckiest man on the planet!"

I am glad to be part of the West Coast connection—Dom DiMaggio, Johnny Paveskovich (Pesky), Ted Williams (there walks the greatest hitter that ever lived), and the lovable Bobby Doerr (who told Ted, "You don't swing up on a high fastball"), who all have had a great love of the East Coast and in particular the Boston Red Sox. Now we have Pedroia and Ellsbury, the new generation—the rivalry, less violent, but no less fierce! In closing, I will say I actually feel sorry for Yankees fans and Red Sox fans because they no longer "listen" but are caught up in the hoopla at the parks, the mascots, the $8 beer, and the $6 hot dogs. Let's start a revolution and bring the rivalry, the game back to the people!!!!

Thank you.

—Chairman Bill "Spaceman" Lee
Earth, 2012

I
HATE
THE YANKEES

JON CHATTMAN, ALLIE TARANTINO
& RICH TARANTINO

TRIUMPH
BOOKS

For future Yankees haters Cyrus, Jaxon, Juniper, and Noah

CONTENTS

INTRODUCTION

*When my friend's dad died, at the cemetery after the funeral,
they had a bunch of flowers surrounding the gravestone, and
in the middle they had a Yankee-hater cap. Not a Red Sox
cap, a Yankee-hater cap, so he can hate the Yankees for eternity. Touching.*

—Brian Kiley, *Conan* staff writer

No Yankees were harmed during the making of this book…
only feelings of a certain loyal fan base were.

Hollywood elites thrust themselves on the bandwagon by donning their crisp caps with interlocking Ns and Ys, even though
they're miles away from the Bronx. Rappers like Jay-Z spit
rhymes about them, fading comedians get tryouts with the
men in pinstripes while so-called ethical New York journal-
ists let their pride overcome their integrity. If that weren't bad
enough, whenever you travel the globe—be it Jamaica, Tokyo,
or the Expos' old town of Montreal—you'd still bump into
someone with a Derek Jeter jersey.

Yes, we live in a New York Yankees world, and with 27 championships, it's hard not to root for the Evil Empire and ride
their store-bought championships. The Yankees are unofficially "America's Team," but there are many of us who equate
cheering for the Bronx Bombers to be as un-American as

singing the Kazakhstan national anthem in Dubya idiot country. There are some of us who stick with our team no matter what—purists at heart who bleed for our team no matter what the record books and wallets say. We're Boston Red Sox fans, and we will go to bat for our team through the ups and the downs, and celebrate our own rich history without throwing it in your face.

Just like rooting for the Yankees is an American tradition, we declare hating the team is part of our nation's pastime. While fans will rant and rave over heroes like Mickey Mantle or Paul O'Neill, we'd rather shine a light under pinstripe blunders like Kei Igawa or Snuffy Stirnweiss and tally the countless ways in which we despise the Yankees captains of yesteryear and inflated ego superstars of today. Join us in an alternate history of the most arrogant franchise in sports history...one that had to create "rules" for a mid-level middle reliever and facial hair fury. Grab a pint on Yawkey Way and read on as we throw Monument Park, pointless achievements, and supposed superstar plays (Jeremy Giambi slides, and he's safe) under the proverbial team bus. Celebrate Beantown with sticking it to a team that in 1990 had a 67–95 record—translating to what's unequivocally the worst collection of human beings ever to wear pinstripes.

Yes, for all their triumphs and trophies, the most successful franchise hasn't been without its swings and misses. Rejoice, Red Sox Nation, as we exploit them in the pages that follow and celebrate the Fenway faithful.

1
YANKEES MOMENTS WE HATE

Pedro tossing 72-year-old bench coach Don Zimmer down to the ground was a highlight of Sox Nation. Losing that game in the end, however, clearly was not. Johnny Damon winning a World Series ring with the Red Sox was an awesome moment in team history. The Caveman winning a ring with the Yankees five years later wasn't. The 1978 season was memorable, but ended sadly on a more memorable home run off the bat of an unlikely hero.

Yes, we can mention Bucky Dent's name until we're blue in the face, and Lord knows we have in this book, but that and those examples are just some Yankees "moments" that kick us in the proverbial gut. Let's face it—throughout their history, the Bronx Bombers have had our number. They've beaten the Sox in way too many pivotal games during the regular and postseason, and have used that old Yankees "magic" to win games they had no business winning for far too long. In this section, we explore the moments that have humbled Red Sox Nation and fed the already ginormous egos of Yankees fans all around the world.

RAGS, NO RICHES

The 1980s were jam-packed with great American sporting events like the Miracle on Ice, Sergeant Slaughter cobra-

clutching wrestling foes, and Greg Louganis' multiple gold medals. However, not much is more American than a Yankees no-hitter pitched on the Fourth of July. Prior to 1983, many great Yankees moments had already transpired on the Fourth of July, including the birth of the Boss, George Steinbrenner, and Lou Gehrig's famous "Luckiest Man" speech. But Dave Righetti would give Yankees fans another memorable day and one Sox fans would like to forget. Long before the Yankees screwed up the career of Joba Chamberlain, there was Righetti, who, in 1981, won the AL Rookie of the Year and helped pitch the Yanks to the World Series against the Dodgers. While L.A. exacted some revenge on the '77 and '78 losses with a World Series win, the Yanks appeared set at the top of the rotation with the young hurler known as "Rags." With Richard Nixon in attendance, Righetti plowed through the first three innings with seven strikeouts against a lineup that included three AL home run champs (Jim Rice, Tony Armas, and Dwight Evans) and two AL batting champs (Fred Lynn and Wade Boggs).

In the field Righetti was protected by third baseman Bert Campaneris (who had the first two hits of the game) and second baseman Andre Robertson (who drove in the first run). In pitching the first Yankees no-hitter since Don Larsen in 1956, Rags faced only 29 batters. The last batter was Boggs, who would only strike out 36 times in '83. Righetti would later admit how fearful he was of the future Yankee stroking a ball for one of his token hits. Righetti would retire Boggs on a slider and would soon be linked with another future Hall of Famer. The following season, Righetti would be rewarded by being chosen to replace Goose Gossage as team closer. In '86 Righetti would set the major league record for saves (46), which would last four years until it was broken by Bobby Thigpen. He would

make two All-Star appearances out of the pen and pick up two Rolaids Relief Pitcher of the Year awards until he had the Yanks reaching for Rolaids with a few too many 3.50-plus ERA seasons. While he never won a World Series as a member of the Yankees, he finally picked up one as the longtime pitching coach of the Giants in 2010. Bam Bam Meulens and Roberto Kelly were also on that coaching staff.

1961*

ASTERISK (THE TALE OF THE MICK, A PRICK, AND FRICK)

> *It would have been a helluva lot more fun if I had not hit those 61 home runs.*
>
> —Roger Maris

Chasing a baseball god's record while fending off your idol would seem like a dream of a baseball summer to most. But for Roger Maris in 1961 it was anything but that. The reigning American League MVP and Gold Glove winner hardly enjoyed any of the magic in the now historical summer of '61. Fresh off of their stunning Game 7 loss at the hands of Bill Mazeroski and the Pittsburgh Pirates, the Yankees, behind the M&M Boys (Maris and his idol, Mickey Mantle) established a record with 240 home runs (since broken by the 1996 Seattle Mariners). Stubborn. Surly. Out of place. No Charisma. Just a few descriptions that history books and fans (who avoided being spit on) have to share about Roger Maris. As the summer wore on and the assault on Ruth's record of 60 home runs continued, the switch-hitting Mantle appeared most likely to break the mark. Fans and opposing pitchers were likely to throw at Maris, the fans preferring any object they could get their

Roger Maris (left) on July 1, 1961, after hitting his 28ᵗʰ home run of the season, with teammate Mickey Mantle, eyeing the camera like it's a bottle of scotch.

hands on, and pitchers baseballs. With Mantle batting behind him, Maris was never intentionally walked the entire season. Probably the only person who proved to be a bigger prick than Maris the entire summer was commissioner Ford Frick. As the Bombers neared Ruth's sacred record, Frick announced they would have to do so before the 154ᵗʰ game of the season, as the Bambino had set the record under the old schedule format. Born in North Dakota, and suffering from the stress of

chasing the Sultan of Swat in front of the city that never sleeps, Maris battled through the season while the Mick lost some time to injuries. In 161 games, Maris would launch 61 homers, while Mickey would hit 54 in 153 games. Pulling out clumps of his hair and chasing a hallowed record was not enough to put behinds in the seats as Maris hit the record-breaking 61st in front of 23,154 on the last day of the season against the Red Sox in the Bronx. Frick's mandate that Ruth's record still be deemed the best was affirmed by his literal, then figurative asterisk that was forever placed with Maris' 61. In recent times, Maris has become a more sympathetic figure as his record has been surpassed several times over by Barry Bonds, Mark McGwire, and Sammy Sosa. The worst being the 1998 season, when the Maris family was dragged through the home run chase only to be hoodwinked like the rest of us by "Big Mac" and "Slammin' Sammy."

BRONX BOMBS

Once again proving that Yankees fans can learn something from obsessive Yankees haters, here's a Home Run Baker's dozen Bronx Blasts that will make your skin crawl. Some are historic (most are obnoxious), but all tape measures listed are by the Bombers.

Speaking of Frank "Home Run" Baker...during the Red Sox championship season of 1918, the Yankees "enjoyed" a fourth-place finish with a 60–63 mark. The Hall of Fame third base-man Baker led the pre-Bambino Yankees with six home runs. This pinstripe-leading total was five less than that of Red Sox pitcher George Herman Ruth. As amazing as it might sound today, on September 24, 1929, Babe Ruth Day was celebrated

at Fenway Park. As you could expect with the Sultan of Swat now playing for the Yanks, they were victorious 5–3. Ruth was a modest 2-for-3. While he did not hit one out of the park, he was appropriately hit by a pitch on his day of honor.

June 3, 1932. New York 20, Philadelphia 13. No, this was not an NFC East matchup between the New York Football Giants and the Eagles. This was the game where Lou "Biscuit Pants" Gehrig became the first modern major leaguer to homer four times in one game. A few years later, on May 24, 1936, Tony Lazzeri totaled three homers (including two grand slams). Throw in a triple and 11 RBIs, and you have a still-standing American League record for "Poosh 'Em Up" Tony.

Fast forward to 1965, the Eighth Wonder of the World is about to open for business. On April 9, in a rare trip to Houston for a spring training game, the Mick broke in the Astrodome by hitting the first home run in the ballpark's history off of Turk Farrell. The next season on September 11, John Miller became the first Yankee to hit a home run in his first at-bat. Miller's first (and only) pinstripe tater was launched at Fenway and was followed by two more first at-bat homer Yankees: Marcus Thames (June 10, 2002, vs. Arizona) and Andy Phillips (September 26, 2004, again at Fenway).

On June 24, 1970, in a doubleheader against Cleveland at Yankee Stadium, Bobby Murcer hit four consecutive home runs. Murcer's five RBIs on the day would only be good enough for a Yankees split. Don Mattingly avoided appearing in a World Series, but in 1987 with Steve Trout, Dennis Rasmussen, and Charles Hudson on the hill, "the Hitman" was not to blame. During the '87 campaign, Donbo was a one-man wrecking

YANKEES

MORE DYNAMIC THAN *THE* YANKEES' M&M BOYS (MANTLE *AND* MARIS):

Jose and Ozzie Canseco: The not-so Bash Brothers were briefly teammates during Ozzie's 24-game career. While the more famous bro Jose helped introduce the world to steroids, Ozzie began his career as a Yankees minor league pitcher and, despite becoming an everyday position player, ended it without ever going yard in the big leagues.

The Wild Samoans: These raw fish–eating bad boys of the squared circle are perhaps the most dangerous duo in the history of the ring. Former three-time world champions, the Samoans dropped their way into the most prestigious group in pro wrestling in 2007 when they were inducted into the WWE Hall of Fame.

The Barbers: Tiki and Ronde Barber were perhaps the National Football League's most well-known two-point conversion. Man, that was a lame football reference. Speaking of lame, while Ronde became a Super Bowl winner with the Tampa Bay Bucs, his identical bro Tiki attempts an NFL comeback after a failed *Today Show* stint.

Barbi Twins: They have rescued kittens and sold a boatload of calendars dating back to the early '90s. Their record-breaking *Playboy* appearances are in fact legendary according to most self-proclaimed Barbi-maniacs!

crew. On July 18, against the Texas Rangers and Jose Guzman, he tied Dale Long's record of eight straight games with a home run (which included 10 homers during the streak). As the season wore down on September 29, Mattingly cranked his sixth grand slam of the season (against Boston's Bruce Hurst).

With the losing ways of Mattingly gone, the Yankees were on the verge of their fifth title in six years when on October 31 and November 1, 2001, Tino Martinez and Scott Brosius enjoyed back-to-back, bottom-of-the-ninth home runs off of Byung-Hyun Kim. In a World Series where Derek Jeter earned the nickname "Mr. November," it was Kim who walked away with the World Series trophy. Not too far removed from his BALCO-induced MVP, Jason Giambi signed a seven-year $100 million-plus deal with the Yankees. On May 17, 2002, he finally earned some level of trust from the Yankees fans when he became the second player in franchise history to hit a walk-off grand slam against the always-ready-to-pack-their-tents Twins. "The Giambino" joined "the Bambino" for the briefest of moments.

On June 8, 2005, and August 4, 2007, Alex Rodriguez hit his 400th and 500th home runs, respectively. He became the youngest player to reach each landmark, and the third Yankee (Ruth and Mickey) to notch No. 500 with New York. On July 31, 2007, the Bombers tallied eight homers for the second time in team history. Even more impressive and irritating is that during the 16–3 win against the White Sox, seven different Yankees blasted the ball out of the park. Led by Hideki Matsui with two, Bobby Abreu, Melky Cabrera, Robinson Cano, Johnny Damon, Shelley Duncan, and Jorge Posada also went yard. Most recently, in 2011 switch-hitter Mark Teixeira homered from both sides of the plate for the 12th time in his career. He broke the previous record set by Eddie Murray, who overtook the record once held by Mickey Mantle. We could list more home runs from the Yankees' long history, but we've already wasted enough time talking about this spoiled franchise.

20-WIN WONDERS

The secret of success in pitching lies in getting a job with the Yankees.

—Hall of Fame pitcher Waite Hoyt

I don't see a better team to have a chance to win 20 games with than the Yankees.

—Rick Rhoden

After his second All-Star selection in 1986, Rick Rhoden fled the NL in hopes of becoming a 20-game winner and world champion with the Yankees. Rhoden knew first-hand the success of the Yanks, having lost in the World Series to them as a member of the Dodgers in 1977 and 1978. While he would become a successful golfer, winning 20 games proved to be elusive. However, Rhoden was onto something when he stated that pitching for the Yankees enhanced one's chances at obtaining 20 wins. Since the Bambino joined the New York Yankees in 1920, the Bombers have been all about the long ball. They've scored so many runs that it is indeed the easiest locale in which to notch 20 wins in a season. Whether it is a budding prospect they burned out, a mediocre middle-of-the-road pitcher, or someone else's star, the Bronx has been the home of 13 pitchers who earned their only 20-win season while with the Yankees.

Bullet Joe Bush (26), 1922. Bush won a World Series with the Babe in Boston and New York. Prior to that, he was a 24-game loser with the Philadelphia A's in 1916, despite managing to toss a no-hitter that season. The Bullet is often credited with inventing the forkball shortly after World War I.

George Pipgras (24), 1928. Pipgras spent nine seasons with Yankees before finishing his career with the Red Sox. "The Danish Viking" had a career season for the '28 champions, leading the league in wins and innings pitched (300²/₃). He was the starting pitcher for the Yanks in Babe Ruth's "called shot" game and became an umpire when his career ended.

Tiny Bonham (21), 1942. Bonham has the Yankees record for most wins by a pitcher named Tiny with 79. During his career year, he led the league with 22 complete games and six shutouts. Tiny appeared in three World Series with the Yankees, and although he pitched a complete-game win in the Game 5 clincher in '41, he lost his other two starts in '42 and '43.

Eddie Lopat (21), 1951. Born in New York City, Lopat was known as "the Junkman." He was part of the Yankees "Big Three" rotation who won five straight championships, yet Lopat managed to win 20 games just once. He won 15 or more games six times and had four World Series wins; however, there probably isn't a Yankees fan under the age of 40 who could name him.

Allie Reynolds (20), 1952. Prior to his 20-win season, "the Superchief" became the first AL pitcher to throw two no-hitters in one season. After posting a .520 winning percentage in five seasons with the Indians, Reynolds would flourish with a .686 winning percentage with the Bombers to go along with seven World Series wins.

Bob Grim (20), 1954. Grim was named AL Rookie of the Year during his lone 20-win season. He was then moved to the bullpen, where he helped the Yankees win a World Series in 1956 and led the league in saves with a measly 19 in 1957.

Bob Turley (21), 1958. "Bullet Bob" was rescued from the Browns/Orioles franchise, where he'd managed to lead the league in walks and strikeouts in the same season in 1954. By 1958 he was once again leading the league in walks, but now that he was with the Yankees, Turley was also a 20-game winner.

Ralph Terry (23), 1962. Terry was the MVP of the 1962 World Series, but he is remembered most for being the goat of the 1960 World Series. Bill Mazeroski owes his Cooperstown enshrinement to Terry, who served up the Game 7 walk-off blast to Pittsburgh.

Jim Bouton (21), 1963. Bouton became more well-known for his baseball tell-all *Ball Four* than for being a 20-game winner for the Yankees. Just like everyone on the Pilots, he spent one year in Seattle. However, unlike his teammates, he turned that porous 1969 season into a controversial, groundbreaking tome.

Fritz Peterson (20), 1970. Fritz pitched during the leanest years in Yankees history. In nine seasons he managed just a .507 winning percentage in pinstripes while never appearing in the playoffs.

Ed Figueroa (20), 1978. The Cy Young of Mustaches was obtained from the Angels with Mickey Rivers for Barry Bonds' dad, Bobby. Figueroa averaged 250 innings pitched over three seasons before his arm was toast. He was out of the league just three seasons after his career year.

Mike Mussina (20), 2008. Nobody has more wins (270) with fewer 20-win seasons in baseball history. The cerebral crossword-

solver notched his lone 20-win season in his finale. "The Moose" managed to have a better career winning percentage with the Orioles (.645) than the Yankees (.631). He also was sub-.500 (5–7) in the postseason on the perennial playoff-bound Yanks. If he does make it to Cooperstown, it should be as an Oriole but will most likely be in pinstripes.

CC Sabathia (21), 2010. It's tough to hate on a guy who helped the small-market Brewers get to the playoffs in '08 by pitching what seemed like every other day. But the record shows that CC (a workhorse for his era) has only won 20 games once and took the most money to accomplish the feat.

PINE TAR GAME

It's not just Red Sox Nation that has a hatred for all things Yankees. There are vignettes throughout baseball history that give other fan bases pause to despise the Bronx Bombers. Take the Kansas City Royals, for example; the once-proud Royals (were you even alive for their 1985 world championship?) shared an intense playoff rivalry with the Yankees from 1976 to 1978. The teams played in three straight ALCSs, with the Yankees taking all three while winning two World Series. The rivalry started when the entire borough of the Bronx emptied onto Yankee Stadium in '76 as Chris Chambliss sent the Royals on vacation with a walk-off homer. Yet the unlikely rivalry was all but faded when Royals relevancy ended (that would be the 1985 season, when former Yankees bomb Steve Balboni hit a Royals record 36 home runs).

In between, one of the zaniest moments in baseball history took place on July 24, 1983, and it included two Hall of Famers,

a volatile manager, and a heaping amount of pine tar. With U.L. Washington on first base (most likely with his trademark toothpick) and the Royals trailing 4–3, Goose Gossage served up what appeared to be a lead-changing home run to George Brett. Billy Martin, in a sober moment of clarity, noticed an excessive amount of pine tar on Brett's bat. The rookie home plate umpire agreed with the Yankees manager and called the All-Star third basemen out. Brett proceeded to out-Hulk Lou Ferrigno. AL president Lee MacPhail listened to the Royals' subsequent protest, and the game was to be resumed on August 18 but without Brett, who was thrown out for his outraged reaction, and Gaylord Perry, who tried to hide the suspect lumber by sneaking it to the bat boy. By the time the game was replayed from the point of Brett's reinstated home run, the Yankees had traded their center fielder, so they played with All-Star pitcher Ron Guidry in the spot once graced by Joe D and the Mick. Even stranger, they placed lefty Don Mattingly at second base where his 25-game hit streak came to an end; he remains the last lefty to appear at second in a major league game. The small-market Royals would win the 1983 contest, and the pine-tar bat used by Brett would join him in the Hall of Fame. But the Royals would suffer through two-plus decades of misery and irrelevance as the Yankees would further brand themselves as large-market mainstays.

JETER: 2009 *SPORTS ILLUSTRATED* SPORTSMAN OF THE YEAR

The Yankees captain finished third for the 2009 Most Valuable Player award voting and also passed Ted Williams for 68th place on the all-time hit list. Before the championship season, Jeter traded in the pinstripes for the stars and stripes

to play for the U.S. in the second World Baseball Classic, won by Japan. Jeter added the 2009 *Sports Illustrated* Sportsman of the Year to his list of major league accolades. Jeter joined a fraternity that includes hit king Pete Rose, as well as 1998 winners Mark McGwire and Sammy Sosa, to name just a few. Jeets beat out two-time winner Tiger Woods, whose reputation was all but ruined by the time 2010 spring training arrived.

PERFECT GAMES

I would rather beat the Yankees regularly than pitch a no-hit game.

—Bob Feller

On October 8, 1956, journeyman pitcher Don Larsen made back-page headlines by pitching the only perfect game in the history of the World Series. Since that day, pitching perfection has been reached a total of 14 times. That means Larsen, a career 81–91 pitcher, has been milking the Yankees ta-ta's for more than 50 years. Larsen went 27 up, 27 down to win Game 5 of the series against the Brooklyn Dodgers, earning a victory that thrust him straight into Yankees immortality, not to mention an unforgettable hug from diminutive Bronx-Bombing catcher Yogi Berra.

Although he was the catalyst in one of the more memorable pin-stripe moments, Larsen pitched for seven different clubs from 1953 to 1967. In fact, just two years prior to perfection, "Gooney Bird" went a dismal 3–21 with the Baltimore Orioles. Following his not-so-perfect season in 1954, he was shipped to the Bronx as part of a 17-player trade. Used primarily as a backup starter and relief pitcher, Larsen did happen to have a more successful run under the watchful eye of Casey Stengel. He finished his

Don Larsen catches an exuberant Yogi Berra (8) after completing his perfect game in Game 5 of the 1956 World Series against the Brooklyn Dodgers.

Yankees tenure going 45–24 over five years, despite his Spuds McKenzie–like partying reputation. Ironically, Larsen's Game 2 start of that '56 series lasted less than two innings in which he allowed four runs on four walks. In recent years, the ageless right-hander has made many appearances at the stadium old and new. One specific Kodak moment that rivals even "the everlasting image" is one in which he and the chairman of the board, Whitey Ford, were photographed on the pitcher's mound childishly filling up Ziploc bags with Stadium dirt.

On May 17, 1998, David Wells pitched the second perfect game for the Yankees, and the team's first by a player with an admitted hangover. Boomer, who has a lifelong public infatuation

TOP 10 YANKEES HEADLINES YOU'LL NEVER SEE

1. Maris Rounds Third, Scores Asterisk
2. Marky Mark (Teixeira) and the Funky Slump
3. Randy Winn Is a Loser
4. Weekend at Bernie Williams
5. Righetti Spaghetti with Balsamic Wynegar
6. America Runs on Shelly Duncan
7. The Joy of Sax
8. Hank But No Hank
9. Christmas Cancelled, Santa Joins Yankees
10. So Easy a Caveman Could Manage the Yankees

with the Bambino, disposed of a Minnesota team that featured an aging Paul Molitor, some guy named Jon Shave, and seven others dressed in Twins uniforms, none of whom ever finished with a career .280 batting average (Matt Lawton, .267; Brent Gates, .264; Marty Cordova, .274; Ron Coomer, .274; Alex Ochoa, .279; Javier Valentin, .251; and Pat Meares, .258). Just a little over a year later on July 18, 1999, David Cone threw the third Yankees perfect game. It was on Yogi Berra Day during a rain-soaked Bronx afternoon when the lifelong hired gun pitched his way into both Yankees history and onto Steiner Sports memorabilia. It took the five-time world champion only two hours and 16 minutes to mow down Vlad Guerrero and the artists formerly known as the Montreal Expos. BFFs Larsen and Yogi were in attendance.

But perhaps the most notable of all Yankee perfect games was on May 9, 2010, in a game in which the Oakland Athletics beat

the Tampa Bay Rays. This game in particular was pitched by Dallas Braden, whom an un-apologetic Alex Rodriguez dissed just 17 days earlier after the star slugger ran across the mound on his way back to first base. A-Rod, who had nothing better to do than scoff at Braden's brief career and losing record, most likely ate crow when the Mother's Day game was logged into the record books as being absolutely perfect.

JEFF MAIER: DEVIL IN THE OUTFIELD

Some of you may remember *Angels in the Outfield* as that 1994 Disney dud that starred Danny Glover and Tony Danza. Perhaps your interpretation of Angels in the outfield features the fleet-footed Gary Pettis. When it comes to the Yankees, angels in the outfield only has one legit meaning, and it begins and ends with the legend of Jeffrey Maier.

Like a bad case of the MTV *Cribs*, the magic happened on October 9, 1996, during Game 1 of the ALCS. Trailing 4–3 in the bottom of the eighth inning to the Baltimore Orioles, it was left up to a young shortstop by the name of Derek Jeter to save the Yankees' day. Taking advantage of the friendly confines, Jeter hit a deep fly ball to right field that prompted Orioles right fielder Tony Tarasco to move onto the warning track with his back against the wall, ready to make the second out of the inning. With a routine fly-out in his sight, it was then that 12-year-old Jeff Maier reached over and clearly deflected the ball into the stands.

The kid clearly made a bone-headed move, which was absolutely unnecessary. Seriously, we needed Jeff Maier like the baseball card industry needed Sportsflics. Although fans are

allowed to catch and keep balls that are hit into the stands, by no means are they allowed to reach over or go onto the playing field and touch a live ball.

In an even greater bone-headed move, it was right-field umpire Rich Garcia who blew the spectator interference call and ruled Jeter's fly-out a home run. Despite his best efforts, Baltimore manager Davey Johnson was ejected for rightfully arguing an awful call, and as Yankees luck would have it, the game was knotted at 4–4. To make matters worse, the Yankees would go onto win the game in the 11th inning on a Bernie Williams' walk-off home run, which was to be an exclamation point on their championship run through Atlanta.

The legend of Jeff Maier continues to resonate in our subconscious and remind us of the selfish and overly obnoxious heartbeat of the Yankees universe. Becoming yet another Yankees casualty, the Orioles postgame protest fell by the wayside as Maier's celebrity rose to unimaginable heights. He was awarded the key to New York City by head cheerleader Rudy Giuliani, becoming a symbol of a generation; a generation of Yankee tools who believe that winning a championship is their God-given birthright.

BIZARRO WORLD

When the Red Sox are unable to oppose the Yankees on the field, the Bombers' crosstown rivals fill in admirably. From the dawn of the Yankees in the early 1900s until the New York Giants and Brooklyn Dodgers fled for the West Coast after 1957, the National League was well-supplied with Yankees haters in New York. After a brief five-year hiatus, NL

ball returned to the "Big Apple" in the form of the New York Metropolitans. In total, the Yankees would face a New York senior circuit nemesis 14 times in World Series history. These faceoffs would come to be known as "Subway Series," and they generated plenty of animosity and vitriol in the direction of the pinstripes.

New York Giants

Quick, ask the person next to you which baseball franchise owns the most wins in the sport's history. Better yet, find someone in a Yankees hat and ask that question. Yankees hat or not, the person you ask will most likely reply "the Yanks," and they would be wrong. With more than 10,500 victories, the New York/San Francisco Giants have collected the most wins. They've done so with 55 Hall of Famers in team history, which is a dozen more than the pinstripes. As a matter of fact, according to Dennis Purdy's *Kiss 'Em Good-bye* entry about the New York Giants, they had a Hall of Famer every season they played in upper Manhattan.

Yes, it's true their franchise started close to 20 years before the Yankees, but their all-time winning percentage is second only to them. Known early on as the Gothams, their 19th-century success shows no shortage of Hall of Famers. To name just a few—Mickey Welch, Buck Ewing, Tim Keefe, Amos Rusie, and Roger Connor (whose career home run record of 138 would be broken by Babe Ruth). As the era of handlebar mustaches faded, the great Christy Mathewson entered the scene. He would be shortly followed by manager John McGraw, and the New York Giants at the turn of the century were off and running. The 1905 World Series may have included the

greatest Fall Classic performance in history. In the five-game series, Christy Mathewson shut out the Philadelphia A's three times, and the other win was a shutout by fellow Cooperstown hurler Joe McGinnity.

While the New York Yankees were busy floundering throughout the 1910s, the Giants frequently outdrew them at the Polo Grounds while finishing first or second in eight seasons. Unfortunately, Rube Marquard, Edd Roush, Waite Hoyt, and Frankie Frisch failed in four tries as NL champs. After prying Babe Ruth from the Sox, the Yankees were now ready for prime time. However, the Giants, with great team defense, won the first two of three World Series against their AL counterparts played from 1921 to 1923. With nine Hall of Famers on their '23 squad, they became the first of the Yankees' 27 World Series victims.

Even more embarrassing was the following year, when the Giants had 10 Hall of Famers and lost to the usually lowly Washington Senators. In the 1930s the Giants were armed once again with Hall of Famers (Bill Terry, Mel Ott, Rogers Hornsby, Carl Hubbell, etc.), and they avenged their Series loss to the Sens in '33. It would be a long dry spell before their next New York World Series victory, as they would submit to the Yankees three more times (1936, 1937, and 1951). The Giants' World Series hopes would be dashed by career bookend performances by Joe DiMaggio. Yet in 1954, behind "the Catch" by Willie Mays, the Giants would win their fifth and final New York World Series in an improbable sweep of the 111-win Cleveland Indians. The rivalry against the Dodgers would travel with the team to the West Coast, but other than an occasional interleague game, the Giants-Yankees rivalry is as forgotten as Roger Connor's 138 career home runs.

Brooklyn Dodgers

Years before three city kids known as the Beastie Boys turned the borough of Brooklyn into their own personal hip-hop playground, the Dodgers were the talk of the town. The National League team, named the "Trolley Dodgers" after the residents of Brooklyn who had to duck and dodge the trolleys that came through the borough back in the day, began their long-lasting rivalry with the Yankees when they first met them in the 1941 World Series. "Dem Bums from Brooklyn" would lose the Series as well as those in 1947, 1949, 1952, and 1953 to the crosstown nemesis Bronx Bombers. Finally in 1955, after much heartbreak, "the Boys of Summer," led by Pee Wee Reese, took down the Yankees in seven games, in the process changing the team's rallying cry from "Wait 'til next year" to "This *is* next year." One year later in 1956, the Dodgers were defeated in what would be the last Subway Series played during the 20th century. In 1958 the Dodgers left Flatbush behind and traded in Ebbets Field for Hollywood, crushing the hearts of many a New Yorker but continuing a winning tradition over the years. The two teams would meet again in 1963. Led by the dominating pitching of Sandy Koufax and Don Drysdale, the Los Angeles Dodgers would sweep the Yankees in four games. Fourteen years later, the two teams would play in back-to-back World Series. In 1977 the Billy Martin–led Bronx Zoo ballclub would ride the Mr. October coattails for their first championship since 1962. In 1978 the Yankees would repeat the feat and beat their West Coast rival Dodgers, all thanks in part to that one lousy Dent home run during the one-game playoff against the Red Sox.

However, the Dodgers would get the last laugh in 1981 behind the brilliance of Fernando Valenzuela, beating the Yankees for

the title and eventually leading them into a downward spiral of not winning a single World Series in the 1980s. It would be 18 years between ticker tape celebrations for the Bronx Bombers, while the Dodgers would again win in 1988, bashing the Bash Brothers behind Kirk Gibson's dramatic duck fart off of Dennis Eckersley and the Oakland A's. In 2007, after leading the Yankees to four championships, Joe Torre accepted a deal to become manager of the Dodgers, leading the 2008 squad to the playoffs while the Yankees would fail to make the postseason for the first time in 14 years. Beginning in 2011, Yankees hero Don Mattingly took over as Los Angeles' manager, trading in his pinstripes for Dodger blue, thus fueling the fire that has been lit since the rivalry began in the fall of 1941.

New York Mets

When the Red Sox aren't posing a threat to the Yankees in the standings (or the other way around), the rivalry between the two New York teams ramps up—especially since the introduction of interleague play in 1997. True, the Big Apple battle is nothing compared to the Sox-Yanks slobber-knocker, but when both teams are in the thick of a pennant race, it certainly gets heated. Case in point: Roger Clemens throwing a broken bat at Mike Piazza in the World Series between the clubs just months after he beaned him. Before we explore the New York rivalry, which the Yankees have soundly mastered, let's take a look at the origin of that other team in Ed Koch town. Ripping off, er, taking, the colors respectively of the dearly departed Dodgers and the Giants, the Mets were created soon after the teams left New York in 1957 to help fill the void of a weeping fan base. The Amazin's were anything but amazing when they debuted at the Polo Grounds in 1962 with the eternally old Casey Stengel at the helm. Stinking up the field worse than any 2008 Shea

FIVE ONE-TIME METS WHO THREW NO-HITTERS WITH OTHER TEAMS

1. **Tom Seaver** (Reds)
2. **Dwight Gooden** (Yankees)
3. **Nolan Ryan** (Angels, Astros, Rangers)
4. **David Cone** (Yankees)
5. **Hideo Nomo** (Dodgers, Red Sox)

YANKEES

Stadium bathroom stall, the Mets found creative, somewhat lovable ways to lose at first but ultimately stole the back pages away from the Yankees with an epic run in 1969. That year, the usual cellar-dwellers became the "Miracle Mets" when stars like Tom Seaver, Tommie Agee, and other players not named Tom propelled them to a World Series victory. For that year and a few after, the Mets arguably owned the city—breaking attendance records in New York. The same would ring true throughout the 1980s when the Mets were typically great, and the Yankees typically stunk up the joint. As we know, in 1986, the bad-boy Mets took over the city with a historical winning season that culminated with a Series win over the Sox. Players like Keith Hernandez, Gary Carter, and Lenny Dykstra won over fans, as did the infamous drinking and drugging tandem of Gooden and Straw. In their history, the Mets may not have a no-hitter thrown, but they do have two championships, four NL pennants, and five NL East titles. They also won consecutive wild-cards in 1999 and 2000.

Speaking of which, in those two years, with the Sox out of the race (although they rode the Yanks all season), the talk in New

York was centered on a possible Subway Series. That came to fruition in 2000, but the Mets didn't show up, and the Yankees led by, um, Denny Neagle, defeated them in five games. That's the problem—often times the Mets don't show up. Therefore, they always play second fiddle to the Yankees because they traditionally throw money at the wrong players (see: Jason Bay, Roger Cedeno, Oliver Perez…the list goes on), mishandle PR nightmares and injuries (see: Vince Coleman throwing a firecracker and Jose Reyes running the bases), and always seem to come up lame in big spots (see: Carlos Beltrán's no-swing in the 2006 NLCS). They also make boneheaded moves from the bottom to the top—whether it's passing on Reggie Jackson in the 1966 draft or moving catcher Todd Hundley to left field. In 1962 nothing was expected and nothing was delivered. In the early 1990s, has-been burnouts took the field, and to no one's surprise, came up Pat Tabler lame. But even with top talent—sans the 1986 season and those that bookend that (if the wild-card were around, they would've become a dynasty in the 1980s)—they fail to capitalize and truly take off. In other words, the Mets battle themselves more then they battle the Yankees. Still, it makes for a great rivalry when the two teams are hot and bothered.

THE STREAK

2,130—gone. 60 and 61—see ya. 714—sayonara. 56—still hangin' tough like a New Kids on the Block comeback. Other than 27 (and counting), 56 seems to be a Yankees magic number that won't go away. In the summer of 1941, Joe DiMaggio broke St. Louis Brown George Sisler's 41-game hit streak for the new modern record of 56 games. Along the way he took down the Yankees record (Roger Peckinpaugh, 29 games

![Joe DiMaggio batting]

Joe DiMaggio lines a single to left in the second game of a doubleheader against the Washington Senators on June 29, 1941. He set a record for hitting safely in 42 straight games on his way to establishing his 56-game mark.

in 1919) and Wee Willie Keeler's all-time mark (44 games in 1897). While the Yankee Clipper is often described as graceful, he once broke his kneecap getting out of a cab after a minor league record 61-game hit streak in the Pacific Coast League. While this discouraged many teams from purchasing his contract, it did not have that effect on the Bombers,

who bought his rights from the San Francisco Seals. In 1937 Joe D had a 22-game hit streak followed by a 21-game hit streak, which started the day after the first ended. Three seasons later, Joltin' Joe would hit safely in 23, but he was only warming up for his assault on the record book in the following season. While DiMaggio's streak was beginning, fellow Hall of Famer and Yankees teammate Bill Dickey saw his 21-game hit streak coming to an end. Dickey's streak lasted about as long as a Zima six-pack did on store shelves during the clear carbonated alcohol's heyday in the early '90s.

Richard Ben Cramer's *Joe DiMaggio: A Hero's Life* elaborates on the hit streak in great detail. With the streak at 15 games, DiMaggio (.330) trailed Ted Williams (.429) by close to 100 points. On the subject of "Teddy Tantrum," Joe D stated, "He throws like a broad and runs like a duck." In Ted Williams' *Hit List*, the Splendid Splinter takes the high road, tabbing DiMaggio the fifth greatest hitter of all-time. Williams explains, "At the plate he was poetry in motion; his fluid swing a thing of beauty." DiMaggio, who had time to take in the classic Joe Louis vs. Billy Conn fight at the Polo Grounds with Lefty Gomez, did face pressure during the streak and struck out an amazingly low five times. In fact, he went over a month (June 8 to July 26) without striking out. However, it was not all roses for the Yankees during this time. The Iron Horse, Lou Gehrig, passed away in the midst of the streak. The streak was full of many trivial bits, some of which make it incredibly spectacular, and others that make it seem plausible. DiMaggio faced many pitchers who went the duration of the game; therefore he rarely faced a fresh arm late in a game. He faced only four Hall of Famers (Lefty Grove, Bob Feller, Hal Newhouser, and Ted Lyons) while his average rose from .304 to .375 during

the streak. He would finish at .357 and never catch Williams for the batting title (.406). But he would pick up his second of three MVPs and be dismissive of the Kid at the end of the season, saying, "Sure, he can hit, but he never won a thing." DiMaggio's streak was played in eight cities, appeared in seven doubleheaders, and he managed to go 1-for-4 in the All-Star Game. The streak ended when Cleveland's third baseman Ken Keltner famously robbed Joltin' Joe twice.

Following this 0-fer, DiMaggio would hit safely in the next 16, a remarkable 72 of 73 games. This streak has long overshadowed Ted William's record of 87 games safely reaching first base. While the two brilliant hitters did have their heated moments, they shared a love for their country, and both lost considerable playing time for service to their country. Upon his retirement in 1952, Marilyn Monroe's future husband was offered $100,000 to play just in Yankees home games. DiMaggio turned it down to appear as Mr. Coffee and as a Simon and Garfunkel lyric.

THE REASON THE F-WORD WAS CREATED

If there were ever a heavyweight title fight for biggest Yankees dagger to the hearts of Red Sox fans, it would undoubtedly be between the home runs by Bucky Dent and Aaron Boone. If you are holding this book, you know all of the painful details and don't need many reminders on the likes of Grady Little or Mike Torrez, but we'll relay some of them, anyway. In 1978 the Sox, who had once held a 14-game lead, found themselves tied for the AL East lead with the Yankees at 99 wins. Despite having a 3-4-5 of Hall of Famers (Rice, Yaz, and Fisk), the last thing the BoSox would win all year would be the coin toss to

A nickname is born: Bucky "Fuckin'" Dent sends an offering from Red Sox righty Mike Torrez over the Green Monster for a three-run, game-winning home run in the 1978 one-game playoff versus the Yankees to determine the AL East title.

get the game to Fenway. But, while the Sox's middle of the lineup would perform admirably, it would be the Yanks No. 9 hitter who played scene-stealer that day. The 5′9″, 170-pound (soaking wet) Dent was such an unlikely hero that manager Bob Lemon considered pinch-hitting for him, but because of

injuries didn't have many options. Good for Lemon, bad for us. The Yankees had obtained the one-tool, one-time All-Star tool from the Chicago White Sox for Oscar Gamble's afro and future Cy Young Award winner LaMarr Hoyt, and up until that one-game playoff, he had hit just four home runs that year. Then Mike Torrez served one more up. (The prior season, Torrez was the winning pitcher in Reggie's famous three–home run World Series performance, by the way.)

After fouling off his foot and cracking his bat, Dent needed to borrow Mickey Rivers' bat, and with his next swing the former Russell Earl O'Dey became forever known as Bucky "Fuckin'" Dent. Fortunately, the home run happened before ESPN, and Red Sox fans were spared the replay through the night and into the winter. Lost in the history of the day is that Dent is not credited with a playoff home run, however his magic would continue into the World Series, where he would be named MVP for hitting .417 with seven RBIs. Eventually, the Yanks traded Dent (.239 in six seasons) for the even more adorable Lee Mazzilli. Dent would only hit 40 home runs in his career, but he would parlay his final-day-of-the-season blast into two Yankees All-Star appearances and one of the least successful Yankees managerial tenures (36–53 over parts of two seasons). Upon his firing (in Boston, of all places), *Globe* writer Dan Shaughnessy compared it to "Neil Armstrong tearing his Achilles doing the moonwalk." Some 25 years after the Dent hit the fan, another unlikely hero summoned the Yankee Gods and stepped up. Yeah, he got a new middle name, too. More on that in a few.... In May 2003 the Yankees had just won their sixth straight regular season series from the Red Sox, and by the trade deadline, they had a 3¹/₂-game lead over the Sox. With their fan base getting antsy since

YANKEES

Nineteen seventy-eight drove me nuts. We had a 15-game lead that just chiseled away. I was at the last game of the season. Mike Torrez, the former Yankee who lived the next town over, pitched. I remember streets were so crowded going out to Yawkey Way after that last day, I was 14, and my cousin was short. We were in a river of people. People were happy but it was tense. We had to play a one-game playoff. My cousin nudged me and pointed to his feet. I looked down, and his feet were off the ground but he was moving. That's how crowded it was. We cut school and went to the game. Bucky Fuckin' Dent.

—John Slattery, actor, *Mad Men*

the Bombers hadn't won the World Series in a whopping three years, the Yanks jettisoned a used-up Robin Ventura to the Dodgers and traded with the Reds for third-generation major leaguer Aaron Boone.

Earlier in the season, Boone had played in the All-Star Game, but by the time the ALCS against the Sox rolled around, he warmed the bench behind Enrique Wilson. In Grady Little's last game as manager, Tim Wakefield was spared the goat horns. Just days before it looked like an apocalyptic World Series might happen between the Cubs and Sox, but Little made sure that wouldn't happen by famously sticking with Pedro Martinez and blowing a Game 7 lead. Moments after Pedro finally exited the game, Boone pinch hit. In the bottom of the 10th inning, his home run reached left field faster than you can say Bubba Trammell, and the Yanks were on their way to their 39th World Series appearance.

In retrospect, the Dent homer remains more painful because the Sox were robbed of a playoff chance, and the 2004 BoSox

erased much of the heartache from the Boone blast. Besides, in 2009 Boone became the first player to ever return to the majors after open-heart surgery—even the most hardened member of Red Sox nation has to tip their cap to him for that. (Or not.)

BUY BUY BABY
(AKA *FREE AGENT SIGNINGS*)

Randy Johnson

Freddie Mercury once sang "I Want It All," and that's essentially been the mantra of the New York Yankees franchise since they started or at least since free agency was born. Sometimes, however, having everything on paper doesn't translate to championship titles. Already with an All-Star at essentially every position and still reeling from headline hog Roger Clemens rocketing to Houston a year prior, Bombers GM Brian Cashman orchestrated a deal on January 6, 2005, for Arizona ace Randy Johnson to join the team. All they gave up was 9 million clams, Brad Halsey, Dioner Navarro, and never-a-good-Yankee Yankee Javier Vasquez.

Forty-two years old but still reliable, Johnson was a sought-after southpaw whom the Yankees had coveted since he mowed them down in the 2001 World Series. With expectations high and media buzzing, The Big Unit proved to be a surprisingly lackluster move. Even before taking the field, Johnson made enemies in the Big Apple. His gruff attitude didn't sit well with fans, who instantly balked at his non-Yankee-like demeanor, or the New York media, who were rubbed the wrong way instantly when, seconds into his Yankees stay, the pitcher had a run-in with a cameraman en route to his press conference.

With expectations high, much like Larry Brown with the Knicks and a sequel to the original *Arthur*, the union between Johnson and the pinstripes was wrong right from the very start. While he pitched well enough to lead the team to play-off berths (he had 34 wins in two seasons), Johnson's stay in the Bronx was as uneventful as a Mike Pagliarulo playing a day/night doubleheader. Johnson would end up returning to Arizona after his two-year stay with the Yankees, and finished his career with the Giants. Altogether, the Big Unit finished with 303 wins, 166 losses, and one dead dove.

CC Sabathia

In 2008, for the first time since 1982, the Milwaukee Brewers made it to the playoffs and the New York Yankees did not. While most of the baseball world was happy to see the small-market Wallbangers make a playoff push, the fat cat Yanks and their spoiled fans were wondering how to spend half a billion dollars and return to their rightful place in October. Shortly after the Phillies took out the Brew Crew on their way to a World Series championship against the Tampa Bay Rays, the Yankees wasted no time pouncing on free agent stud pitchers CC Sabathia and A.J. Burnett like Rex Ryan on an Atlantic City buffet line. As if that spending spree wasn't enough, they outbid the Red Sox and Nationals for Mark Teixeira to replace iron-glove-and-thong-wearing Jason Giambi. With the arrival of 2009, and Joe Girardi's uniform No. 27 collecting mothballs, the Yankees once again bought themselves another world title as CC, A.J., and Tex played an important role in defeating the defending-champion Phillies and becoming the first team with a $200 million–plus payroll to win the World Series.

DRAFT DODGERS

When it comes to drafting amateur players, the New York Yankees are more Mickey Klutts than Mickey Mantle. In 1965 baseball became the last of the four major sports to institute a draft to distribute incoming amateur talent in a fair manner. One of the driving reasons for creating a draft was to level the playing field so that wealthy teams like the Yankees did not monopolize all of the game's young talent. Prior to this, the Yanks would just sign amateur free agents as they did with Mickey Mantle in 1949. Once the draft was instituted and they had to wait their turn, they were often left with players like Mickey Klutts (fourth round in 1972). Since '65, the Yankees have hit below the Mendoza Line in drafting and promoting players to their major league roster. Early in draft history, the Yankees got off to a good start, selecting some regulars. Ron Blomberg (first rounder in 1967) became the first designated hitter in baseball history for the Yankees, for whom he "played" seven seasons. Thurman Munson (first rounder in 1968) became Yankees captain, league MVP, and seven-time All-Star before his untimely death. However, you'd have to fast forward from the Summer of Love to the height of Grunge in 1992 to find the next first-round pick that mattered in the Bronx. After the Brien Taylor debacle of '91, the Bombers used the No. 6 overall pick on future captain Derek Jeter. More recently, former Yankees first rounders Joba Chamberlain and Phil Hughes have become on-again, off-again starters/bullpen men. Beyond the first round, it's tough to find anyone not named Ron Guidry who was drafted by the Yanks and had a substantial career in the House That Ruth Built. The evidence is clear the Bombers have little use for drafted players other than as trade bait. The Yankees have had a propensity

to trade prospects for veteran players. Among the All-Stars the Yanks tabbed in the first round who became All-Stars are: Willie McGee, Scott McGregor, Pat Tabler, Carl Everett, and Ian Kennedy. In subsequent rounds, you'll find there are better players the Yankees traded away (Al Leiter, LaMarr Hoyt, Fred McGriff, Hal Morris, J.T. Snow, Mike Lowell) than kept (Dan Pasqua, Dave Eiland, Jim Beattie, Kevin Maas, and to be fair, 19th-rounder Don Mattingly). You can see the laziness in the Yanks front office. Have others draft and develop major league talent and then sign the player from their original franchise. The Yankees took an interesting approach in showing unusual restraint in 2011; they did not trade prized draft pick Dellin Betances. Nor did they ship out international free agents Jesus Montero and Manuel Banuelos. The last time they showed such restraint, the Boss was exiled from baseball and the Yankees held onto the pair of Andy Pettitte (22nd) and Jorge Posada (24th). Also in 2011 they used draft picks on players like Dante Bichette Jr., Samuel Stafford, Jordan Cote, and Matt Duran. It is more likely that the road for these players will be blocked by a huge free-agent signing because that is the Yankees way.

BILLY CRYSTAL BALLS

Up until March 12, 2008, Billy Crystal's greatest baseball performance was the silent film baseball mime routine he performed during one of his one-too-many Academy Award hosting gigs. On that day, he donned uniform No. 60 (his age) and proceeded to stretch out his hammy with new BFF Derek Jeter. The audacity of his leading off as designated hitter against the Pittsburgh Pirates was surely pitcher Paul Maholm's biggest nightmare as a pitcher (certainly a bigger

MOVIE TITLES THAT PERSONIFY THE YANKEES

1. *The Usual Suspects*
2. *The Fellowship of the Ring*
3. *The Good, the Bad, and the Ugly*
4. *For a Few Dollars More*
5. *Money Train*
6. *Limitless*
7. *Million Dollar Baby*
8. *The Empire Strikes Back*
9. *Jackass 3D*
10. *Rich Man, Poor Man*

nightmare than *Forget Paris*). As the costar of *My Giant* dug into the batter's box, all thoughts of integrity of the game, his wearing a New York Mets hat in *City Slickers*, and owning a 2001 Arizona Diamondbacks World Series ring as a part owner became a distant memory. While his at-bat lasted six pitches (sorry, Billy, one meek foul ball won't make it on the back of a baseball card), history will show that Crystal didn't look Maaaaahvelous, and Johnny Damon remains the only player ever to replace him in a major league game.

THE GOLDEN THONG

More infamous than a 1989 Billy Ripken Fleer card and just as pointless as a King Kong Bundy five count, the Jason Giambi

golden thong will go down in history as the most useless baseball accessory since Bobby Valentine's fake mustache.

In the summer of 2008, three years removed from apologizing to Bomber loyalists without using the "S" word, Jason Giambi finally told the truth. In a move just as lame as his brother Jeremy not sliding during the Jeter flip play, older brother Jason admitted to donning a tiger-striped golden thong under his pinstripes when he needed to break out of a slump. Of course, the former Bomber took it one step further, announcing that he shared the goods with hitless teammates wanting to get back on track.

When it comes to superstitions, the golden thong is like a rabbit's foot on steroids. But despite allegedly sharing the slump-breaking butt floss with Bernie Williams, Derek Jeter, and Robin Ventura, the former Yankees slugger finished his Bronx tenure without ever winning the World Series—which, of course, is the baseball equivalent of a Wonka golden ticket.

These days Giambi has yet to hang up the cleats or his thong, for that matter. And, speaking of the Giambino's undergarments, we can only imagine if the golden thong would have had the same effect on Tanyon Sturtze.

2

WE HATE YANKEES
PLAYERS AND LEGENDS

*When I was a little boy, I wanted to be a baseball player and
join a circus. With the Yankees I've accomplished both.*

—Graig Nettles

The Yankees are a team rich in history and well, just rich, and
for decades, they have been the team to beat every season.
There may be 30 teams in baseball, but there's only one Yankees, and the organization runs its business that way. They
require all players be clean cut, well groomed, and play the
fundamentals. They require all players give 110 percent, and
when they do and still come up short, their owner throws
them under the bus.

The Yankees are beloved by a fan base of loyal followers (old
school fans who stuck out the bad years) and new bandwagon-
ers who couldn't tell you yesterday's lineup, never mind who
played center field for the team in 1968. The Yankees are an
astonishingly successful franchise that buys the best to beat
the best and stand above the rest. Because of all of this, the
team has a long line of players whose walking of the proverbial
company line infuriates us.

Derek Jeter plays the game the right way. He puts his team first and his personal stats a distant second. He leads by example, and helps motivate his team by simply performing at a high level. He's dedicated and a proven winner. He's got the Gold Gloves, five World Series titles, and, according to the YES Network, is the only hitter to ever reach 3,000 hits. He's the kind of player you love if he's on your team, and the kind of player you loathe if he's not. That trait explodes when you factor in such a player wearing Yankees pinstripes. Jeter is not the only player who we hate in Boston.

Throughout their history, the franchise has had its share of players who get under our skin on so many different levels. We hate Bucky Fuckin' Dent because he—of all people—sent the Sox home in 1978. Similarly, we hate Aaron Fuckin' Boone because he—of all people—sent the Sox home in 2003. But there are players who consistently annoyed us for years—not just because they became a one-hit wonder at our expense.

Some players we hate because of their past personal connection to our franchise (i.e., Clemens, Damon), while others simply rub us the wrong way because of their sheer arrogance (well, Clemens again). There's Yogi Berra, a respected backstop who hit a ton, but ended up becoming an American sweetheart because he uttered ridiculous non-sequitur ramblings known as "Yogisms." Give it a rest, Yogi. Babe Ruth did well in Boston, but became a legend when the Sox sold him to the Yankees. Ruth annoys us because all we'd heard pre-2004 was the dreaded "Curse of the Bambino." Please.

This book would be *Lord of the Rings*–style long if we went on to name every single player we hated, but below you will read a

handful that made us gag, from Phil Rizzuto to Don Mattingly and beyond. Sure, there are some Yankees who manage not to rub you the wrong way in Boston. They are a select few, and you won't read about them here.

WADE BOGGS, 3B

We cried with Wade Boggs when he wept during Game 7 in the visitors dugout in Queens. We cried harder 10 years later when the third baseman rode *Seabiscuit* to a World Series title with the enemy Yankees. Before joining the Evil Empire, Boggsy won five batting titles and, over 11 seasons with the team, batted .338. Following his first sub-.300 season (.259), he was granted free agency and signed with the Yankees over the Dodgers because they threw more money and years at him (hmm…where have I heard that before?).

With the addition of Boggs, the Yanks had two old mustachioed studs on each side of the diamond who quickly vaulted the team back above .500 after a four-year hiccup. The 1993 squad was good enough for a wild-card spot, but unfortunately for Buck Showalter's Bombers, MLB wouldn't add the wild-card until a year later. The following season, Boggs was his old self (.342) and the Yankees were cruising to face the Montreal Expos in the '94 World Series until labor strife resulted in a lost World Series. No doubt Boggs cried over that. He and the Bombers would say good-bye to Don Mattingly and a 2–0 ALDS lead over the Mariners in one Ken Griffey Jr. slide. But in 1996 Boggs got his World Series ring. We cried. After leaving the Bronx, Boggs signed with the then-hideous Tampa Bay Devil Rays (with equally hideous uniforms) and collected his 3,000[th] hit. The third baseman's post-baseball career has some

out-of-left-field moments. He requested to go into the Hall of Fame with a Rays hat on (Bud Selig knew better), inducted Mr. Perfect into the WWE Hall of Fame, and has been spotted in Cosby-esque sweaters. The Rays have since retired his number, but the Sox haven't as of yet. The fowl taste of the noted "chicken man's" horse riding is still too bitter for Red Sox Nation to swallow.

ALEX RODRIGUEZ, ~~SS~~ 3B

Dubbed as the most important basketball injury in the history of baseball, Aaron Boone was released from his Yankees contract shortly after tearing his knee during a pick-up game on January 16, 2004. No word on whether shirts or skins won the game, but history tells us that the most infamous torn ACL in the annals of sports led to the most talked about acquisition in the Red Sox–Yankees rivalry since Babe Ruth was shipped to the Bronx in 1919. Not settling for an Enrique Wilson/Miguel Cairo platoon at third base, the Yankees, hot off a World Series loss to the Florida Marlins, acquired the services of the great Alex Rodriguez. Considered to the best shortstop in the league, A-Rod, as he is known throughout the universe, took one for the team. In a bold move not to offend Derek Jeter, the game's greatest player ever made the smooth move to the hot corner.

After spending his first few years in Seattle's hitter-friendly Kingdome, Rodriguez signed to play with Texas in 2000 for 10 years, $252 million. The contract was the richest in history at the time, which left the power-hitting shortstop earning $63 million dollars more than the second-highest-paid player. Following some record-breaking seasons and a few last-place

TOP FIVE LOVE AFFAIRS INVOLVING A-ROD

1. A-Rod and Kate Hudson
2. A-Rod and Madonna
3. A-Rod and Jeter
4. A-Rod and Cameron Diaz
5. A-Rod and A-Rod

finishes, Texas began feeling offers to relocate A-Rod to a new zip code. Initially, the Rangers agreed to send him to the Red Sox, but the deal was nixed when it was ruled by radio personality Mike Francesa to be unfair to the Yankees. Actually, it was the MLB Players Association that vetoed the deal because of a voluntary reduction in Rodriguez's salary.

Learning that Rodriguez was available, it was the New York Yankees who came in and snatched the future Hall of Famer from the Rangers in exchange for Alfonso Soriano. It should be noted that Rodriguez never had to take a pay cut after the trade, thus finalizing the biggest off-season move in the Boston–New York rivalry since Harry Frazee sold Babe Ruth to the Yankees. After which, of course, the Sox were left playing damage control with a disgruntled Nomar.

Speaking of Ruth, when Rodriguez made his pilgrimage to the Bronx, he had to change his jersey from No. 3 to No. 13 since the Bambino's digits were already retired. Since the trade, A-Rod has continued his torrid pace through the record books, as he became both the youngest to reach 500 and 600 home runs. His greatest blast however was on July 24, 2004,

during his first season in New York when he was plunked by a pitch. The beaning led to a bench-clearing brawl and one of the most iconic shots in sports of Red Sox captain Jason Varitek shoving his fist in A-Rod's face (see page 21 of *I Love the Red Sox*—the upside-down section of this book—in the "Red Sox Moments We Love" chapter).

Certainly not one to shy away from controversy (please insert Toronto strip club jokes here), Rodriguez once again was in the thick of things during Game 6 of the 2004 ALCS. With Derek Jeter on first in the bottom of the eighth inning, A-Rod managed to hit a slow dribbler between the mound and first base, which was fielded by pitcher Bronson Arroyo. As Arroyo reached to make the tag, he was slapped, and the ball was knocked loose, scoring Jeter all the way from first on what was first officially ruled an Arroyo error. After a meeting of the minds, the umpires ruled that Rodriguez was out for interfering, and Jeter was summoned back to first base. So what did we learn from all this? Well, we already know there is no crying in baseball, there is certainly no betting, and thanks to A-Rod there is definitely no slapping. So, with a little help from digital cropping, every time we Google image search this moment you can see A-Rod running up the first-base line with a purse. Thanks, Photoshop.

While news spread that A-Rod and Jeter were no longer in a bro-mantic relationship, the 14-time All-Star was also coming to grips with the fact that he and Madonna were "just friends." A *New York* magazine article even reported that the superstar was involved in a deal with the Chicago Cubs that included part-ownership of the team. Thankfully, cooler heads prevailed, and while Alex Rodriguez was dotting i's and crossing

Alex Rodriguez slaps the ball out of pitcher Bronson Arroyo's glove as he tries to apply the tag during Game 6 of the 2004 ALCS. Though the ball came loose, A-Rod was eventually ruled out because, well, that's just a wuss move.

t's on his 10-year, $275 million contract, the Red Sox were tapping the Rockies in the World Series.

In the winter of 2009, after denying use of performance-enhancing drugs, A-Rod—or as the Fenway faithful dubbed him, A-Roid—admitted to using steroids during his days with the Texas Rangers. Maybe Jose Canseco was right all along about the fastest man to 600 round-trippers. A-Rod did say it

10 BIGGEST BONEHEAD A-ROD MOVES

1. Knocking the ball out of Arroyo's hand
2. Calling "I got it" in Toronto
3. World Series interruption to announce opt out
4. Steroid Gammons interview
5. Loyalty to cousin Yuri
6. Pa-Pa-Pa-Poker face
7. Madonna
8. Kate Hudson
9. Super Bowl popcorn with Cameron Diaz
10. Moving to third base

was due to "an enormous amount of pressure," or, as we like to call it, the inability to perform in clutch situations.

Dating back to Game 4 of the 2004 ALCS, Rodriguez had come up to bat with 38 runners on base over a span of 61 postseason at-bats, stranding every single one of them in an 0-for-29 October drought.

Despite finally earning his South Bronx street cred and carrying the pie-tossing Yankees to a World Series in 2009, Alex Rodriguez may very well be the most disliked Yankees player in the Yankees–Red Sox rivalry—Yankees fans included.

Regardless of his on-the-field accolades and his off-the-field drama, there is no denying that he is the top player in the major leagues today not named Albert Pujols. That being said, Boston fans are truly grateful for the shortstop by committee of Orlando Cabrera, Edgar Renteria, Alex Gonzalez, Alex

Cora, Julio Lugo, and Marco Scutaro, and even more grateful that the deal for A-Rod never went down in the first place.

PHIL RIZZUTO, SS

I heard the doctors revived a man after being dead for four-and-a-half minutes. When they asked what it was like being dead, he said it was like listening to New York Yankees announcer Phil Rizzuto during a rain delay.
                    —*Late Night* host David Letterman

Growing up in the '70s and '80s, most kids in the New York area knew Phil Rizzuto as the announcer who would give shout-outs and Holy Cows during the games and would be seen shilling (and visibly reading from the teleprompter) for the Money Store during commercials. How fitting that a Yankees legend advertised a place called "The Money Store," since in some circles, that term is used to describe the new Yankee Stadium.

In Yankees lore, the Scooter was much more than TV pitchman. While he may have lovingly miscalled many Yankees moments in the booth and annoyingly referred to people as "huckleberry," he led the Yankees over the Sox many times as a player. The diminutive shortstop batted over .300 in only two seasons in his Hall of Fame career (his 1941 rookie season and 1950 MVP season). However, he surpassed the .300 mark in four of his team's nine World Series title runs. Ted Williams famously stated the Red Sox would be in much better standing if they and not the Yanks had "the Little Squirt" on their team. The small-ball genius and bunting whiz became a master of digression. Scooter followed a Yankees tradition of

meaningful games called by half-witted announcers with unnecessary catchphrases. Whether he was talking about where he could get a scrumptious cannoli or how he could leave the game early to beat traffic on the G.W., Rizzuto was charming to Yankees listeners and nauseating to any other baseball fan listening. As his 40-year broadcasting career drew to an end, the Bombers presented the aged Scooter with an actual cow, which proceeded to bump him to the ground.

SCOTT BROSIUS, 3B

Did Scott Brosius even know he was Scott Brosius with the Yankees? Sure, he put up decent numbers as a member of the Oakland A's for seven years, but did he really have to come off more like Nettles and less like Blowers? Taking a page from Gob of *Arrested Development* fame, "C'mon!"

Brosius was the player to be named later in a trade the Yankees made to rid themselves of a roasted Kenny Rogers after the 1997 season. In 1998 the infielder made fans forget all about Wade Boggs by delivering key hit after key hit and ending the season with 19 home runs and a career-best 98 RBIs. He also won the World Series MVP that year, and a year later earned a Gold Glove. Yes, the presumed weakest link in the plentiful Yankees lineup turned out to be yet another weapon in the team's overpriced arsenal, and he helped them finish first every year he played with them (despite his numbers returning to normal after 1998). To make matters more annoying than the B-52's "Rock Lobster" chorus, he always seemed to be a thorn in the Sox's side by hitting 15 home runs and more than 40 RBIs in his career against the team.

To make Sox fans feel a little better, Brosius' biggest home run as a Yankee ended up not mattering much. Just one night after Tino Martinez homered off eventual Boston scrub Byung-Hyun Kim in Game 4 of the 2001 World Series, Brosius hit a two-out, two-run home run off the same deflated pitcher to tie Game 5 in the bottom of the ninth and set the stage for yet another textbook Yankees extra-inning win. Thankfully, "Brosius the Ferocious" couldn't save the Yankees from losing pivotal Games 6 and 7 in Arizona.

DEREK JETER, SS

The captain has gone where no Yankee has ever gone before, and in doing so, Derek Jeter became the first person named Derek Jeter to collect 3,000 major league hits. Since his debut in the Bronx in 1995, Derek Jeter has rewritten the Yankees record books all while displaying pride, class, dignity, and that old-fashioned winning tradition. While Jeter plays the consummate professional persona to a tee, the interlocking N and Y remains the No. 1 fashion accessory among active hooligans and bad guys. I guess we can overlook that as long as good old No. 2 is in the lineup, ready to show off his clutch hitting and Gold Glove fielding. These two superior skills that only a player like Jeter can possess are what helped earn him 12 All-Star selections and entry into the elusive Kalamazoo Central High School Athletic Hall of Fame.

In a move that likely did not go over so well in the Tony Fernandez household, manager Joe Torre announced that Derek Jeter would be the team's starting shortstop on Opening Day of 1996. He hit his first home run that game and finished the

Derek Jeter gets a little chin music from Boston's Derek Lowe in Game 7 of the 2004 ALCS in New York. Jeter later singled in the at-bat, driving in a run, which is part of why we hate him (though, of course, the Sox won!).

season with Rookie of the Year honors and of course a Yankees pennant.

The Jersey-born star would help lead the Yankees to four more tickertape parades with grace under pressure, a knack to make that great play when it counts (nice slide, Jeremy), and the ability to make any Red Sox fan vomit.

After the damn dynasty of the late '90s, Captain Clutch found yet another chance to shine on the big stage. On October 31, 2001, Game 4 of the World Series went into extra innings, leading to an improbable home run from Jeter just after midnight. The game-winning blast earned him the nickname "Mr. November." Despite his late-inning heroics, El Capitan was 3-for-12 (.250) during November baseball, and the Yankees would eventually lose in seven games to the Arizona Diamondbacks.

In 2003 Burgermeister Meisterburger—oops, we mean George Steinbrenner—named Jeter the first captain of the club since Don Mattingly's ring-less run ended in 1995. One year later the leader of the free world would earn ESPN web gem cult status by making a dramatic over-the-shoulder snag followed by a launch into the third row of seats. The catch ended the inning, left Jeter with chin lacerations and a bruised face, but thankfully did nothing at all to help the Yankees' chances of being on top of the baseball world.

It would not be until 2009 that Jeter and his spoiled Yankees fan base who expect to win every season retook the mountaintop. It was a banner year for the captain, who also went home with *Sports Illustrated*'s Sportsman of the Year award.

After the 2010 season, Jeter found himself in unfamiliar territory because, for the first time in his life, he was a free agent. Despite some rough patches, he finally reached an agreement with the Yankees on a three-year contract with a fourth-year option. The Yankees, who were bidding against themselves for his services would have had a hard time explaining to fans why Jeter was getting his 3,000th hit with the Cincinnati Reds.

On July 9, 2011, Jeter became the first player in pinstripes to ever reach the 3,000-hit milestone when he homered off of Tampa Bay's David Price. Luckily, he managed to hit his 3,000th hit to the only person in the stadium who was willing to just give him the ball. Throughout his record-breaking career, the great Derek Jeter has even made cameo appearances in such films as *Anger Management* and *The Other Guys*. We haven't seen better Yankees acting since Triple Crown threat Clu Haywood's breakout performance in 1989's *Major League*. Quite certainly, there is not an endorsement deal he doesn't like. Appearing in everything from Nike to Skippy ads, Jeter has endorsed just about everything under the sun except perhaps for wearing a Cosby sweater and whoring for Jell-O pudding pops.

1927 YANKEES

During 1922, in Babe Ruth's third season with the New York Yankees, "the Bambino" took a team of all-stars (which included Bronx teammate Bob Meusel) to compete against the Kansas City Monarchs. The Monarchs proceeded to take both games of the late October doubleheader with help from Newt Allen, John Donaldson, and Bullet Joe Rogan. When you consider the pre–Jackie Robinson times of the 1920s, it is tough to consider the 1927 Yankees as the greatest collection of ballplayers,

YANKEES

MURDERED ROW:
A CAPTIVATING EXPOSÉ ON SOME
PRETTY LOUSY YANKEES TEAMS

Not every season is a World Series winner, as this pothole-filled trip down memory lane will prove.

The **1912 New York Highlanders** (50–102) were so bad that they ditched the name and became the Yankees the following season. Amazingly, this remains the last 100-loss team of the franchise. With hitting leaders like Birdie Cree (.332) and Guy Zinn (six homers), it's easy to see why there is very little Highlanders-era memorabilia hanging at Yankee Stadium. The 1913 name change didn't immediately help, as the Bombers celebrated the occasion with their worst win percentage ever as the Yankees at .377 (57–94).

The **1925 New York Yankees** (69–85) finished seventh out of eight AL teams, in large part because of the Babe's "bellyache." You can't surround the Babe with players named Pee Wee Wanniger and expect big things, especially when the Bambino was limited to just over 350 ABs from what has long been rumored to be a battle with venereal disease. The Babe did manage 25 homers. However, oft-forgotten Yankees star Bob Meusel led the team with 33. The grander story that history would take from this subpar season was an injury to Wally Pip that would lead to the Iron Horse's charge to greatness.

continued

The **1966 New Yankees** finished only a half game behind the Red Sox. How then do they find themselves on this list? Easy. The Red Sox finished in ninth place in the 10-team American League, which placed the Yankees in dead last. The Yankee basement-dwellers were only five years removed from their historic season of '61. Maris and the Mick combined for 115 HRs in '61, but only 36 in '66, which helped the team finish 26½ games out of first. Mel Stottlemyre, who would later become famous as the Yanks' pitching coach, spent the year becoming the last Yankees pitcher to lose 20 games in one season. Jim Bouton went 3–8 while collecting notes for his infamous book, *Ball Four*.

The **1990 New York Yankees** (67–95) are unequivocally the worst collection of human beings to wear Yankees pinstripes. Led by ringless Don Mattingly, this squad managed to have *THREE* players with 100-plus at-bats hit below .200 (Deion Sanders .158, Steve Balboni .192, and Mike Blowers .188). Jesse Barfield led the team with 25 home runs, edging out rookie Kevin Maas' wild finish with 21. Stump Merrill and Bucky Dent managed a pitching staff that saw some remarkable feats. Relief Pitcher Lee Guetterman led the team with 11 wins. This was made possible because Tim Leary was busy leading the league with 19 losses and setting a Yankees record with 23 wild pitches. Let us not forget the magic of Andy Hawkins. Hawkins pitched a no-hitter against the White Sox on July 1. However, the Yankees lost 4–0.

The **2008 New York Yankees** (89–73) somehow missed the playoffs despite outspending everyone once again. They remain the only interleague-era Yankees squad not to make the playoffs. This collection of non-winning Yankees was the culmination of eight seasons of Bronx Blueballs. Giambi. Abreu. Pudge Rodriguez. Sexson. Mussina. Pavano. All stars of the 2000s who would leave the Bronx ringless.

but that is exactly what most baseball fans call that particular "Murderers' Row" of Yankees talent. While Major League Baseball was still about 20 years from integration, Babe Ruth and Lou Gehrig continued to move the national pastime further from the dead-ball era and the Black Sox scandal. In 1927 Ruth and Gehrig combined for 107 of the 439 home runs hit in the American league. This barrage of home runs led to 110 wins, a 19-game first-place margin over Cornelius McGillicuddy's Athletics, and a severe case of whiplash for Yankees skipper Miller Huggins. According to an article in the *New Yorker* (August 6, 1927), much of the good fortune of Murderers' Row could be attributed to pickled eels. It seems that when the Iron Horse wasn't busy clobbering home runs (47) he could be found in the vicinity of Harlem fishing for eels. Described as "naturally clumsy" but able to "overcome much of his ineptness," Gehrig would catch the eels and have them pickled by his mother whenever he was urged by his slumping teammates.

It's hard to figure when the 1927 Yankees were ever slumping. While they didn't play against the great black ballplayers of the time, they were 18–4 against the last-place Red Sox. This head-to-head record was only surpassed by their 21–1 record against the hapless St. Louis Browns. About the only team that was somewhat competitive against the '27 Yanks was the Tribe; Cleveland won 10 of 22 against the Bombers. The Yankees did not have to battle through several rounds of playoffs like today's editions must; their first-place finish vaulted them right to the World Series against the Pittsburgh Pirates. The 1927 World Series involved 11 Hall of Famers between the Yankees (Ruth, Gehrig, Tony Lazzeri, Earle Combs, Waite Hoyt, and Herb Pennock) and Pirates (Paul and Lloyd Waner, Joe Cronin, Pie Traynor, and Kiki Cuyler). Despite just a

one–Hall of Famer advantage, the Yankees swept the Bucs in four behind two homers and a .400 batting average from the Bambino. It is most likely that Gehrig did not go fishing for eels during the Series.

MOONING THE ROCKET

Forget the fact he shaved to look good for reporters while his Sox were blowing Game 6 of the 1986 World Series. Forget the fact he couldn't wait to leave for Toronto in 1996 and became an arrogant Yankee two years later. Forget that he may or may not have taken steroids and perjured himself in a court of law and public opinion. The reason we hate Roger Clemens is because he tarnished his dozen years of devoted service to the Sox by wearing out his welcome and sticking it to the team every chance he had after leaving. True, the Sox didn't exactly do their best to re-sign "the Rocket," but this is a Sox book not a Clemens book, and he's an easier target.

Clemens could've gone down as the best Sox player of all-time (his numbers were ridiculous), but his ego got as inflated as his bank account, and that's what we'll remember him by. If Clemens were a more likable person, it'd be a whole lot easier to focus on his pre-Yankees days. But we digress. Let's take a stroll down memory lane to a time where the mere mention of his name made us giddy rather than grate on our nerves.

Clemens was drafted 19th overall by the Sox in 1983 and made his debut in the bigs just a year later. Within two years, the Rocket was viewed as the best pitcher in the game not named Dwight Gooden and excited not just Sox fans but the entire

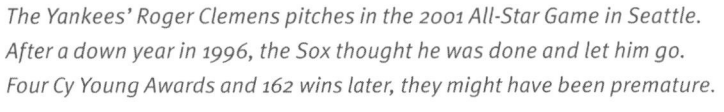

The Yankees' Roger Clemens pitches in the 2001 All-Star Game in Seattle.
After a down year in 1996, the Sox thought he was done and let him go.
Four Cy Young Awards and 162 wins later, they might have been premature.

MLB. In 1986 Clemens had arguably the best season a pitcher has ever had in the game. With an impressive (to say the least) 24-win season, Clemens picked up not only the Cy Young Award but the American League MVP and helped lead the team to the World Series. That same year, he became the first pitcher to ever strike out 20 batters in a nine-inning game (he did it again 10 years later with the Sox).

Often arrogant and outspoken—not to mention reckless (he beaned a lot of batters each year), fans could still rally behind their ace throughout his 13-year run in Boston because he always kept them in the game. But by 1996, the righty's numbers weren't exactly what they had been, so the Sox chose to let him go. General manager Dan Duquette stated at the time that the pitcher was in the "twilight" of his career. Boy, was he wrong.

After winning 192 wins for the Sox (to tie Cy Young for the club record), Clemens signed a four-year $40 million contract with the AL East rival Toronto Blue Jays in 1997. In each of his two seasons with the Jays, the pitcher won the Cy Young Award and Triple Crown. And, naturally, in his first start against the Sox in 1997, he struck out 16 and shut the offense down. Seeing Clemens in a Blue Jays uniform was strange enough—but to see him don pinstripes hurt the most.

In 1999, a year that Sox fans would rather forget, Clemens was traded to the New York Yankees in exchange for David Wells, Homer Bush, and Graeme Lloyd. Who made out better on that deal? Certainly not the Blue Jays. Anyway, in his first two years with the Bombers, Rocket got two World Series rings but didn't really pitch like he did as a Canuck or in

Boston. In 1999 he pitched to a 14–10 record with a whopping 4.60 ERA. (To his credit, he had a strong postseason.) The next year, Clemens pitched a little better with a 13–8 record and 3.70 ERA. That postseason, he set an ALCS record for strikeouts in a game by striking out 15 Mariners in Game 4 of the ALCS.

Clemens didn't pitch like Clemens for the Yankees until 2001, in which he started the season 20–1. He ended up finishing with a 20–3 record and won his sixth Cy Young Award. Clemens dueled Curt Schilling in Game 7 of the 2001 World Series against the Arizona Diamondbacks. He got a no-decision, and the D-backs went on to win the Series.

In 2003 Clemens announced he'd retire at the end of that season. On June 13, 2003, he earned his 300th win and 4,000[th] strikeout against the Cardinals. As the year ended, Major League Baseball celebrated Clemens' career by paying tribute to him. When he came to Fenway for his "last" game of the regular season, he was met with a standing O. He returned to Fenway in the infamous "Down Goes Zimmer" game in which Pedro Martinez shoved Popeye to the ground. In that epic showdown, Clemens bested Martinez. And for the rest of the postseason, Clemens was met with more cheers for his farewell tour.

After all the cheers and vomit-inducing homages that took place in 2003, Clemens unretired, spurned the Yankees, and joined his Yankees pal and teammate Andy Pettitte as a member of the Houston Astros. That season, he posted an 18–4 record and earned his seventh Cy Young. With retirement once again looming, Clemens returned in 2005 to Houston

for a record $18,000,022 salary. That season, he posted a 1.87 ERA, a 13–8 record, and got his 4,500th strikeout. After pitching well in the postseason, the Astros fell to the White Sox in four straight games due largely because Clemens' hamstring couldn't hold up.

In 2006 the "will he or won't he?" game continued. Finally, on May 31 of that year, it was announced he was coming out of retirement again. He pitched to a 7–6 record and a 2.30 ERA. In 2007 he once again sat out part of the season and on one "magical" day—at least according to Suzyn "Goodness Gracious" Waldman—Clemens returned to the Yankees via George Steinbrenner's box to tell fans at Yankee Stadium he was returning.

Making over $1 million a start, Clemens pitched to a 6–6 record and a 4.18 ERA. His hamstring injury held him from making as big an impact as he probably had in his mind. Clemens hasn't pitched for the majors since then, and has been met with controversy ever since.

We all know his name appeared on the Mitchell Report. We all know former Yankees trainer Brian McNamee has said he gave him anabolic steroids and human growth hormones. We all know a federal grand jury indicted him on six felony counts of perjury, false statements, and obstruction of Congress. We know he's vehemently denied everything since and that his trial was declared a mistrial.

Whether or not Clemens took steroids to enhance his game play is irrelevant to us. We simply don't like him because ever since he left Boston (and even before), he's just an utterly

unlikable person who puts himself over his team any day of the week. Rooting for Roger Clemens to succeed is like rooting for the star high school quarterback with an already hot cheerleader girlfriend to get lucky with another hot blonde at the prom. In other words, you just can't.

Clemens was an "ass" as former manager Cito Gaston once called him long before his name came up with Mitchell and McNamee. There was the time he got tossed after arguing during a pivotal game in the 1990 ALCS. There was the 2000 World Series game in which he threw Mike Piazza's broken bat at him. And there were all the times Clemens threw at Yankees batters before he became a Yankee and was deemed by that organization as a headhunter.

Amazing talent, an amazing jerk—that best defines what Clemens means to us.

KEVIN MAAS

He was supposed to be the Roger Maris to Don Mattingly's Mickey Mantle; instead Yankees M&M wannabe Kevin Maas literally crapped the Bomber bed, finishing his career with a pedestrian .230 batting average, 65 home runs, and 169 runs batted in.

His Yankees fairy tale began in 1990 when he hit 21 home runs in 79 games—however, if there is a record for most meaningless home runs hit in meaningless games then the record-holder must be Kevin Maas. During his not-so-historic run, the Sultan of Squat hit more solo homers in a losing effort than anyone ever. So much for living happily ever after.

YANKEES

27 YANKS WITH NO CHANCE AT A YANKEEOGRAPHY

1. Lee Guetterman
2. Ken Phelps
3. Steve Kemp
4. Clay Parker
5. Chuck Cary
6. Steve Karsay
7. Greg Cadaret
8. Eric Plunk
9. Oscar Azocar
10. Francisco Cervelli
11. Gary Ward
12. Henry Cotto
13. Cecilio Guante
14. Lenn Sakata
15. Bobby Meacham
16. Orestes Destrade
17. Armando Benitez
18. Luis Aguayo
19. Claudell Washington
20. Andy Stankiewicz
21. Deion Sanders
22. Scott Kamieniecki
23. Sterling Hitchcock
24. Kenny Rogers
25. Chris Chambliss
26. Dave Eiland
27. Chan Ho Park

During his amazing second-half run in 1990, the Yankees scored a run in each game that Kevin Maas hit a home run. Maas did manage to hit a home run off the great Nolan Ryan, and while his homer off of Charlie Hough was not as historic as Reggie's World Series tot off the knuckleballer, Maas did provide thrills for one of the worst Yankees teams ever. The Bombers did manage to play near .500 ball in games in which Maas homered (9–10).

In Maas' final homer game, Prince Fielder's dad went deep twice. They were Cecil's 50th and 51st, when hitting 50 homers still meant hitting 50 homers. Despite his record-breaking four-baggers, his one-hit-wonder season makes Right Said Fred's "I'm Too Sexy" seem like a greatest hits album. Speaking of one-trick ponies, it's clear that Kevin

Maas had the same impact on the Yankees that Kevin Federline had on the music industry.

With his 15 minutes clearly in the rearview mirror, the once-promising first baseman now works as an investment adviser and certified financial planner, making the occasional appearance at Old Timer's Day, reminding fans of his brief glimpse of Yankees power.

He was touted to be the next Don Mattingly, but he clearly became the first Kevin Maas.

REGGIE JACKSON

He'd give you the shirt off his back. Of course, he'd call a press conference to announce it.

—Catfish Hunter on Reggie Jackson

When it comes to the sports world, the word *overrated* has been used throughout the years to describe an athlete or event that is given way too much credit and hype. For example, the "Next One," Eric Lindros, was supposed to be God's gift to hockey, but instead the overrated power forward traded in hat tricks for belly flops. One particular event that will go down as one of the most overrated moments in sports was the buildup surrounding American decathletes Dan O'Brien and Dave Johnson before the 1992 Summer Olympics. "Dan and Dave" went the way of the buffalo, which saw a merchandise campaign from Reebok go from advertising gold to a disappointing bronze. Perhaps the most overrated athlete and event in sports is none other than "the straw that stirs the drink," Reggie Jackson.

For all his clutch hitting in the postseason and his trash-talking throughout all seasons, Reggie Jackson, with his .262 career average and his all-time leading 2,597 strikeouts, was a first-ballot Hall of Famer. To make matters worse, the strike-out king chose to wear a Yankees cap despite only playing for the Bombers for five of his 21 years in the major leagues. It's really too bad Reggie didn't strike out with Hall of Fame voters as much as he did on the field. Only Reggie Jackson can say he rode a three-homer World Series game and a tumultuous relationship with the boss all the way to Cooperstown.

Born Reginald Martinez Jackson and rechristened "Mr. October" by the late Thurman Munson during the 1977 World Series, Reggie's three-dinger clincher was cooked up by Burt Hooton, Elias Sosa, and Charlie Hough for the Game 6 meatball wedge they served up.

He once said, "I didn't come to New York to be a star, I brought my star with me." That is because nobody ever had more mustard on their hot dog than the 14-time All-Star. In a time before peanut allergies, Reggie Jackson released a chocolate bar with so much caramel pea-nutty goodness, it was easy to forget how often he struck out. On the other hand, it was not easy to forget the poisonous relationship between Reggie and skipper Billy Martin. On June 18, 1977, during a televised game at Fenway Park, Jim Rice hit a ball into shallow right that Reggie weakly attempted to field. Martin became so furious that he yanked Jackson from the game before the inning was over, which led to an ensuing dugout squabble between disgruntled player and hot-tempered manager. Boston fans on hand for the game could not be happier that the Bronx Zoo was burning right before their very eyes.

YOGI BERRA

You can't compare me to my father. Our similarities are different.

—Dale Berra, *Baseball Almanac*

If you Google "Yogi Bear quotes," the popular search engine will most likely ask, "Did you mean Yogi Berra quotes?" While it's easy to mistake the cartoon bear with the 5'7" catcher, there is no way to confuse the ultra-successful 10-time champion Lawrence Peter Berra with his one-time (really?!?) champion son Dale Berra. To Yankees fans, Yogi Berra is the lovable, charming reminder of the late 1940s to 1960s Yankees dynasty, whose witticisms bring a smile to your day and whose timely hitting produced 12 World Series home runs. To Yankees haters, Berra is an annoying, bad-ball swinging, Yoo-Hoo pitchman, who managed to win three MVPs and whose 16 World Series appearances (two as manager) are only surpassed by his nonsensical views on life and forks in the road. While Yogi is widely known for his catching prowess and baseball smarts, he also played more than 400 games in the outfield. The designated hitter didn't exist when Yogi played, but he was most likely designated driver a time or two, considering the drinking habits of some of his Yankees teammates. Yogi not only caught Don Larsen's Game 5 World Series no-hitter in 1956, he hit two Game 7 home runs to propel the Yanks to title No. 17. Yogi's Yankees legacy was not without lowlights. His well-documented fallout with the Boss lasted at least a decade until Steinbrenner finally apologized. Many years from now, most will likely think that Yogi had a hand in every Yankees title. Maybe by then, Dale Berra will have finally gotten a word in.

YANKEES

10 YOGISMs YOGI WOULD NEVER SAY BUT WE WOULD

1. Jeter hit a ball 1,000 times three times.
2. When you reach a dead end, make a left.
3. My best toilet humor comes in the bedroom.
4. I always set my watch to Old Timers' Day.
5. When I wear my socks, they're on my feet.
6. Frank White is black and Bud Black is white.
7. If you reach a fork in the road, ask for a spork.
8. I got to first base with her last night but there was a rain delay.
9. I only take the morning after pill in the evening.
10. I only use coupons on Daylight Savings Time.

PAUL O'NEILL

Paul O'Neill was like that spoiled kid who cries in a toy store when his parents don't buy him another present. Whenever things didn't go his way on the field, the beloved Yankee would throw a temper tantrum in the dugout and shout at the umpires. Unlike a tot manipulating his mom or dad to purchase another action figure or doll, observers cheered O'Neill on while he cried over sour grapes. Yes, Yankees fans loved their star—whether it was fighting for what he believed in, hitting in the clutch, going Mike Tyson on some water coolers, or always being at the center of a rally.

The former kickball player came over to the Yankees from the Cincinnati Reds in November 1992 in exchange for the once-untouchable, then very-touchable prospect Roberto Kelly. While Kelly only stayed in the Queen City for two years and

never lived up to his potential, O'Neill far exceeded expectations in the Bronx. A career .259 hitter before joining the Bombers, O'Neill hit over .300 almost every year he was with George's team. A Yankees favorite through the 2001 season, the man they called "the Warrior" earned four more rings than Giambi and had more power in his bat than Roy Hobbs did in his "Wonderboy." In particular, O'Neill was a thorn in the Red Sox's side, batting .305 against them and bopping a whopping 19 home runs and 69 RBIs off their pitchers.

Yes, if you were a fan in the Bronx, you loved him. If you weren't, you wanted to spank him or flip him the bird. It's funny, as a ballplayer, the once-permed outfielder used to show charisma and an engaging personality that matched his play on the field. As a commentator, he's the antithesis—he's as stiff as one of those cardboard cutouts of the obnoxious Lotto guy standing outside your local deli.

DON MATTINGLY

The term "lovable loser" is not often associated with Yankees lore, but it's hard to argue that it's a fitting description of former Bomber and 1985 AL MVP Don Mattingly. Despite winning nine Gold Gloves, three Silver Sluggers, six All-Star selections, and once homering in eight straight games, Donbo's career (1982–1995) was perfectly sandwiched between two Yankees World Series appearances, and in Yankeeland that doesn't add up to much. In his final act as a Yankee, Mattingly batted .417 in the 1995 ALDS but was shown the door with the acquisition of Tino Martinez. That's why it's tough to hate on the former Yankees captain. It seems no matter how good he is or was, he'd always fall behind somehow or

have an asterisk next to his legacy. Case in point: he is the only Yankee with a retired number to not win a World Series. In the late '90s, as fans were taking their "Hitman" posters off the wall, a slew of fading stars achieved what Mattingly couldn't—winning a World Series as a Yankee. Among them are Denny Neagle, Chad Curtis, and Tim Raines. Pouring on the could've-but-didn't, Mattingly's non-winning Yankees ways continued into his coaching career from 2004 to 2007, so it's no surprise he was bypassed for Joe Girardi (a three-time winner as a Yankees player) in 2008. Adding insult to injury, he finally replaced Joe Torre…in Los Angeles, smack in the middle of the worst divorce since Burt and Loni.

BABE RUTH

I room with Babe Ruth's suitcase.

—Teammate/roommate Ping Bodie

No one will ever know for sure if in fact the Bambino called his shot on that brisk October afternoon in Chicago's Wrigley Field. However, what we do know is this, he blasted home runs and he blasted them with relative ease. It's almost as if opposing pitchers were serving the Babe meatballs while the rest of the league just watched in awe as heroic blast after blast left his Louisville Slugger and ascended on its final trip into orbit. The most astonishing Babe stat is this: when he smashed 60 home runs in 1927, he single-handedly had 14 percent of all home runs in the league that year. In other words we cannot deny his greatness and the impact he has left on our national pastime. He was a slugger of legendary proportions, but there is one very over-sized Ruthian myth that cannot be overlooked when it comes to the prolific career of one George Herman Ruth. For

all the "called shots," the lone MVP hardware, the two All-Star Game appearances, and the .342 lifetime batting average, not once in his 22-year playing career did he ever pick up a hammer and nails and build a house in the middle of the South Bronx.

"The Babe" was a lot of things. He visited sick kids in the hospital, he hit a baseball exceptionally well for a guy who spent his playing days hovering around the 250-pound mark. He was even a fantastic pitcher (six years on the Boston mound

Say it ain't so, Babe: Ruth shakes hands with New York governor Nathan L. Miller, while Yankees owners (from left) Colonel Tillinghast L'Hommedieu Huston (actual name) and Jacob Ruppert pose with their prize catch prior to the Bombers' first appearance in the World Series, against the crosstown rival New York Giants, October 6, 1921. The Giants won the Series five games to three.

resulted in a 94–46 record with a 2.28 ERA and three World Series championships for the Red Sox). However, one thing that Babe Ruth was not was a well-respected and highly regarded carpenter able to build a 60,000-seat, three-tiered stadium. He rewrote the record books many times over and will forever be the face of the 20th-century sports universe. But let's not forget that, despite being sold to the Yankees for a record $100,000 at the time, the Colossus of Clout finished his career in the Bronx with a dismal 4–3 World Series record.

Seven-hundred-fourteen home runs later and leaving behind a larger-than-life aura, it should be noted that Ruth's immortal No. 3 was issued eight more times before Yankee brass decided it was unfit to disrespect the man who single-handedly ushered in the live-ball era. In a related note, right fielder Cliff Mapes, a lifetime .242 career hitter will be remembered as the only New York Yankee in history to wear both Babe Ruth's No. 3 and Mickey Mantle's No. 7.

Finally, let the record books show that utility infielder Luis Sojo, who is often described as a decent contact hitter with limited power has just as many Yankee rings (four) as the iconic Ruth does. Okay, the Sojo comparison is a bit of a stretch on our part, but what other major league legend holds the dubious distinction of being the only player to be caught stealing to end a World Series? George Herman "Babe" Ruth, the Sultan of What.

WE STILL LIKE *MATT* DAMON

Johnny Damon left his beard and his balls in Boston. Following the 2005 season—a somewhat down year in power

production for the reliable two-time All-Star, Damon left the Sox and shed his trademark "idiot" attire of long hair and over-grown facial hair in favor of the clean-cut company in the Bronx. Watching the spectacle the Big Apple media made of our former "homeboy" was as hard to watch as an Al Leiter bunt attempt. Cameras followed him and his wife as he got a shave and haircut at a pretentious city salon, and his pinstripe press conference that followed was no doubt a dark day in Boston. It felt so wrong—like watching a reunion show of *The Golden Girls* with the cast of *Designing Women* instead.

Before the betrayal, Damon made his presence known in Boston almost immediately after he signed with the team (after a one-hit-wonder season in Oakland) in 2002. The outfielder was quickly admired by the Fenway faithful for his grittiness, clutch hits, and run-scoring skills, and it remained that way for his entire four-year run. Obviously, his crowning achievement came as a pivotal member of the "idiot" squad who won it all and broke the "Curse of the Babe" in 2004. Who can forget his ALCS Game 7 effort in which he hit two homers (one grand slam) in a game and choke-clinching victory over the Yankees?

Damon also hit well in the Series sweep of Albert Pujols and the Cards, and solidified his place as one of Boston's finest acquisitions of all-time and one of its best teams ever. Then 2006 came, and he stabbed us in our red-and-navy backs. True, the Sox likely played hardball with re-signing him, but rather than give them a hometown discount, Judas, er, Damon, took the money and ran to Cashman country. Adding insult to injury? Damon won a World Series with the Yankees in 2009

Former Red Sox center fielder Johnny Damon, clean shaven and no longer an "idiot," grimaces after Boston's Josh Beckett strikes him out in the first inning of a game on May 9, 2006, at Yankee Stadium.

and vetoed a trade back to Boston in 2010 when he was playing for Detroit. How'd that work out for you?

While it wasn't as big as the Babe leaving Boston or as anti-climatic as Dice-K opting for former Yankee Tommy John surgery, Damon's departure was the biggest slap in the face in Boston since the Brits dumped tea in our waters. Et tu, Damon?

THE CORE FOUR PLUS ONE MORE

"Evil Empire" is a term that was used during the Reagan Administration to describe the Soviet Union at the height of the Cold War. It's also the title of the rap-metal group Rage Against the Machine's second album. For the purpose of this book, it was also a nickname given to the Yankees by Sox president Larry Lucchino a few years back. It's clear the CEO was upset at the time, but let's be brutally honest here, losing the Jose Contreras sweepstakes isn't necessarily a bad thing, is it?

For years, the Yankees have had free rein on any superstar they deemed worthy of donning the pinstripes and a seemingly giant bankroll that helped them obtain said player with an even larger and astronomical contract. Of course, not every All-Star at every position during the most recent dynasty was bought by the highest bidder or in every case the New York Yankees.

This particular bunch of homegrown Bombers is often referred to as the Core Four. Since this is undoubtedly a Yankees Hater book and we simply enjoy hating on the damn dynasty, we have taken the liberty to one up the Evil Empire and refer to them as the "Core Four Plus One More." Let us take a closer look, shall we?

Derek Jeter: Since the mid-'90s, the shortstop position has been defined by two simple words, Derek Jeter. In fact, there may very well have been a campaign to universally rename the position after the Yankees captain. Of course, we can neither confirm nor deny that, nor can we confirm that the lyrics to the old baseball classic "Take Me Out to the Ballgame" are being reworked as we speak to accommodate the Bronx Bombers and there four gazillion loyal fans. So don't be surprised next season if "Take Me Out to the Yankee Game" is played throughout all major league baseball stadiums during the seventh-inning stretch. The sacred position has stood the test of time as far as Yankees lore is concerned. Hall of Famer Phil "Scooter" Rizzuto, as well as the forgettable Bobby Meacham who played Derek Jeter throughout most of the 1980s, once patrolled the former shortstop position. This guy can't do anything wrong, either. In all seriousness, the only scandal he was ever remotely involved in was in the winter of 2010 when his lingering free agency had to share back-page headlines with text-messaged snapshots of Brett Favre's Jet junk. Sadly, the Jeter regime is coming to an end, and the beginning of a new era in Yankeeland begins, not seen since 1995 when Tony "Flipper" Fernandez patrolled the South Bronx infield, gas was only $1.09 a gallon, the world's first cloned sheep made headlines, and Justin Bieber turned one. You know, come to think of it, there hasn't been this much hype for a 3,000th hit since Bernie Mac played with the Brewers.

Andy Pettitte: Only member of the Core Four to leave the quartet only to return when he found out that the AL East powerhouse set its sights on becoming the first team in MLB history to win the division and wild-card in the same season.

Obviously, if this were to happen, a dream match-up during the ALCS would be the Yankees playing against the Yankees. Bomber fans should rejoice throughout the universe because during next postseason the Yankees could essentially be playing with themselves. Of course, high-tailing it out of the American League and following Roger Clemens to Houston weren't the only things that separate the postseason's winningest pitcher from the rest of his Core teammates. In 2007 the big lefty flushed his Cooperstown dream down the toilet when he and Yankees champion teammates Glenallen Hill and Chuck Knoblauch appeared in Senator Mitchell's report on the illegal use of steroids in baseball.

Mariano Rivera: It's safe to say that Mariano has secured a spot among the Mount Rushmore of Yankees legends. Of course, Mickey Mantle is rolling in his grave right about now, but as Michael Kay's head continues to grow, so does the storied career of arguably the best relief pitcher in the history of MLB. Would you be at all shocked if one day the decision was made to retire No. 42 at every ballpark in honor of Mariano Rivera? We wouldn't want to hurt the Yankee reliever's feelings or any Yankee feelings, for that matter. So, in that case, Jackie Robinson was a great ballplayer, but let's be honest, he never played for the Yankees. But the reality is this: for all the saves, milestones, and accolades that have come Mo's way, the only thing he will be remembered for is the blown-save, duck-fart, walk-off courtesy of the Diamondbacks' Luis Gonzalez in Game 7 of the 2001 World Series. Try editing that out of your Yankeeography. *Yes!*

Jorge Posada: Only member of the Core Four to take himself out of the lineup, which occurred during the 2011 season

against the Sox on national television. Speaking of 2011, how come Lance Berkman only looks like fat Elvis when he's wearing pinstripes? Back to Jorge and his Tom Berenger–like achy knees, although he may have caught some meaningful games during his storied Bronx lifespan, you won't see him on the receiving end of any pie shots from glorified cream pie tosser A.J. Burnett or any Yankees pitchers, for that matter. Sadly for him, his Yankees era will most likely not end with cream pies, and Sox fans couldn't be happier when we say don't let the Gate 4 door hit your ass on the way out.

Joe Girardi: He ended the Yankees' long and treacherous nine-year championship drought, he sported braces because of a promise to his five-year-old daughter, he even helped a distressed young lady involved in a one-car accident just hours after winning the World Series. He then changed his number to 28 to signify his goal to win the 28th title for the Yankees, an obvious act of class, tradition, and honor displayed among pinstriped royalty. Yes, we can safely say that Joe Girardi is indeed cooler than the other side of the pillow. However, as cool as he is, was, or ever will be, he shall be remembered for being the one who eventually breaks up the Core Four completely, because somewhere down the line someone is going to have to pencil Eduardo Nunez into the Derek Jeter position forever. So enjoy your dynasty-schmynasty now, Joe.

DYNASTY SCHMYNASTY

Whenever you hear the word *dynasty*, it conjures up grainy black-and-white images of Yankees heroes of the past proudly running the bases in full pinstriped regalia. Or you may recall scenes of a prime-time soap opera centered around Blake

NEW NICKNAMES FOR YANKEES STARS

1. Mr. Vanilla (Derek Jeter)
2. The Whiner (Paul O'Neill)
3. Mr. January (Kei Igawa)
4. Mr. Glass (Nick Johnson)
5. A-nnoying (A-Rod)

YANKEES

Carrington, which starred the iconic trio of John Forsythe, Linda Evans, and Joan Collins. Thankfully, this is not a book centered around Aaron Spelling TV dramas—in other words, let's shift focus to another dynasty built in the South Bronx in the late 1990s. Just as irritating as having to sit through an episode of Michael Kay's *CenterStage* during a Yankees rain delay, we are quite often made to believe that this particular dynasty was won only by the homegrown quartet of Jeter, Posada, Rivera, and Pettitte. However, the truth is the Bombers' title run was clearly not won by the Core Four alone. In fact, if not for the Yankees' very own iconic quartet, who knows what the Yankees trophy case would look like at this point? Chuck Knoblauch somehow finished a major league career with four World Series rings, several throwing miscues, a few key Yankees hits, and one Mitchell Report name-drop. Olympic gold medal winner Tino Martinez replaced Don Mattingly not only on the field but also in the hearts of Yankees fans. He earned Yankeeography cred by playing a huge part during all four Yankees championships. Finally, Bernie Williams, who is atop many Yankees all-time postseason record books recently traded in his bat and balls for a classic guitar. Despite collaborations with Bruce Springsteen and Jon

YANKEES

TOP 10 YANKEES TEAMS OF THE 2000s

10. **2000 Yankees**—The Yanks' first title of the 2000s was also the owner of the fewest wins in a season for the Bombers this decade. With just 87 wins, the Yanks backed into the playoffs only to win the Subway Series and bat-throwing competition against the Mets.
9. **2007 Yankees**—The team that cost Joe Torre his job! A measly 94-win team eliminated in four by the Tribe and a swarm of flying ants in the ALDS.
8. **2002 Yankees**—This squad was no match for the Rally Monkey-ing Angels. The Angels took the Yankees in four (and eventual World Series), even though the Giambino batted .357 in the series.
7. **2006 Yankees**—*D* is for Detroit and Destiny! The Tigers, armed with Yankees and Mets castoff Kenny Rogers, get the greasy upper hand against the Yanks in a four-game victory. Future Yankee Curtis Granderson plays a pivotal role in sending the Yanks to early vacation.
6. **2004 Yankees**—Leading 3–0 over the cursed Red Sox, this squad costs itself the No. 1 spot by becoming the first *and* only team to ever then lose the last four in a seven-game series in baseball.
5. **2010 Yankees**—Annual playoff sweep of Twins precedes Yanks being blindsided by the Rangers. This takes place in the summer the Yanks lose "the Boss" and Bob Shepard. *continued*

4. **2005 Yankees**—95-win team once again owned by the Angels. At least this series went five games.

3. **2003 Yankees**—Aaron Boone dramatics could not be replicated against the Florida Marlins, who to this day have yet to lose a playoff series.

2. **2001 Yankees**—This team lifted the city after 9/11 and is fondly remembered. However, they couldn't finish off the D-Backs in Arizona as Mariano's bullpen failures proved costlier than Byun-Hyung Kim's.

1. **2009 Yankees**—The best team money could buy! Cashman finally gets it right, giving the new stadium a firm foundation for years to come.

Secada, Bernie is yet to officially retire since his last game in 2006, and thus the greatest center fielder in team history not named DiMaggio or Mantle remains in Yankee limbo.

DWIGHT GOODEN AND DARRYL STRAWBERRY

These days, it's the New York Mets ownership and their TV network that's been milking the 1986 season. But, back in the 1990s, it was George Steinbrenner. Without a World Series championship in his grasp since 1981, the shrewd Yankees owner tried to bring some of the Amazin' magic from a decade prior to the Bronx. Sadly for everyone, he succeeded.

Next to Roger Clemens, Dwight Gooden was the most iconic pitcher in the 1980s. A stud pitcher, whose rise in the big leagues was among the biggest in baseball history, ended up falling from grace due to a heavy reliance on the white stuff.

After the Mets gave up on their former ace, Steinbrenner swooped in and signed him in 1996. Naturally, the Mets' garbage became the Yankees' treasure when Doc-K tossed his only career no-hitter for the Yanks that year. Steinbrenner picked up one-time Mets superstar Darryl Strawberry later that season. Together again in New York, only with different uniforms, the duo would win a Series with the Yankees in 1996. Strawberry would actually win two more rings with the team. Gooden returned to the Yanks and finished his career on a relatively high note in 2000.

Doc and Straw winning titles in the Bronx, and seeing them become lovable Yankees made us almost as sick as seeing them celebrating a World Series victory against the Sox in 1986.

3

WE HATE YANKEES PRIDE AND TRADITION

I root for the Red Sox because they give their fans the opportunity to experience every possible human emotion. I hate Yankee fans because they believe they're entitled to success.

—Alastair Ingram
lead Red Sox columnist, RantSports.com

We get it, Yankees fans—you have more titles than us. You have 27—at least at the time of this printing—and have such a storied history that it's hard to believe the world isn't a Yankees fan. That latter isn't as prosperous a notion as you'd think given the fact the Bronx Bombers have a worldwide network of international bandwagon-jumpers.

See, the world is full of Yankees fans, and the "Bronx" ones are the worst. Every chance they get, they'll throw it in your face. They'll point to their ring finger as if to say "we have 27." Speaking of which, it's always "we" with them—as if they're on the field. It's a test of patience to listen to sports radio in New York where listeners call in and propose "we" trade for a marquee player for a song. "If we traded Ivan Nova and Nick Swisher could we get Albert Pujols?" Okay, we made that

> *They infest everywhere. Every stadium is going to be infested with Yankees fans. No mosquito repellent, nothing works on them.*
>
> **—Torii Hunter**

question up, but chances are you'll hear one of those arrogant, aimless questions directed at an arrogant, aimless Yankees-rooting announcer.

And if you're going to a game to see your team at Yankee Stadium, and that team isn't the Yankees—stay home. Rooting for the opposing team—be it Boston or Kansas City—at the House That Ruth Didn't Build—is as appealing as being on the receiving end of an Anthony Weiner Tweet. If you've got the cap of another team at Yankee Stadium, God help you. More so than any other fan base, they will do everything in their power to ruin the experience for you, whether it's tossing beer your way or spending nine innings telling you how much you and/or your team suck.

Given all of that, it's hard to admit it, but we hate Yankees pride more than the fans, although it's a close race (think tortoise finishing first over…another tortoise). Once you get past the history of the Yankees in terms of rings (how arrogant are those "Got Rings?" T-shirts?), the Yankees and Red Sox are on a pretty level playing field. Both franchises are usually at the top of their division, playing meaningful games in September, and boasting some of the biggest stars in the game—many of which are homegrown. Both franchises don't have their players' names on the back of their home uniforms (Sox have them

on the road jerseys), because they know the unis stand for so much more than just one individual player.

In addition, both franchises are usually at the top of every free agent's list to sign with—although the Sox didn't join that party until recently. But there is a huge difference between the Yankees and our Sawx: the Red Sox executives run the team very seriously but don't ever take themselves half as seriously as the blowhard Yankees do. Management doesn't care if players go out to all ends of the night partying so long as they come to the park prepared to give 110 percent. Ownership doesn't care if their players have goatees, Buckner mustaches, full beards, or (we're guessing) nose-piercings. A player's worth isn't tied to the "professional" look and feel the Company Men of the Yankees is. (Sox players can wear their jerseys untucked, and it's not the end of the world.)

Aside from technicalities, another big difference between the Yankees and Sox are how general managers usually will bow down to the oh-so-great Yankees and trade away their best players in exchange for a box of balls and, oh yeah, a whole lot of cash to cover said best players' remaining salaries. In that way, the Yankees are the biggest sponge the world has ever seen: absorbing bad contracts and once-great ballplayers faster than you can say "Square Pants."

From bowing down to backing down, the other biggest frustration is how other teams feed into the Yankees mystique—especially in the postseason. The "ghosts," as Derek Jeter reportedly once told Aaron Boone before he slammed the 2003 ALCS game- and series-winning home run, always come out to scare

the other team and help propel the team to victory. Yeah, right. The Yankees are never as good as some opponents (talking to you, A's and Twins!) make them look sometimes. Oftentimes, it's butterflies and paranoia that can lead to a Yankees victory—like it did when Grady left in Pedro. Clearly, Martinez let thoughts of Monument Park get the best of him. Sometimes aura and fear win games—the actual players are irrelevant.

This barely scratches the surface. Seriously, a whole book could be written about the pointlessness of dragging old former Yankees or scrubs out of their beds or bedpans for Old Timers' Day, but we digress.

Read more on hating Yankees fans, pride, and tradition below...

YANKEE STADIUM
(THE NEW ONE LOOKS LIKE THE OLD ONE)

It was on February 6, 1921, when the New York Yankees announced the purchase of 10 acres of land in the South Bronx. The future home of the Yankees was purchased from the estate of William Waldorf Astor for $675,000 and on April 18, 1923, the world's first triple-decked ballpark was ready for action. Of course it was the Great Bambino who hit the stadium's first home run en route to a 4–1 win against the Red Sox, but despite the Babe's popularity and clout that ushered in "The House That Ruth Built," it was in fact "The House that White Construction Company Built."

Unfortunately for them—as well as architects Osborn Engineering, who designed the original stadium in 1923, and

10 BOOKS NO RED SOX FAN WILL EVER READ

The Yankee Years
by Joe Torre & Tom Verducci

The Goose Is Loose
by Goose Gossage & Richard Pate

Munson: The Life and Death of a Yankee Captain by Marty Appel

The Perfect Yankee: The Incredible Story of the Greatest Miracle in Baseball History
by Don Larsen

Designated Hebrew: The Ron Blomberg Story
by Ron Blomberg & Dan Schlossberg

Ladies and Gentleman, the Bronx Is Burning: 1977, Baseball, Politics, & the Battle For the Soul of the City by Jonathan Mahler

The Big Bam: The Life & Times of Babe Ruth
by Leigh Montville

Joe DiMaggio: The Hero's Life
by Richard Ben Cramer

O Holy Cow: The Selected Verse of Phil Rizzuto by Phil Rizzuto

The Yogi Book: "I Really Didn't Say Everything I Said" by Yogi Berra

Praeger-Kavanaugh-Waterbury, who were in charge of the remodeling in 1973—the Babe to this day gets all the credit. Finding out the Babe didn't actually build the house was like

finding out that the almighty Wizard of Oz was only the man behind the curtain. Known as the "Cathedral of Baseball," the original stadium was host to more World Series games than any other park. Of course, despite all the champagne celebrations, the Stadium was also host to the most undesirable public bathrooms this side of Grand Central Station. The historic home of the Yankees has also been a landing pad for other sports and entertainment events. As many as 30 championship boxing fights were fought at the stadium, three Papal Masses were held, and it was an early home for the New York football Giants.

The nostalgic ballfield of the Bombers has been the scene of many of the game's greatest moments. The Babe's 60th home run in 1927, Don Larsen's perfect game on October 8, 1956, and Roger Maris' record-breaking 61st in 1961. Of course, we all know where we were for these memorable moments, much like we knew where we were during the infamous O.J. white Bronco chase in the spring of '94. Speaking of infamous, no Yankee Stadium montage would be complete without footage of a Wade Boggs World Series horse-ride celebration or a Chris Chambliss home run mêlée. Although we like to focus on the Jim Abbott one-armed no-hitters of the world and of course the 2000 Subway Series highlighted by a hot-tempered Roger Clemens throwing out the game's first pitch, or in this particular case the game's first charred bat.

Known for its famous façade and not so friendly location on the west side of the Bronx, the stadium has been making lasting memories, including those with or without pinstripes. It was on November 12, 1928, that Knute Rockne delivered his "Win one for the Gipper!" speech, which helped guide Notre

Dame over Army 12–6. In the summer of 1936 the world witnessed Germany's Max Schmeling knock out American Joe
Louis in the 12th round; and in an unforgettable rematch two
years later, the Brown Bomber avenged his loss with a first-
round knockout in front of a raucous Bronx crowd.

Perhaps one of the most solemn moments in the Stadium's existence occurred on August 17, 1948, when more than 100,000
mourners paid their respects to Babe Ruth, whose body lay in
state at the main entrance. Amid the countless World Series
won and lost by the Bombers, October 4, 1955, marked the
only World Series championship won by the Brooklyn Dodgers in a 2–0, Game 7 victory led by should-be Hall of Famer
Gil Hodges and slick fielding help from Sandy Amoros. Sure,
the Yankees may have played in many great games at the stadium, but on December 28, 1958, Johnny Unitas and the Baltimore Colts were victorious over the Giants in what is known
as "the Greatest Game Ever Played."

History was made on September 25, 1966, when the smallest
crowd in stadium history (413 diehards) watched the last-place
Yankees lose to the Chicago White Sox. Perhaps another low
blow to the Bomber jewels occurred on June 16, 1997, when
the Bombers and New York Mets played in the first regular
season interleague series between the two clubs, which was
highlighted by an Amazin' Dave Mlicki shutout victory.

In 2006 the Yankees, after years of talking about moving the
team to Jersey or maybe Mars (we wish), began construction
on a new $2.3 billion stadium across the street. In 2008, as
millions of fans said good-bye to Yankees ghosts and Bob
Sheppard, it was finally time to say hello to inflated parking

prices and frickles. As memories past and present loom large on the sacred grounds of both stadiums old and new, we can only imagine how many fried pickles the Babe would have consumed back in the days of the Murderers' Row.

IRRITATING VOICES OF THE YANKEES

John Sterling

Tim McCarver, aka "Captain Obvious," can rest easy. He's not the worst sportscaster in baseball history in our book. That distinction belongs to a brownnoser in the Bronx who's notorious for miscalling plays, nicknaming any player in pinstripes no matter how hard their last name is for him to pronounce, and telling stories that have no point…and sometimes no end.

Since joining the booth in 1989 (who can forget the days of Balboni and nights of "Pags"?), John Sterling has accomplished something arguably no other person in the baseball universe has: he's given Yankees and Red Sox fans something to agree on. Ask anyone from Beantown or some diehards in the Bronx, and they'll tell you, when it comes to calling a game, Sterling is the….*ah…ah…ah*…worst. The best radio announcers paint an unbiased picture of the going-ons across the diamond, and place the listener or viewer right in the middle of the action. Not Sterling. What the "Yankeeography" host with the very least does is play the role of super fan who tells you what's going on in the game only when it doesn't interfere with pointless stories he likes to tell to his equally foaming-at-the-mouth partner Suzyn Waldman (more on her sorry "goodness gracious" ass later). When not bantering like a long-winded used car salesman (do they make laxatives for the mouth?), the "Sterlster" spends most of each broadcast

thinking up logically illogical explanations for a recent Yankees slump and coming up with those annoying nicknames like "the Melkman delivers" and "the Grandyman can" and catchphrases like, "You're on the Mark, Teixeira," and, "It's another A-bomb from A-Rod."

Yes, the man who actually started his career calling basketball games and was part of many a Braves broadcast has made a career out of delivering nails-on-a-blackboard trademark calls like, "It is high, it is far, it is gone!" Well, to take a page of the Yankees talking head's book, each time he announces a game, he "cuts on and misses."

Bob Sheppard

Once dubbed the "Voice of God" by *Naked Gun* star Reggie Jackson, the iconic Bob Sheppard served more than five decades as Yankees public address announcer, introducing every Bombers immortal from Alvaro Espinoza to Paul Zuvella.

With more than 4,500 games under his belt, not to mention 22 pennant-winning seasons and 13 world championships, one can argue that Sheppard lingered in the stadium booth almost as long as a Stump Merrill fart (which was longer than his managerial career). The game's most recognized public address announcer was also part of six no hitters, including three perfect games and, of course, one epic choke job back in 2004 (hey, what we can say? it's a Yankees hater book). On that note, it should also be known that the first player ever announced by Sheppard was a guy by the name of DiMaggio— Dom DiMaggio to be exact. Dom may not have a section of the West Side Highway named after him, but he was the first to be name-dropped by the voice of the Yankees.

The Bombers won the game and, from there, his career was well on its way. Among his other accolades was his 50-year PA gig with the New York Football Giants and, of course, his microphone's "induction" into the National Baseball Hall of Fame. Deciding to call it quits on the heels of the Thanksgiving weekend of November 2009, just 11 months shy of his 100th birthday, one can only imagine the look on the Native Americans' faces when a young Bob Sheppard provided introductions for the Pilgrims as they arrived at Plymouth Rock in 1620 for the original Fall Classic. One of only two people to be awarded both a World Series and Super Bowl ring, Sheppard continues to work, even though, sadly, he left us in July 2010. Even in the afterlife he welcomes a new generation of Yankees fans to the Stadium each and every game as well as announcing Derek Jeter at-bats, which in essence gives new meaning to being dubbed the "Voice of God."

Suzyn Waldman

Long before she became a brown fixture under George Steinbrenner's nose, Yankees announcer Suzyn Waldman had a successful Broadway career that included a role in *Man of La Mancha*. If we "dreamed an impossible dream," she'd be off the air and the Yankees would move to Sheboygan. But we digress. It's actually quite fitting that Waldman got her start on the Great White Way, considering each game she calls is a bigger train wreck than the *Spider-Man* musical.

Waldman joined the booth with Sterling in 2005, and the two quickly became the world's worst tag-team partnership next to only wrestling's pairing of Honky Tonk Man and Greg "the Hammer" Valentine (aka Rhythm and Blues). The one-two punch of Tweedle-John and Tweedle-Suzyn has translated to

10 THINGS THAT MAKE SUZYN WALDMAN SHOUT, "GOODNESS GRACIOUS!"

1. A hit
2. A walk
3. A balk
4. A home run
5. The original cast recording of Rent
6. A bunt
7. A wild pitch
8. Roger Clemens appearing in George Steinbrenner's "bawx"
9. A strike
10. A strikeout

YANKEES

endless babbling, which always takes center stage over any homer hit over the center-field fence. The Massachusetts native (for shame) shows her love for the team ad nauseam, has a more annoying voice than reporter Penny Crone, and makes excuses for anything that goes wrong with the golden franchise. She also refers to all players by their first names only—as if she's BFFs with them. Who knows? Maybe she does shots with Jorge Posada after he hits the showers. Actually, who cares?

And, while there's no question that Waldman has meant a lot to the Bombers (she supposedly helped end the feud between "the Boss" and Yogi) and is a historic figure in the sports broadcasting world (she's among the first female full-time

color MLB commentators ever), her legacy may actually be an over-blown announcement she made when alleged juicer Roger Clemens announced at Yankee Stadium that he was returning to the team in 2007. "Roger Clemens is in George's box, and Roger Clemens is coming back. Oh, my goodness gracious…of all the dramatic things I've ever seen," she told radio listeners, as if Neil Armstrong sold crack on the moon. There was that Lou Gehrig retirement speech which, we're guessing, was the second most dramatic thing she's ever seen.

The bottom line is the most popular franchise in all of sports has a tandem more suited to announce a mid-sixties recreational league softball game than a major league monopoly. Goodness gracious, indeed.

IF YOU BUY IT, THEY WILL COME
GEORGE "THE BOSS" STEINBRENNER

> *What does George [Steinbrenner] know about Yankee pride?*
> *When did he ever play for the Yankees?*
> —Manager Billy Martin

In 1973 a Cleveland ship-builder named George Steinbrenner bought the New York Yankees for a reported $8.8 million from CBS. The team was the baseball equivalent to the *Titanic*—they'd hit an iceberg and were sinking fast, having not won a championship since 1962. Since the early '70s, the Boss, as he is so eloquently called among Yankees fans, opened up his bottomless checkbook and never looked back. Starting with Jim "Catfish" Hunter and followed by Reggie Jackson, these two free agents helped the Bombers win the crown in 1977. Of

course, it wasn't always sunny in the Bronx, and this was never more evident than when manager Billy Martin yanked Reggie from a game against Boston for failing to run hard after a fly ball. Billy and George never really saw eye to eye and, despite yet another title, the manager was given the pink slip. Martin would eventually have five separate stints as skipper, and because Steinbrenner changed managers like we change underwear, it would be another 18 years before gold at the end of the baseball rainbow. The Boss also had a penchant for letting go of promising pinstriped prospects only to replace them with over-the-hill superstars. This, of course, didn't bode so well for the spoiled fan base that expected to win every single season.

Despite his God-like image, Steinbrenner was by no means a saint. In fact, he was suspended not once but twice by Major League Baseball. His first suspension was in relation to illegal contributions to President Nixon's reelection, and his second was when he paid an investigator to get dirt on former Yankee Dave Winfield. Ironically, the latter of the two suspensions enabled the Yankees to keep many of their young gems while George ceded control of the club. Who knows if the Yankees would have traded the Core Four if Steinbrenner weren't spending these three years in baseball Siberia?

After being reinstated, the Yankees made a return to the play-offs and would win four more times during Steinbrenner's spending spree, with the nucleus of his farm system intact. With his intimidating presence and his uncanny ability to criticize his players to the press, George was still able to turn the club into a billion-dollar business as well as earning a recurring role on *Seinfeld*—thanks to Larry David.

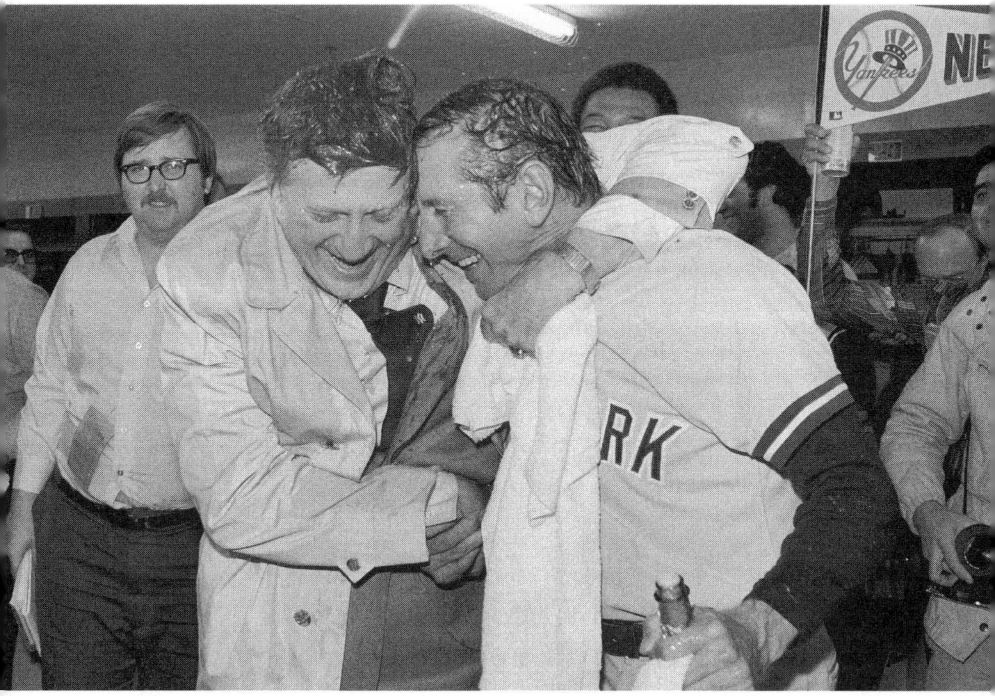

George Steinbrenner gets on-again, off-again manager Billy Martin in a head lock after the Yankees won the 1977 ALCS against the Kansas City Royals. Martin has cleverly doused himself with champagne to cover up the smell of bourbon.

Despite alienating the great Yogi Berra, who then refused to set foot in Yankee Stadium for over a decade, the world's most famous sports owner managed to call the even greater Hideki Irabu a "fat pussy toad." Sure, Irabu never lived up to his main event status, but at least he left the Bronx with a ring, while somewhere in Maryland, Mike Mussina weeps.

George was larger than life, and thankfully for New Yorkers, so was his wallet. That is why the Yankees changed their spring training facility from Legends Field to George M. Steinbrenner Field. No doubt George is the Yankees' greatest

legend because measuring at an astonishing 7' wide by 5' high, the recently erected Steinbrenner shrine towers among the other tributes of former Bombers. The structure clearly outshines the lesser-sized plaques of Yankees come and gone such as Mantle, Munson, and DiMaggio. So, despite the weight that Babe Ruth carries both on the field and off, it's no surprise that the bronzed George Steinbrenner will live forever and can probably be seen from Uranus.

FREDDY SEZ, "NO MASCOTS"

Who needs running sausages or big-head presidents when you have Freddy Sez and 27 world championships? That is the $1 million question when it comes to the New York Yankees and their history of mascots—or lack thereof.

According to the dictionary, the word *mascot* is defined as a person, animal, or object adopted by a group as a symbolic figure, especially to bring them good luck. Throughout its existence, our national pastime has seen its share of loveable and enduring figures. Among the elite include the Philly Phanatic, Mr. Met, Bernie Brewer, Mr. Redlegs, Wally the Monster, and of course the world-famous San Diego Chicken.

Sadly the team with the most champagne baths earns a zero in the mascot department. In 1979 fans who ventured into the upper deck of Yankee Stadium were introduced to a furry character often mistaken for an over-sized muppet that loosely resembled former Yankee and Red Sox pitcher Sparky Lyle. His name was Dandy, and his Yankees stay was as anticlimatic as yet another seven-footer by the name of Randy Johnson. Although Dandy was a bigger Yankees bust than Carl Pavano

YANKEES

PINSTRIPE PILEDRIVER

March 31, 1985: Yankees great Billy Martin is guest ring announcer for the main event at the inaugural WrestleMania.

April 2, 1989: Donned in a battered and torn bomber sweatshirt, The Brooklyn Brawler is unable to help his mentor Bobby "the Brain" Heenan defeat the Red Rooster.

October 11, 2003: Pedro Martinez steals a page from the Monday night wars and face-plants bench coach Don Zimmer during Game 3 of the ALCS.

March 31, 2007: "Mr. Perfect" Curt Hening is inducted into the wrestling Hall of Fame by his good friend and Yankees horseback rider Wade Boggs.

June 21, 2009: Curtis Granderson, formerly of the Detroit Tigers, appears at TNA's PPV event Slammiversary as guest belt holder.

December 21, 2009: Johnny Damon's last appearance as a Yankee was as guest host of WWE's *Monday Night Raw*.

and Kevin Brown combined, he will for the record remain the only official mascot in team history. In fact, his time in the Bronx was so brief that the only furry memories that remain from the '80s is the mascot underneath Dale Berra's nose.

We should take into account that, over the years, the Bombers have unofficially recognized several other mascots to their enduring fan base. Until his demise in the fall of 2010, Fred Schuman roamed throughout the stadium leading the Yanks to several titles with help from his cake pan and lucky spoon. With one eye on the game and, well, with one eye on the game, Freddy Sez will be remembered most for his handpainted signs and his love for everything Yankees.

In 1996 and the several years that ensued, Don Zimmer joined the club as bench coach and became unofficial mascot when he started donning army helmets instead of the traditional ballcap.

Complete with their obnoxious roll call at the beginning of all home games, the Bleacher Creatures have quickly become baseball's most notorious collection of insulting fanatics. More obnoxious than those Raceway park commercials, the Creatures are a mixed bag of Yankees loyalists both young and old that cannot afford the good seats but can afford to be extremely annoying.

These days, some 30-plus years after belting three dingers in a single World Series game and some 20-plus years since his assassination attempt on the Queen of England, Reginald Martinez Jackson, better known simply as Reggie, has been playing the role of special assistant to the principal owner. In other words, it is a nice way of saying that the former Mr. October is now unofficially the new mascot for the team formerly known as the Bronx Zoo.

So despite their pinstripes, façade, and winning ways, the New York Yankees are seriously lacking in one department: mascots! And, for the record, Michael Kay and Rudy Guiliani do not count.

MANAGE THIS

Probably the only thing more unnecessary than 1990's *Rocky V* was 1988's Billy Martin. Martin, best known in his playing days as a temperamental middle infielder, became well known

as a temperamental manager while with the Yankees. His well-documented Bronx Burnin' feuds with Reggie Jackson and George Steinbrenner made him larger than life, but in many ways he was…overrated. Martin only hoisted the World Series trophy once as a manager in 1977. In his bid to repeat, he was fired with a .553 winning percentage after calling Reggie a "liar" and the Boss a convicted felon. After making nice with the Boss, Martin was brought back whenever the Yanks were on the ropes throughout the 1980s. This all came to a sad end when Martin died on Christmas Day in 1989 just three years after the Yankees retired his number.

Joe Torre played 2,209 major league games without ever playing in a World Series, and his managing career seemed to be heading in the same direction after mediocre stints with the Mets, Braves, and Cardinals. So, when the quick-to-fire George Steinbrenner pegged the baseball lifer Torre as Yankees manager for 1996, nobody suspected the second-longest tenure for a Bronx manager was about to begin. With Torre pushing all the right buttons and Steinbrenner finally chilling out, the Yankees embarked on winning six pennants and four World Series titles. The 1971 NL MVP snatched the 1996 and 1998 AL Manager of the Year awards when it seemed like he was doing something other than sitting next to Don Zimmer and not just sending out a fantasy lineup. While successfully managing the many egos that entered the Yankees clubhouse, Torre was often criticized for annually overusing his bullpen. Torre's farewell was handled poorly, and he was not even mentioned during the ceremonies at the closing of Yankee Stadium in 2008. Torre has since repaired his Yankees rift, and you can expect his No. 6 to be retired, which would leave Nos. 1 through 10 unavailable for future Yankees.

The Yankees braintrust in 1999, Joe Torre (left) and Don Zimmer, aka Darth Sidious and Jabba the Hut.

MINOR LEAGUE YANKEES

The Trenton Thunder. The Columbus Clippers. The Staten Island Yankees. The Kansas City Athletics. The Nashville Sounds. All have served as minor league affiliates to the Yankees at various points in franchise history. If you are thinking the Kansas City Athletics were actually a major league team and the second incarnation of the current Oakland A's, you would be correct. However, the K.C. A's essentially were a farm system for the Bombers during their brief history in the Midwest. In 1954, as New York's stranglehold on championships and pre–draft day prospects was dwindling, the Yanks principal owner arranged for one of his business friends, Arnold Johnson, to buy the once-proud Philadelphia A's from the Connie Mack

family. The new ownership quickly moved the Athletics to Kansas City, where a one-sided partnership and years of baseball futility was about to begin. From 1955 to 1960, the Yankees rarely traded with anyone other than the A's, and during the six-season span, the Bombers finished first five times with two World Series titles. In that same span, the A's finished dead last twice and never higher than sixth in the eight-team American League. If that wasn't bad enough, the Yankees won it all again in 1961 and 1962 in large part because of the 94 homers in those two seasons from Roger Maris, who the Yanks received in a trade from…the Kansas City A's. In the winter of 1959, the Yankees received Roger Maris, outfielder Kent Hadley, and the A's starting shortstop Joe DeMaestri for a few washed-up Yankees (yeah, you, Don Larsen) and a player in Casey Stengel's doghouse (but not Casey Stengel's actual dog). Maris would quickly adapt to life in New York with two MVP seasons as one-half of the M&M boys with Mickey Mantle.

Whether it was a reliable starter (Art Ditmar, 47 wins in five Bronx seasons; or Duke Maas, 26 wins in two and a half Yankees seasons), a starting infielder (Clete Boyer, 882 hits in eight seasons as a starting third baseman/shortstop), bench help (Bob Cerv or Harry Simpson), or a veteran relief pitcher (Ryne Duren, 43 saves; or Bobby Shantz, 19 saves), the A's were only a phone call away and willing to accept scrubs. This shady arrangement ended when Arnold Johnson passed away in 1960. Yet, because of all the assistance, the Yanks continued to win well beyond that season. In 13 unlucky seasons in Kansas City, the A's lost 100 or more games four times and finished in the bottom half of the AL every season. About the only thing the A's ever did right in K.C. was when they brought in 58-year-old former Kansas City Monarch Satchel Paige to

pitch with fellow future Hall of Famer and then 19-year-old Catfish Hunter in 1965. Two years later, Hunter would be joined in K.C. by Reggie Jackson. The two would move with the franchise to Oakland and win three titles before taking their act to the East Coast. We're confident you know how that one ends.

THE $200 MILLION MEN

In the early 2000s you could visit the city of Montreal and find more Yankees hats worn or in shops than hometown Expos caps. After their late '90s success and growth of their YES Network, the Yankees brand was clearly marked in all four corners of the globe. Unlike other sports that try to even the playing field for small-market teams, the no-salary-cap Yankees have a perpetual window of opportunity in baseball. Under the current wild-card system (with potential for a second wild-card team in coming seasons), it would be almost impossible for the Bronx Bombers to ever miss the playoffs. However, it would be foolish to think the Yanks are outspending everyone with great ease. The Boston Red Sox, often second in standings and payroll, have built themselves into a marquee landing spot for free agents. The Tampa Bay Rays have built themselves into a credible opponent (2008 American League pennant) through deft drafting and prudent signings. While the Toronto Blue Jays and Baltimore Orioles wish they were in the AL Central on a yearly basis. The Yankees do not hide the fact that they will spend, spend, spend. After missing the playoffs entirely in 2008, they plunked down a half billion dollars in contracts to Mark Teixeira, CC Sabathia, and A.J. Burnett in mostly outbidding themselves. A quick look at the Top 10 Highest Payrolls in Baseball History (courtesy of *USA*

YANKEES

OOPS! FAVORITE YANKEES SIGNINGS

1. Kei Igawa
2. Brien Taylor
3. Hideki Irabu
4. Carl Pavano
5. Danny Tartabull
6. Kenny Rogers
7. Damaso Garcia
8. Jaret Wright
9. Chris Hammond
10. Tim Leary

Today Salary Database), reveals that the Yankees payroll actually went down after signing those big three, but that the pinstripes own the monopoly on highly paid teams:

1. 2008 New York Yankees: $209,081,577
2. 2005 New York Yankees: $208,306,817
3. 2010 New York Yankees: $206,333,389
4. 2011 New York Yankees: $202,689,028
5. 2009 New York Yankees: $201,449,189
6. 2006 New York Yankees: $194,663,079
7. 2007 New York Yankees: $189,639,045
8. 2004 New York Yankees: $184,193,950
9. 2011 Philadelphia Phillies: $172,976,379
10. 2010 Boston Red Sox: $162,447,333

It's no wonder a middle-class family in New York can't take their family to a game without skipping a week of groceries. Those who defend the Yankees would be quick to point

out that the Yankees don't win the World Series every year. However, they have been involved in the roll of the dice that is the MLB playoffs every year but one since the institution of the wild-card in 1995. Other teams have fleeting chances because they can't re-sign key stars and role players or lack the resources to cover up bad decisions (Kei Igawa, Chuck Knoblauch, Randy Johnson, to name a few). In other sports or for other baseball teams, they are stuck with mistakes. On the other hand, the Yanks can cover up mistakes by spending even more. MLB's feeble attempt to level the playing field is the luxury tax system. Since there is no salary cap, if a team payroll exceeds a certain amount (determined annually), they pay a tax to the league. Depending on how often you surpass the tax, it gets higher. Needless to say, the Yankees surpass it every year and gladly pay the tax to retain their competitive edge. The Yankees are one of only four teams in baseball history to have paid the tax (shelling out over $170 million, or 95 percent of all the luxury tax money ever collected). With the strongest union in sports, this system is unlikely to change. As stated earlier, it appears that MLB will allow another playoff team in the near future, so be prepared to root hard against the Yankees in the playoffs for the next century.

GRUMPY OLD MEN, AKA OLD TIMERS' DAY

Every year at Yankee Stadium, fans are treated to a two- to three-inning game between washed-up has-beens and never-will-bes dressed as Yankees looking for that one final curtain call under the South Bronx sun. It is a clear reminder of how much we cannot stand the interlocking NY cap and the sad players grasping for the one last nostalgic trip in pinstripes. Do fans honestly care that much about Pat Kelly or Brian Boehringer?

It is like watching a Yankees game in slow motion, something we can certainly do without. Of course, to make matters worse, the player introductions for the last decade or so have been conducted by radio play-by-play stooge John Sterling and YES Network's very own Michael Kay. This babbling duo is perhaps better known as being the Lenny and Squiggy to the Yankees' Laverne and Shirley. Think the only thing worse than sitting through an Old Timers' Game is having to watch a Babe Ruth movie starring John Goodman? How about when the Bombers carted out the starting lineup from 1923, among others, during the closing ceremonies at the old stadium in 2008? Rumor has it that Casey Stengel was played by a former batting practice catcher, but thankfully Tino Martinez played himself during 2011's annual Yankees train wreck.

The glorious tradition of such a noble event started in the late 1930s, when individual days were set aside for Lou Gehrig and Babe Ruth. Sadly, with doom approaching, fans were given a last chance to show there respect to the luckiest man on the face of the earth and the only fat man more famous than Santa Claus.

The collection of out-of-shape sluggers are split into two teams (Bombers and Clippers), with player introductions usually out-shining anything whatsoever left in the former Yankees' gas tanks. So, if you enjoy watching overweight men in there fifties and sixties reliving their youth, you may want to catch a pick-up softball game at the local sandlot, because at least then you know the brews will not cost you $10 a pop. Speaking of expensive bar tabs, if Mickey Mantle were alive and knew Homer Bush was starting on Old Timers' Day, he would've blew off the game faster than Jeter did the 2011 All-Star Game.

RETIRED NUMBERS

On January 22, 1929, the Yankees announced that they would have numbers on the backs of their uniforms on a permanent basis. This new trend would spread to a few other teams, and by May 13 of the '29 season, the Yankees would be 4–3 losers against the Indians in the first game that included two teams with uniform numbers. Even though most people could tell which one was Babe Ruth, he wore No. 3 for his spot in the lineup. Batting ahead of the Babe and wearing Nos. 1 and 2 were Earle Combs and Mark Koenig, respectively. In the cleanup spot and No. 4 was the Iron Horse followed by No. 5 Bob Meusel, No. 6 Tony Lazzeri, and No. 7 Leo Durocher. Bill Dickey wore No. 10 for the 1929 season but would eventually switch to No. 8. The Red Sox joined the number fad in 1931, and by the following season, the entire league was on board.

Ten years later, the Yankees began another tradition in numerology...the retired number. The Yankees have retired 16 numbers, which doesn't include any players from the recent dynasty. They might have to eventually resort to large letters or triple-digit numbers. While No. 42 has been retired by everyone for Jackie Robinson, it'll be re-retired by the Yankees for Mariano Rivera. There are only two other instances where a number is retired by a team twice (Yogi Berra's and Bill Dickey's No. 8 for the Yanks, and Andre Dawson's and Rusty Staub's No. 10 for the Montreal Expos). In tribute to those double retired numbers, here's a few more the Yanks should re-retire or just plain retire:

No. 1 Snuffy Stirnweiss. Snuffy Stirnweiss was a Fordham Prep star in the Bronx who signed as an amateur free agent

YANKEES

YANKEE–FEN FACTS

- In 2010 Don Zimmer was inducted into the Red Sox Hall of Fame. He still awaits that same call from the Yankees.
- In 1997 Mike Stanley went to the Yanks for Tony Armas and Jim Mecir—the last trade between the two clubs.
- Bob Stanley is the only Red Sox hurler to pitch in both the Bucky Fuckin' Dent and Bill Buckner games. It's no wonder he was known as "the Steamer."
- Bill Lee and Terry Francona were teammates on the 1981 Expos.
- On June 19, 1977, Carl Yastrzemski—second only to Jarrod Saltalamacchia for having the longest surname in Boston—hit the longest homer in Fenway History (about 460 feet) off Yankees forget-me-so Dick Tidrow.
- On April 11, 2005, the Sox received their World Series rings in front of the opposing New York Yankees at Fenway, who ended up losing the game. Curse schmurse.
- 2007 World Series MVP Mike Lowell, who also played on the 2003 world champion Florida Marlins, was drafted in the 1995 Major League Draft by the New York Yankees.
- In back to back seasons (1981 and 1982) the Yankees used second-rounders on John Elway and Bo Jackson.

continued

They used the 52nd overall pick on Elway, six spots
ahead of baseball Hall of Famer Tony Gwynn.

- Boston's Bruce Hurst served up Don Mattingly's record
  sixth grand slam of the 1987 season.
- Did you know that Bucky Dent's real middle name is
  Fuckin' Earl?
- Casey Stengel hit the first postseason home run in
  Yankee Stadium history while a member of the New
  York Giants.
- Hideki Matsui became the third player in MLB history,
  along with Babe Ruth and Lou Gehrig, to bat .500 or
  above and hit three home runs in the same World
  Series in 2009. Two months later he was an Angel.

with the Yankees in 1940. Snuffy made his debut in 1943 and
was a regular by the next season. The 175-pound infielder led
the American League in runs, hits, triples, and stolen bases in
1944 *and* 1945. Stirnweiss was named an All-Star during the
1946 season. Snuffy was part of three Yankees world championships. He would've been part of the 1950 title team, but
the Yanks snuffed out that chance by exiling Stirnweiss to the
St. Louis Browns.

No. 2 *Mike Gallego*. Rickey Henderson once said, "If they
are gonna pay me like Gallego, I'm gonna play like Gallego."
A finer tribute could not be found, unless you are counting a
Yankees retired number. From 1992 to 1994, Gallego warmed
up the No. 2 jersey in the Yankees dugout. With more than
1,000 plate appearances as a Yank, Gags managed to hit 19
Bronx Bombs and bat .262. Gallego never made an out for

the Yankees in the postseason. In contrast, Derek Jeter, who would later wear No. 2 for the Yankees, made more than 400 postseason outs.

No. 3 *Twinkletoes Selkirk*. If you thought Babe Ruth won the most titles as a Yankee wearing No. 3, you were wrong. In 1934 George Herman Ruth played his last game as a New York Yankee. In the Bronx dugout, rookie George "Twinkletoes" Selkirk admired his No. 3. In 1935 Ruth slugged his final six home runs with the Boston Braves, and Selkirk donned No. 3 for the Yankees. Twinkletoes would go yard 103 times wearing *número tres* from 1935 until he retired in 1942. Along the way, Selkirk would be named an All-Star twice and win *five* Yankee rings compared to the Bambino's four.

No. 5 *Nick Etten*. From 1943 to 1945, Joe DiMaggio was out of baseball rising to the rank of sergeant in the United States Air Force. The Yankees honored him by issuing his No. 5 to Nick Etten. During Joltin' Joe's three-year absence, Etten won one World Series in 1943, led the league in home runs with a paltry 22 in 1944, and paced the AL with 111 RBIs in 1945. When the Yankee Clipper returned in '46, Etten was given No. 9, which would later be used by Roger Maris. Etten would be gone from baseball by 1948 and forgotten by Yankees fans shortly afterward.

No. 8 *Aaron Robinson*. Yogi Berra and Bill Dickey are not the only Yankees catchers to wear No. 8 and win a World Series. Aaron Robinson achieved this in 1947, one season after Bill Dickey wore the number as a Yankees manager. As a matter of fact, Yogi was on the '47 roster but was sporting No. 35. Robinson batted .270 with five home runs in roughly half a season

behind the plate wearing No. 8. He batted an un-Yogi-like .200 in the World Series but picked up the ring nonetheless.

No. 11 Chuck Knoblauch. The meat in the Tino-Jeter sandwich, Chuck Knoblauch played an integral part in the Yankees dynasty during the 1990s. Okay, maybe not Jeff Nelson integral, but integral nonetheless. Knoblauch is known best in recent years for his supporting role in the Mitchell Report and for pegging Keith Olbermann's mom in the head with one of his now-infamous miscues at second base. Here is one mind-blowing stat sure to be etched into Chuckie's plaque in Monument Park: he has more World Series rings with the Yankees than Don Mattingly, Dave Winfield, Jason Giambi, and Alex Rodriguez combined (Knoblauch 4, Yankees Greats 1).

No. 26 Paul Zuvella. While 1986 holds many countless memories to Mets fans, Yankees fans hold June 30, 1986, close to their hearts. On this date, the Bronx Bombers pulled the trigger on a deal that would bring Paul Zuvella to the Stadium. "Zuvie," as Joe Girardi probably would've referred to him, arrived with *the* Claudell Washington from the Atlanta Braves for the original Ken Griffey and "Andre 1986" Robertson. Zuvella proceeded to steal the headlines from the '86 Mets with his .083 average in 57 plate appearances. His lone extra-base hit was a double, and what a double it was. Zuvella most likely followed that at-bat with an out because he was really good at doing that.

No. 31 Dave Winfield. They don't call Dave Winfield "Mr. May" for no reason. In nine seasons with the Yankees, Winfield out-homered (205 to 144) and out-RBI'd (818 to 461) fellow Hall of Famer Reggie Jackson in pinstripes. The placement

of one zero after a decimal point shouldn't matter when retiring numbers. So we'll toss aside the fact that Reggie hit .450 in the 1977 World Series win, while Winnie batted .045 in the 1981 World Series loss.

No. 43 *George Frazier*. In the Yankees' storied history, it takes a lot of balls to lose three games in a single World Series, but that's what George Frazier possessed. With the Yankees leading the 1981 World Series against the Dodgers two games to none, George Frazier did his best Joe Frazier vs. George Foreman impersonation and was repeatedly knocked down. With a 17.18 ERA, Frazier managed to lose three of the final games of the series as the Dodgers took the title in six. In $3^2/_3$ innings pitched, Frazier dominated by allowing nine hits and five walks.

No. 44 *Mike Ferraro*. After Reggie Jackson bolted back to the West Coast, signing with Gene Autry's Angels, the Yankees issued his famous double-digit number to three coaches: Jeff Torborg, John Stearns, and Mike Ferraro. Ferraro was the last to don the uniform before Jackson readopted the Yanks as his team to make his annual appearances in spring training and in October.

4

YANKEES GAMES WE HATE

There's a reason Bucky Dent's middle name is a curse word. Ditto for Aaron Boone. Those two underachievers infamously ended the Sox playoff hopes in 1978 and 2003, respectively. Scrubby players aside, it's happened way more often than we'd care to remember. Too often, the Sox's World Series aspirations are crushed at the hands of their rival New York Yankees. But pivotal losses to the Bronx Bombers haven't been reserved for the playoff run only. There have been far too many "Boston massacres" courtesy of the Yankees. These games epitomize how intimidating the Yankees can be, and what underdogs the Sox often find themselves. These five gut-wrenching games cut to our core, tested our resolve, and make us only hate the Yankees more.

TUESDAY, APRIL 18, 1923
vs. BOSTON RED SOX

Back in 1923 some 70,000-plus baseball fans swarmed to the Bronx to catch a glimpse of the new show in town. After being told they were no longer allowed to play home games at the Polo Grounds, the Bombers had to build a house of their own to accommodate the inflated ego and waistline of George Herman Ruth. There was no denying that the Bambino was the

main event at the inaugural game at the new home built a quarter mile from the National League's New York Giants. Fittingly enough, the first game at Yankee Stadium, which still had that new car smell, was against the Boston Red Sox. Beating Boston was a top priority, but adding insult to injury was the Babe's three-run home run in the bottom of the third inning, which happened to be the first of many at Yankee Stadium. The homeboys beat the away-boys 4–1 on Opening Day of the 1923 season, a season in which the Yankees also would go on to to beat their former landlord Giants for the World Series. So, although the former Red Sox pitcher will be remembered for hitting the first home run at Yankee Stadium, the power-hitting right fielder also was charged with the team's first error when he dropped a fly ball in the fifth inning.

MONDAY, JUNE 19, 2000
AT *BOSTON RED SOX*

The Yankees, channeling the spirit of 1927, handed the Red Sox their most lopsided home defeat ever on a Monday night in Fenway that, much like the constant reminder of Joe D's hit streak, we would rather erase from our memory. Sadly, though, it happened, and aside from a 27–3 spanking from the Cleveland Indians on July 7, 1923, this is no doubt one of the more embarrassing losses to rock the Red Sox organization in some time. To make matters worse, the usual suspects all pitched in. Derek Jeter, Jorge Posada, and Scott Brosius all hit the long ball, had a few hits apiece, and scored a bunch of runs. Shane Spencer (Kevin Maas Light) went 3-for-5 and was only a single away from the cycle. Finally, adding insult to Fenway injury was a home run by pinch-running specialist Felix Jose. We try to forget that round-tripper as much we try

I'm a Bostonian, my wife's a New Yorker, my son's a New Yorker, and they're both Yankee fans. When Grady left Pedro in the game, I almost threw my TV out the window. I was in New York and I could hear people cheering in the streets, and I thought, Tomorrow's going to be a long day.

—John Slattery, actor, *Mad Men*

to forget the 16 runs New York scored in the final two innings of the game to make it a 22–1 final. If there was ever a time to invoke the slaughter rule, this was the game to do it. This was certainly a Sox stinker that smelled just as bad as one-time Celtic Shaquille O'Neal's role in *Kazaam*.

SUNDAY, SEPTEMBER 2, 2001
AT *BOSTON RED SOX*

Spending his entire career in the ultra-competitive American League East from 1991 to 2008, right-handed pitcher Mike Mussina's big-league journeys can be summed up in one simple phrase: "close but no cigar." He posted 270 career wins (30 away from the exclusive 300 club), six top-five finishes for the Cy Young Award, and two World Series appearances (2001 and 2003) without a championship. It did not stop there, however, for the one-time 20-game winner whose flirtation with perfection has been well documented. In 1997, after retiring the first 25 Cleveland Indians, it was a single in the ninth by Sandy Alomar Jr. that halted Mussina's bid for history. One year later against the Detroit Tigers, Mussina once again fell short of perfection after a Frank Catalanatto double with just four outs to go.

On September 2, 2001, Mussina was once again on the cusp of history. This time, though, was much sweeter because not only was it going to happen in Fenway against the archnemesis Boston Red Sox but it was also going to be the fourth perfect game in New York Yankees history. Amazingly, the game remained scoreless until the top of the ninth when a pinch-running Clay Bellinger scored the game's lone run off of Sox pitcher David Cone, when Enrique Wilson grounded out to first. In the bottom of the ninth, after Shea Hillenbrand and Lou Merloni were sent packing, respectively, Carl Everett pinch-hit for Joe Oliver with just one out remaining. Everett, who was 1-for-8 with seven strikeouts against Mussina on the season, ended the silence at Fenway as well as the perfect game attempt with a clean hit to left field. As Trot Nixon grounded out to end the game, assuring a 1–0 Yankees win, one thing was certain: Mike Mussina avoided perfection just as well as Domino's Pizza avoided the Noid. Thankfully for Yankees haters across the universe, Moose's lapse in perfection continued during Games 1 and 5 of the 2001 World Series against the two-headed monster of Curt Schilling and Randy Johnson, then known as the Arizona Diamondbacks. Mussina posted an 0–1 record and a 4.09 ERA in 11 innings of work. Though the game was lost, thanks to Carl Everett, Mike Mussina is still the greatest pitcher to never win a Cy Young, a World Series, or pitch a perfect game.

THURSDAY, JULY 1, 2004
vs. BOSTON RED SOX

Only the Red Sox and Yankees can play a game in the beginning of July that begins and ends with a playoff-like atmosphere. After 13 innings, 37 players, and one memorable dive into history, it was a game that has no doubt found a permanent home on the

Derek Jeter dives into the seats behind the left-field line after making an over-the-shoulder catch of a Trot Nixon pop fly in the 12th inning of a Yankees–Red Sox game on July 1, 2004. The catch preserved the tie, and the Yankees went on to win the game 5–4 in the bottom of the 13th.

YES Network airwaves over the years. It was another Sox-Yanks match-up for the ages, loaded with plenty of drama (Gary Sheffield was beaned not once but twice), a couple of Manny home runs (including a leadoff blast in the top of the 13th inning), and the defining play of the career of Yankees captain Derek Jeter. During the postgame, former idiot Johnny Damon said the game was "already an instant classic." With the game tied at 3 in the top of the 12th, Boston had runners on second and third with two out. Little did Trot Nixon know that he was about to hit the most famous pop fly in Yankee Stadium history. After his over-the-shoulder catch, Jeter launched himself over the third-base wall, landing three rows into the left-field seats. The

dive into the stands ended the inning and sent the game into the bottom of the 12th. The Red Sox took the lead behind a home run from Yankees destroyer Manny Ramirez, setting up a dramatic comeback behind three unlikely Bomber bats. After two outs were in the books, Ruben Sierra got a single, followed by a game-tying double from Miguel Cairo. With Jeter on his way to the hospital (he looked like he'd lost a split-decision to Marvelous Marvin Hagler), the Yankees were on the way to a 5–4 victory after Cairo scored on pinch-hitter John Flaherty's single.

The Yankees won the battle, but they did not win the war, by the end of the month the Red Sox would go on to trade their very own All-Star shortstop Nomar Garciaparra in a four-team deal at the trade deadline, obtaining shortstop Orlando Cabrera from the Montreal Expos and first baseman Doug Mientkiewicz from the Twins. Mientkiewicz would eventually catch the last out in the 2004 World Series clincher. The July 1 game, which left the captain with a bloodied chin, swollen cheek and bruised shoulder, helped pave the way to a resilient Red Sox team that would unleash a Boston beat-down of their own, leaving an unhappy New York club and their fans with a historically bruised ego.

FRIDAY, AUGUST 7, 2009
vs. BOSTON RED SOX

After five hours and 33 minutes, Alex Rodriguez ends a scoreless tie after 14½ innings with a two-run blast in the 15th off of Junichi Tazawa well past midnight. Pie-tossing A.J. Burnett and the hero of the 2003 Florida Marlins, Josh Beckett, both pitched brilliantly before each handed the reins over to their respected bullpens. A-Rod's first homer in three weeks ended the longest scoreless match between the two rival franchises,

YANKEES

THE LUCKY 13: TEAMS THAT BEAT *THE* YANKEES *IN THE* WORLD SERIES

2003 Florida Marlins—Florida remains undefeated in six playoff series behind the hitting efforts of "Mr. Marlin" Jeff Conine and Juan Pierre.

2001 Arizona Diamondbacks—Big Unit and Schilling earn all four wins for Arizona in best World Series of the 21st century.

1981 Los Angeles Dodgers—In strike-shortened season, Yanks take first two in New York before shorting out and losing next four.

1976 Cincinnati Reds—One season after needing seven games to defeat the Red Sox, the Big Red Machine sweeps the Bombers.

1964 St. Louis Cardinals—Bob Gibson strikes out 31 Yanks during epic seven-game series.

1963 Los Angeles Dodgers—Sandy Koufax throws two complete-game victories in four-game sweep of 104-win Yanks.

1960 Pittsburgh Pirates—Yanks outscore the Pirates 55–27, but Bill Mazeroski cements Hall of Fame legacy with Game 7 game-winner.

1957 Milwaukee Braves—Lew Burdette gives up two runs in three complete-game wins, and Hall of Famer Warren Spahn collects the other win in the last baseball title in Milwaukee.

1955 Brooklyn Dodgers—After losing five World Series to the Yanks, Dodgers get off the snide before bailing out of the boroughs. *continued*

> **1942 St. Louis Cardinals**—Stan is not quite "the Man," but the Cards are good enough to take out the Yankees in five.
>
> **1926 St. Louis Cardinals**—Babe Ruth hits the only four Yankees homers in the Series, but fellow Hall of Famer Pete Alexander picks up two wins and a save.
>
> **1921 and 1922 New York Giants**—Frankie Frisch and High Pockets Kelly (with help in 1922 from Heinie Groh and Casey Stengel—yes, that Casey Stengel) become the first and only team to win back-to-back World Series versus the Yanks.

passing the previous mark of 13 on September 24, 1969, a game in which the Sox won 1–0 in 14 innings. Tazawa, about as useless as the Ickey Shuffle was during a touchdown celebration, gave up the bomb to Rodriguez in what was the pitcher's major league debut. This one stung—certainly not as badly as the already mentioned Dent and Boone ding-dongs—but it left a bad taste in our mouths that only grew when the Bombers won the whole thing in October 2009.

HONORABLE MENTION

Honorable mention as far as games we hate is reserved for October 1, 1961, a game in which the Yankees' Roger Maris broke the then single-season home run record, hitting his 61st round-tripper of the year off of Boston's Tracy Stallard. It was the game's only run, which resulted in a Bombers win in the season finale. Of course, we no doubt hate this game, but apparently so did Yankees fans, who were clearly angry that the Bambino's sacred gopher-ball record went down as sadly as Brien Taylor's career after a December 1993 fistfight.

BIBLIOGRAPHY

Books

Bruce, Janet. *The Kansas City Monarchs: Champions of Black Baseball.* University Press of Kansas, 1985.

Cramer, Richard Ben. *Joe DiMaggio: The Hero's Life.* New York: Simon & Schuster, 2000.

Montville, Leigh. *Ted Williams.* New York: Doubleday, 2004.

Purdy, Dennis. *The Team-by-Team Encyclopedia of Major League Baseball.* New York: Workman Press, 2006.

Purdy, Dennis. *Kiss 'Em Good-bye: An ESPN Treasury of Failed, Forgotten, and Departed Teams.* New York: Ballantine Books, 2010.

Shaughnessy, Dan. *At Fenway: Dispatches from Red Sox Nation.* New York: Three Rivers Press, 1996.

Williams, Ted and Jim Prime. *Ted Williams' Hit List:The Best of the Best Ranks the Best of the Best.* New York: Contemporary Books, 1996.

Newspapers/Magazines

New York Daily News
New York Times
Boston Globe
USA Today
Sports Illustrated
The New Yorker
Team Media Guides—Boston Red Sox, New York Yankees

Web

Baseball Almanac (www.baseball-almanac.com)
Baseball Biography Project (http://bioproj.sabr.org)
Baseball Reference (www.baseball-reference.com)Retrosheet (www.retrosheet.org)
Sons of Sam Horn (www.sonsofsamhorn.net)Wikipedia (www.wikipedia.org)
Red Sox vs. Yankees (www.redsoxvyankees.com)

ACKNOWLEDGMENTS

Jon Chattman, Allie Tarantino, and Rich Tarantino would like to thank the following: Triumph Books, notably Tom Bast and Adam Motin, Alex Lubertozzi, and the following talent that were interviewed or provided original quotes specifically for this book: Kevin Millar, Bill Lee, Ellis Burks, Bronson Arroyo, John Slattery, Daniel Epstein, Ken Casey, Jerry Trupiano, and Brian Kiley. Special thanks to Lorraine Fisher of MLB Network, Jeff Pearlman, and the bloggers, tweeters, and fans of Red Sox Nation who helped add some more passion to the book.

JON CHATTMAN THANK YOU:

My wife Alison amazes me. Not only does she put 110 percent into everything—her job, her family, and our marriage—but more amazingly, she's patient and supportive with all of my self-made work obligations, Facebook obsessions, and this and every book I write. She also humors me by going to various ballparks—minor or major. I love her—quoting Buzz Lightyear—"infinity and beyond," and I know she'll be the perfect mother to Noah Sawyer, whom I will love unconditionally and share my disdain for the Yankees with. I'd like to thank my Tarantino brothers from another mother for collaborating on this book with me during so many nights of way-too-much junk food, Cyrus Mac photo ops, and "triple like" status messages. Rich, you're a true friend and great tag-team writing partner. Thanks for your tireless efforts getting this book off the ground and for always being there, even when I'm not mentally all there. Allie, my former co-counselor, our friendship has grown so much since I sported pork-chop sideburns. This book wouldn't be anything without your most impressive baseball knowledge, and off-topic, your coauthors were *Seabiscuit*. I'd like to thank my parents Gary and Patti for being my biggest fans since I burst out of the womb (after a way-too-long labor, as they will tell you or anybody) at over 10 pounds. I wouldn't be able to write this book had my dad not turned me on to baseball in the first place and had my mom not taught me that it was okay not to finish first sometimes. Thanks to my sister and delightfully chronic Facebook responder, Alissa, and her husband, Jake, who have done a fine job raising my nephew, Ryan, a loving boy, an avid baseball fan, and an admirer of my writing (he "read" the Roscoe Orman chapter of my last book repeatedly). Thanks to Barbara and John Correira

for always opening up their home to Alison and me and never being arrogant Yankees fans. They're also wonderful parents to Nate. Nate, if you're reading this, I'm very proud of you…now show Mommy and Daddy. Thanks to my brother-in-law, Wesley Black, for serving our country so proudly and for supporting my work. Thanks to friends who have supported my career by showing it the most—notably John Miele, Carol Nordgren, Keith Troy, Andrew Plotkin, and James Mullally. If this book ends up needing a theme song, I'm calling you, James. Lastly, I'd like to thank Carol Shiffman for all of her support at the Music Conservatory and beyond throughout the years. Her leadership, kindness, and friendship will be so sorely missed. Thanks also to everyone at the Conservatory for their support well beyond the Recital Hall walls. I'd like to dedicate this book to my brother-in-law, Mark Hogg. He was a Yankees fan, but he was never big-headed about it. More importantly, he was a good man who always went the extra mile for Alison and me. True, he may not have liked this book, but I could guarantee if he was here now, he'd tell me he appreciated that I took the time to write it. You're missed, bro.

ALLIE TARANTINO THANK YOU:
Thanks to my wife, Shira, who, through patience and magic, has put up with my baseball obsessions. She has traveled the country coast-to-coast to visit ballparks and an occasional bird sanctuary. In the spring of 2003, I proposed to her on the Golden Gate Bridge and we celebrated the occasion by taking in a San Francisco Giants game. By the fall, Shira and I were married on the night the Marlins beat the Yanks in Game 6. A friend of mine remarked, "It makes sense that the Yankees are losing the World Series on the night of your wedding." Our best creations yet are our son Cyrus and daughter Juniper. Cyrus' first stadium visit was Citizens Bank Ballpark and his first batting stance impersonation was Ryan Howard. Juniper's home birth was an incredible story that deserves a book of its own. Thanks to my parents, Ralph and Diane, who fostered a love for baseball. They have always attended my games, took us to countless games at Shea and Yankee Stadium, and shared in many fun and passionate conversations on baseball. Thanks to my sister, Angela, and her husband, Mike. They are trying to raise their boys, Michael, Matthew, and Nicholas D'Ambrosio as Yankees fans despite influence from their uncles. Thanks to my father-in-law, Ray Goodman, for adding seats from Veteran Stadium to our collection. Thanks to my brother, Rich, and close friend, Jon, for including me in this labor of baseball and Red Sox love. I triple liked the Fenway Research, Facebook Pedro Forum, and Suzyn Waldman YouTube replays. Thanks to Erica,

Alison, and Shira (again) for putting up with their husbands throughout the busy summer of writing. Thanks to Jaxon, Cyrus, Juniper, and Baby Chattman. We look forward to watching you play ball in the years to come. I would also like to extend a big thank you to all of the following: Aaron Goodman, Lisa Cannavo, David Nodiff, Dave Barkin and the Milwaukee Brewers, the Dymeks, Cheryl Hajjar, Jeff Ackerman, Bobbi Wittenberg, Gregg Licht and everyone else at the Wood. Franco Miele, John Fogliano, Mike Sgobbo, Eileen Johnson, Lorna Ferrara, Mike Izzo and the rest of my Ward Family. The coolest inter-rivalry couple I know, Randi Steiner and Mike Fetterer. Ken Walsh for recommending me to Elmwood, which changed my life. The six reasonable Yankees friends I have: Jerry Raik, Bobby Begun, Beth and Chris Reed, Cidalia and Jerry Vincitore. Creative friends who have inspired me over the years, Max Steiner, Nathan Smith, and Chris Barone. My contributions to this book are in memory of Paul R. Spinner and "Uncle" Vinny Lepore, whose love and knowledge of baseball I always admired.

RICH TARANTINO THANK YOU:
I want to dedicate this book to the memory of my Uncle Vinny LePore. Thanks for sharing your love for the national pastime with me and for being a great person as we ventured to "the Dump" on our way through "Cape Cod, New York." I hope my son, Jaxon, grows up with the same passion for baseball that you shared with me. Special thanks to my wonderful wife, Erica, for her patience, love, and support and because nothing compares to living with a Yankees fan from the Bronx in the Bronx. Thanks to my friend and writing mega-power, Jon Chattman. Thanks for another ride. Let's not give up on Fake Holidays, and next time let's not mix the guacamole with the bugles and adult beverages. Thanks to my brother, Allie Tarantino, for swinging at my crappy pitches on Seventh Street and also for rolling a 66–1, you knocked this one out of Fenway Park. Thanks to Jaxon for being the best kid on the planet. Just remember that whatever Mommy says, you do not have to wear pinstripes. Thanks to my parents, Ralph and Diane Tarantino, nothing happens without you guys, love you both more than you can ever know. Thanks to my sister Angela, brother Mike, and the D'Ambrosio boys, Michael, Matthew, and Nicholas. Thanks to Joey and Rachel Amori and Rich Kosiba for your endless friendship. Thanks to "Papa" Frank Rodriguez. Also, thanks to Maria and Lou Pagan, Mike, Josie, Max, and AJ, and my entire family. Thank you for everything. Finally, this book is for Grandma Mary, hopefully one day you will get your hands on this one and maybe then I might be deserving of "getting the pin."

ABOUT THE AUTHORS

Jon Chattman once ate a Reuben sandwich with wrestling icon Randy "Macho Man" Savage, and invited Hall of Famer Gary Carter to his bar mitzvah, but that barely scratches the surface of his many accomplishments. A noted author, pop culture enthusiast, event promoter and media expert, Chattman has been blogging on the *Huffington Post* since 2008 and founded the humor celebrity and music site thecheappop.com in 2005. Over a 15-year span, Chattman has interviewed all walks of pop culture from TV icons and music stars to sports Hall of Famers to Oscar-winning actors and directors. His writings have appeared in the *New York Post*, *Wizard*, *Ultimate Marvel Magazine*, and *TV Guide*, to name a few. In May 2009 he released *Sweet 'Stache*, a humor book on notable celebrity mustaches with coauthor Rich Tarantino. Chattman and Tarantino are currently working on that book's follow-up, *Battle Royal in the Sky*, a humorous homage to pro wrestling over the past 25 years. Outside of his writing experience, Chattman is a media expert who serves as director of communications for the Music Conservatory of Westchester. His efforts there and elsewhere led to his selection as a "Rising Star—Westchester's Forty Under Forty" by the Business Council of Westchester. An avid baseball fan since the womb, Chattman lives in Westchester with his wife and baby, Noah Sawyer.

Allie Tarantino is an elementary school teacher who shares his love for writing, reading, and baseball with his students. Details from his visits to two dozen major league stadiums can be found on his blog www.alliebaseballtour.com. His many trips include a visit to Olympic Stadium to see the Milwaukee Brewers play the Montreal Expos. He hopes to one day return baseball to Montreal so his website www.lastexpostanding.com can become obsolete. Allie's hatred for the Yankees most likely started when he was snubbed by Lou Piniella at Yankee Stadium for an autograph. However, the moment was saved when Hall of Famer Jim Rice interjected and signed his scorecard. His love for baseball is directly attributed to his parents, Diane and Ralph. They frequently took the family to the ballpark, while his dad introduced him to Cadaco All-Star Baseball and APBA. Allie and his dad are frequent competitors these days on Whatifsports.com. Allie owns an extensive collection of Boston Red Sox and Milwaukee Brewers memorabilia, his

Rich Tarantino, Jon Chattman, and Allie Tarantino

favorite American and National League teams, respectively. His baseball card collection includes rookie cards of Robin Yount, Kirby Puckett, and a signed Little League card by an eight-year old Mark Zuckerberg. Allie is a successful elementary school girls basketball coach who has won seven New Rochelle city championships. He spent three years as an assistant coach and statistician for the New Rochelle High School varsity baseball team. Allie looks forward to bringing his growing family on annual trips to Fenway Park and Citizens Bank Ballpark. He lives with his wife, Shira, and children, Cyrus and Juniper, right in the middle of the Red Sox–Yankees rivalry in Connecticut.

Rich Tarantino is a noted author and sports enthusiast. He is the coauthor of *Sweet 'Stache: 50 Bad Ass Mustaches and the Faces That Sport Them* with Jon Chattman. Currently working on that book's follow-up, *Battle Royal in the Sky*, a humorous homage to pro wrestling over the past 25 years, Tarantino is also an educator teaching within blocks of the House That Ruth Built. Tarantino lives in New York City with his wife, Erica, and their son, Jaxon, and has been following baseball for more than 30 years, right around the time he started the Sid Monge Fan Appreciation Club in his parent's backyard. Among his most cherished memories growing up

were when he met Baltimore Orioles legend Ben McDonald in the visitors dugout of Yankee Stadium, his "Bash Brothers" poster hanging over
the bottom bunk, and having no idea where he was when Dave Righetti
pitched a no-hitter in 1983. Tarantino is a lifelong baseball fan who currently resides in the Bronx while his heart belongs on Yawkey Way with
Red Sox Nation.